Seeking Victory on the Western Front

ALBERT PALAZZO

Seeking Victory
on the
Western Front

THE BRITISH ARMY
AND CHEMICAL WARFARE
IN WORLD WAR I

University of Nebraska Press
Lincoln and London

Library of Congress Cataloging-in-Publication Data
Palazzo, Albert, 1957–
Seeking victory on the western front:
the British army and chemical warfare in
World War I / Albert Palazzo.
p.   cm.
Includes bibliographical references and index.
ISBN 0-8032-3725-1 (cl.: alk. paper)
1. World War, 1914–1918—Chemical warfare—Great Britain.
2. Great Britain. Army—History—World War, 1914–1918.
I. Title.
D639.C39P35   2000
940.4'144—dc21   99-42637
CIP

For Lissa

Contents

Illustrations

Tables

Acknowledgments

Projects of this nature require the assistance of a great number of people. This work is no exception. It took its first form at The Ohio State University, Department of History and a debt of gratitude is owed to the faculty, particularly Drs. Williamson Murray, Allan R. Millett and John Guilmartin. Its present version was composed in the comfortable environment of the Australian Defence Force Academy, University College, University of New South Wales. I would like to thank Drs. Peter Dennis and Robin Prior at the School of History, ADFA. Most important, I must extend my appreciation to the staffs of numerous repositories whose assistance considerably eased the labors of this researcher.

I would like to thank the following institutions and individuals for the granting of permission to use their collections and to quote from materials in their possession: the Trustees of the Liddell Hart Centre for Military Archives; the Australian War Memorial; the Imperial War Museum; the National Army Museum; The Liddle Collection; and the Royal Artillery Historical Trust. My thanks also go to the National Library of Scotland and to the Rt. Hon The Earl Haig, as holder of his father's copyright, for permission to quote from the Haig Papers; and to M. A. F. Rawlinson for permission to use the Rawlinson Diary and T. C. Hartley for permission to use the Hartley Papers, both of which are held by the Churchill Archives Centre. For Rawlinson's Fourth Army Records held at the Imperial War Museum, Crown copyright is reproduced with the permission of the Controller of Her Majesty's Stationery Office.

Financial support for this project was provided by a number of institutions. At The Ohio State University the Department of History and the Center for International Studies provided considerable help, as did the School of History at the Australian Defence Force Academy. Alpha Phi Delta Fraternity has my gratitude for a series of National Scholarships. The Australian War Memorial's offer of two grants-in-aid greatly eased the burden. I must also acknowledge the financial commitment and ongoing encouragement of the Joel M. Yarmush Fund.

Friends and family have played a significant role in the conception, development, and preparation of this work. I am grateful to Mr. Colin

Denis and Ms. Julie Hart for the countless conversations and reflections we have shared on the Great War, and to Dr. Jim Folts for his support and encouragement. I must thank my young children—Albert, Thomas, Margaret, and William—for their many gifts and for ensuring that this work retained its perspective. Finally, I must recognize my most ruthless critic, untiring supporter, and unfailing collaborator, my wife, Melissa Benyon, to whom this book is dedicated.

Gas Abbreviations

BB	Mustard Gas
CBR	Phosgene (50 percent) and Arsenious Chloride (50 percent) *or* Phosgene (60 percent) and Stannic Chloride (40 percent)
CG	Phosgene
DA	Diphenylchloroarsine
DM	Diphenylaminechloroarsine
HS	Mustard Gas
JBR	Hydrocyanic Acid (55 percent), Chloroform (25 percent), and Arsenious Chloride (20 percent)
JL	Hydrocyanic Acid (50 percent) and Chloroform (50 percent)
KJ	Stannic Chloride
KSK	Ethyl Iodoacetate
NC	Chloropicrin (80 percent) and Stannic Chloride (20 percent)
PG	Chloropicrin (75 percent) and Phosgene (25 percent)
PS	Chloropicrin
RP	Red Phosphorus
SK	Ethyl Iodoacetate (75 percent) and Ethyl Alcohol (25 percent)
WP	White Phosphorus
Blue Star	Chlorine (80 percent) and Sulphur Chloride (20 percent)
Green Star	Chloropicrin (65 percent) and Sulphuretted Hydrogen (35 percent)
Red Star	Chlorine
Two Red Star	Sulphuretted Hydrogen (90 percent) and Carbon Disulphide (10 percent)
White Star	Chlorine (50 percent) and Phosgene (50 percent)
Yellow Star	Chloropicrin (30 percent) and Chlorine (70 percent)

The Western Front, 1914–18

Seeking Victory on the Western Front

Introduction

Gas achieved but local success, nothing decisive; it made war uncomfortable, to no purpose. – James Edmonds

If the war had gone on until 1919 you would have won by gas alone. – Fritz Haber

Since its appearance in World War I, chemical warfare has been marked by controversy. The comments of Brig. Gen. James Edmonds, the general editor of Britain's official history of the war, and those of Fritz Haber, the Nobel Prize–winning German chemist and father of gas warfare, suggest the widely diverging conclusions that knowledgeable people could come to on the efficacy of gas as a weapon. While the true assessment undoubtedly lies somewhere in between Edmonds's and Haber's extreme opinions, both men advanced conclusions that are legitimate when examined from their culturally different viewpoints. Haber, a scientist and the product of modernist Germany, saw gas as an independent device that could help transform war into an activity dominated by technology; Edmonds, an officer and the product of a British army that valued tradition and moral values, saw gas as a weapon that would violate the primacy of man in battle.

The distance between the opinions of Haber and Edmonds is so great that it demands further investigation into just how significant gas was in World War I. Edmonds was responsible for writing many of Britain's official histories of the western front and had access to both the documents on the conflict and the officers who experienced chemical warfare firsthand. Haber was not only a leading promoter of gas but helped direct the organization of Germany's chemical warfare efforts at all levels. Both individuals had the resources and experience to make a sound evaluation of the value of gas, yet they came to opposite conclusions. It would be easy to dismiss their divergent judgments on any number of grounds. Prostrate Germany, rather than admitting to the nature of its defeat, might seek comfort in the belief that it had lost due to the enemy's superior technology. Conversely, victorious Britain might prefer to assign Germany's loss to the superior British force of arms and will. For historians it has evidently been simpler to accept Edmonds's and Haber's diametrically opposite conclusions as insignificant aberrations when placed in the context of a conflict as vast as World War I. Unfortunately, scholars have thereby failed to assess the true relevance of gas and have made no investigation of the contexts in which the combatants made their decisions regarding its use.

Scholars have not been alone in this failure. The contemplation of chemical warfare tends to produce within individuals a visceral reaction of terror, abhorrence, and perhaps even shame. All warfare and weapons are by definition morally offensive, but gas, along with nuclear and biological warfare, occupies a special niche that society identifies as beyond the pale of acceptable human behavior even in the extenuating circumstances of war. War gases kill by denying their victims the ability to breathe, a violation of one of man's most essential and instinctive functions. Consequently, survival on the chemical battlefield requires specialized equipment and a high degree of training and discipline. Furthermore, the increased lethality of modern chemical agents compared to their World War I ancestors and the vulnerability of civilians to these weapons of mass destruction have only served to increase the call for their prohibition. The entry of chemical agents into the arsenal of the terrorist and the repertoire of the movie producer has only heightened awareness of the vulnerability of noncombatants to attack.

The result of these attitudes is a body of literature on chemical warfare that is copious yet strangely specific, a product of the influence of moral attitudes upon the direction of scholarship.[1] While the moral ambiguity of the effects of gas, the need to achieve its disarmament, and the desire to outlaw its use are all important issues, the emphasis placed on them by scholarly and popular writers has resulted in an overly narrow investigation of the subject. Little has actually been said or written about the process by which armies actually decided how to use the weapon or about the success of any particular application of it. The following discussion will redress this imbalance by studying how the British army incorporated the use of gas into its operations on the western front during World War I, how chemical warfare developed from a novelty in 1915 to an approved component of the British method of waging war by 1916, and how, despite Edmonds's protest, it made a significant contribution to the eventual British victory in 1918.

By examining the evolution of chemical warfare, this work will also address the broader issue of how the British army sought and achieved victory during the war, a subject that until recently has largely been ignored. Warfare on the western front presented the combatants with enormous problems, and victory typically went to the side that accurately interpreted the true nature of the difficulties and then quickly incorporated the correct solutions into its method of waging war. The last 100 days of the war demonstrated that it was the British army that had most successfully undertaken this process. The role of gas in achieving this success will be presented, and will employ chemical warfare more broadly as a means for studying the mechanisms by which the British analyzed the problems of the western front and how they thereby found victory.

Oddly, it is only during the last decade that historians have attempted to discover how the British incorporated the techniques that later brought victory. Until recently the scholarship of the Great War has focused heavily on the personalities and emotions of the conflict. Vitriolic memoirs or fictional accounts by veterans in the 1920s and 1930s usually seized the high ground in their descriptions of the war, and often couched it in terms of the wanton sacrifice of an entire generation by an incompetent and uncaring generalship. The recollections of David Lloyd George and his vituperative and self-serving attacks upon Field Marshal Sir Douglas Haig and other senior British officers, along with the pedantic writings of B. H. Liddell Hart and scholars such as Alan Clark, Denis Winter, and Martin Samuels, all fail to recognize the accomplishments of the British army and instead have limited themselves to attacking its generals.[2] The result of this limited focus is a mentality that equates the Great War, and especially Britain's performance in it, with utter futility and avoids examining the more complex picture. Historians have recently begun to provide a more searching interpretation of British military methods in World War I. The present study hopes to contribute to this more wide-ranging inquiry and to a reassessment of the performance of Britain's military leadership.

This reassessment is long overdue. While personality plays a part in all conflicts, World War I was in actuality a highly technical struggle in which modern weapons and changing technologies became methods of combat of paramount importance. Although the western front posed many difficulties for the attacker, the principle problem was the defender's ability to dominate the battlefield with overwhelming firepower. It was defensive firepower, more than anything else, that created the deadlock in France and made World War I into a prolonged and bloody struggle. Victory would go to the side that learned first how to overcome the firepower of the defense. This work will study the place of chemical warfare in British offensive techniques and how the British employed gas to control or negate the firepower of the defense, thereby reviving the effectiveness of the attack.

Additionally, there is another often misconstrued aspect of British performance in the war that will be considered. Both scholars and the general public have frequently focused their attention on the British emphasis on morale and the related concepts of discipline and offensive spirit, all at the expense of technological achievement.[3] This perception, advanced despite contradictory examples such as the development of the tank, has identified the British army as dominated by a man-centered rather than a technology-centered culture. The result is the erroneous image of an army that promoted moral values above all other strengths in their fighting force. While morale-oriented issues do form an important part of any army's system, the reality is that the British were equally comfortable developing new weapons, devices, and tactics to solve the problems of the western front. Conversely, despite the highly technical nature of the Great War and all conflicts since, morale remains today a vital ingredient in the ability of any army to achieve its objectives. The British were able to balance the demands of an increasingly mechanized war with their longstanding emphasis upon morale to create an army that incorporated the best attributes of both—an achievement that proved to be a significant reason for its eventual success.

When presented with new weapons, military institutions must decide whether, and how, to incorporate them into their method of waging war. The process involves both a mechanical assessment of the weapon's worth and a more abstract determination of its place within the corporate mentality of the institution. The implementation of change requires two steps, one intellectual—innovation—and the other practical—adaptation. Although these two terms are frequently associated with each other, it is important to realize that they represent two separate and distinct processes. Here innovation is used to mean any changes in how an army perceives the nature of war and in how it plans to achieve victory. For most armies innovation typically involves a reassessment of its doctrine. Adaptation, on the other hand, is the modification of tactics, weapons, organization, or any other aspects of an army's operation that attempt to enhance its ability to implement its principles. The differences between innovation and adaptation are analogous to the differences between strategy and tactics.

A detailed charting of the way by which the army added gas to its weaponry will show how the British army underwent a dual process of innovation and adaptation. It will explore the cultural background of the British army's decision-making process and place gas operations within a cultural context that demonstrates the institutional ethos that guided commanders in the selection of gas options. It will then address the practical side of chemical warfare's evolution within the British army—the invention of devices, substances, and tactics—and the integration of gas into the army's operations.

It should therefore be clear that the following is more than just a study of chemical warfare; it is an attempt to use gas as a means to study broader issues affecting the complexity of warfare on the western front. It touches on a number of concepts: innovation, adaptation, tradition, technology, culture, and the quest for victory. However, each of these themes is really a single thread of a more subtle fabric: how the senior leadership of the British army interpreted the problems of combat on the western front, the solutions they devised to address those problems, and how they incorporated these solutions into their method of waging war. It was the successful completion of these three steps that created the British fighting machine of 1918 that was able to secure victory through the defeat of the German army on the field of battle.

CHAPTER I

Confronting the Western Front

The conditions are not at present normal . . . they may become normal some day – Sir William Robertson

The conditions of modern, industrial war presented enormous obstacles to commanders in charge of operations on the western front. The stalemate of the trenches, the continuous and therefore unflankable line stretching from Switzerland to the English Channel, and the attacker's frustration at not being able to achieve a quick and war-winning decisive victory were all symptoms of the scale and complexity of conflict that no commander had ever faced. However, the most significant impediment that leaders had to overcome to achieve victory was the defender's use of firepower to dominate the battlefield and thereby prevent the attacker from achieving a favorable decision. It was the defender's ability to interdict no man's land with a barrier of bullets and shells that made the attacker's task so difficult. One can therefore express the conduct of the campaign on the western front, the litany of failed or inconclusive attacks, and the great toll of dead and wounded in their most simple form: the quest for the means by which to reestablish the potential of the attack and thus to restore decisiveness to battle.

Although the problem of the superiority of defensive firepower was an extremely complex one, its existence did not come as a total surprise to the combatants. One of the more important factors in the Anglo-Boer War was the greatly increased killing power of modern rifles, machine guns, and quick-firing artillery. Commenting on the war in South Africa, Col. C. E. Callwell noted that it was not the mode of Boer fighting—mounted infantry—that was significant.[1] Rather, the lessons lay in the weapons the Boers employed and their increased firepower. The events of the Russo-Japanese War added to the growing debate within the British army over the efficiency of modern weapons but, unfortunately, the lessons derived from that conflict served more to obscure rather than illuminate the best future course of action. In Manchuria, Japanese successes appeared to many British observers to be as much a result of boldness and determination as of superior firepower. However, while the ensuing analysis over the effectiveness of modern weapons shifted the British focus, in part, to the intangible factors of war, it did so in the context of using, for example, superior morale as a means to counter the effect of defensive firepower.[2]

By August 1914 all the combatants of the Great War were still only at the earliest stages of understanding the effects of modern weapons on the battlefield and in finding a solution to the superiority of defensive fire. As the combatants soon discovered, the means to counteracting the benefit that these weapons provided for the defender required not only time and blood but also the development of new tactics, technologies, and weapon systems, as well as the incorporation of these features into an army's intellectual framework for waging war. The British army's eventual success at adapting to the realities of modern weapons and developing methods for employing offensive firepower to destroy or neutralize defensive firepower led to the end of stalemate between the attacker and the defender and in 1918 resulted in the British defeat of the German army on the field of battle.

Prewar observations had also suggested that modern war could degenerate into a struggle of attrition if a combatant failed to secure victory in a conflict's opening campaign. The armies in World War I had built into their mobilization schedules plans for massive, decisive offensives at the commencement of hostilities. The failure of these operations meant that the opponents had to face the titanic and exhausting struggle they feared.[3] Although the British employed attrition, they did not believe it was the only way to achieve victory. Instead, throughout the war they struggled to establish the conditions by which they could restore to war the characteristics that they perceived as "normal." Robertson believed, as his comment above suggests, that the dominance of the defender was an aberration, a temporary impasse whose resolution lay in the application of methods that would return war to its "natural" condition, wherein the attacker could win a decisive victory. By mid-1918 the British, through the integration of new means and approaches in their method of waging war, succeeded in Robertson's goal of returning conflict to a more "normal" condition.

This chapter will address the British perception of the nature of modern war and the methods by which they intended to wage the conflict. It will establish the intellectual framework surrounding the British decision-making process by defining and exploring three key concepts: ethos, decisive victory, and superiority. The chapter will also examine the principles which governed the British method of war-making and will demonstrate that Britain's military strategists never wavered from their prewar conception of how to wage a modern conflict. The chapter will thus lay the foundation for subsequent chapters by establishing the interpretive limits of the British army's approach to war. It will also show that all the operational decisions of the army's leaders conformed to an established and unchanging code of conduct and to a universally accepted perception of the nature of modern war.

Doctrine or Ethos

All military institutions, if they are to deal successfully with the evolving nature of war, must possess an intellectual structure that facilitates change. Military professionals and scholars identify doctrine as the underlying system that an army uses to modify its methods and disseminate new ideas throughout its corporate culture. Further, military commentators generally insist that an army's possession of a well-conceived and universally accepted doctrine is mandatory for the preparation and waging of war. Its absence is a damning condemnation of that military institution's leadership and effectiveness.

The identification of doctrine as the standard by which to measure the professionalism of a military institution is particularly troubling for scholars of the British army because, as a number of historians have observed, the British did not have a doctrine prior to or during the course of the Great War. Shelford Bidwell and Dominick Graham comment on its absence in *Fire-Power*, as does Tim Travers in *The Killing Ground*. In fact, as late as 1992 a senior British officer could point out that the army had only recently accepted the need for doctrine.[4] The officer corps of the World War I era would not have objected to this conclusion. During the years before the war the general staff weighed the possibility of developing a doctrine and actively decided against it. Yet the army's lack of a doctrine was not the result of accident, neglect, or ignorance, but was a deliberate policy decision.[5]

Doctrine is a military concept that is difficult to define, although certain key principles are evident. Bidwell and Graham identify doctrine as the "study of weapons and other resources and the lessons of history, leading to the deduction of the correct strategic and tactical principles on which to base both training and the conduct of war."[6] In a recent essay Brian Holden Reid suggests that the aim of doctrine is not to create rigid dogma but rather to attempt to inculcate a military institution with a common framework of tactical understanding.[7] Jack Snyder sees doctrine as a "set of beliefs about the nature of war and the keys to success on the battlefield." Snyder continues that doctrine "helps to provide a simple, coherent, standardized structure both for strategic thought and for military institutions."[8] John Gooch considers doctrine to be "the bridge between thought and action. It interprets the higher conceptualization of war, embodied in strategic theories and operational plans, into working guidelines for action. In a word, doctrine articulates war."[9] Timothy Lupfer defines doctrine as "guidance for the conduct of battle approved by the highest military authority."[10]

Each of these scholars has identified doctrine as the distillation of ideas into a framework that an army uses to train its forces to achieve maximum battlefield potential. They stress uniformity and an acceptance that commanders must train the entire army within a consistent system following standardized goals, so that the degree of success during training exercises is measurable and readiness reports are comparable. The British did not use such terms in their training, nor in analyzing the capabilities of their forces. Yet, despite the absence of doctrine, the British did succeed, and it was their army that dealt the Germans the terminal blows that led to the Armistice. Historians have been shortsighted in their insistence on doctrine and perhaps could have probed more deeply to determine whether it is possible for an army to base its intellectual structure on a foundation other than doctrine. Instead of doctrine one must identify a different, and perhaps more important, construct to assess the strengths and weaknesses of the British army and its leaders. Indeed, the army had no doctrine, but it possessed instead a unifying philosophy, or, more accurately, an ethos, that provided an equivalent structure for the decision-making process and was the basis for all operations. In ways much more dramatic and all-encompassing than doctrine, ethos provided the British with effective operational and tactical guidelines around which they developed, modified, and inculcated their method of waging war.

In practical terms, ethos obviated the need for doctrine. Ethos provided the continuity of thought that welded the army into a whole; it was based upon the cultural values of the nation and was accepted by members of the officer corps, not only among the senior ranks and general staff but also among junior officers, NCOs, and those of other ranks. Culture played a particularly important role in the British army for it was culture, rather than doctrine, that determined the British method of war-making. Castigating the British army for its failure to create a doctrine obscures the fact that the British did have the means for interpreting the war and guiding their responses to its challenges.

Ethos can be defined as the characteristic spirit and the prevalent sentiment, taste, or opinion of a people, institution, or system.[11] To be identifiable, a people's ethos must meet several criteria: it must be representative of the values of the society; it must include a significant part of the population, particularly those in positions of power and influence who are able to shape the culture; it must be enduring; and the state must possess the desire to maintain it and instill similar values in the next generation. While there is a temptation to equate ethos with tradition, ethos is not a static state of irrational beliefs that isolate a society or prevent the evolution of ideas. Only in extreme cases does ethos act as a barrier to change—usually in cultures that are determined to resist change at all costs, or in leaders who see a political benefit in excluding the outside world, as the government of Japan during the Tokugawa period did when it isolated the country from western influence for nearly 250 years.

The hallmark of British society in the years before World War I was the challenge to the existing order by new ideas, inventions, and experiences, as modernism made its assault upon British culture. It was a tumultuous period, and issues such as Irish separation, the women's vote, and the reform of the House of Lords convulsed the nation. Conservatives resisted but generally, if reluctantly, gave way. Samuel Hynes has identified a standardized response to the introduction of the new theories of modernism. During those tense years before the war, whenever they appeared the pattern was the same: "the New behaved brashly, insolently, or violently, and the Old responded with an arthritic resistance."[12] One part of society sought stability while the other fought for change. Yet Britain did slowly change, for its ethos was not rigid; change gave the nation a mechanism to assess new genius and to shape the adaptation of novel ideas into a recognizable and comfortable form so they could be incorporated into the existing order.

The institution of the army also contained the necessary elements to create a viable, sustainable, and dynamic ethos, thus the army mirrored society by also undergoing a struggle with change during the years leading up to the war. The army derived its ethos by borrowing its values from the broader culture, institutionalized it by imposing it upon the vast majority of the officer corps, particularly at the senior levels, and assured its continuance by incorporating mechanisms to pass it on to the next generation. The army's ethos revolved around certain intangible qualities such as a preference for amateurism, a parallel aversion to professionalism, and an emphasis on the character of the individual. More directly, the army identified particular values such as loyalty, self-confidence, physical courage, obedience, moral virtue, and sacrifice as representative traits of its ethos. This emphasis comes through repeatedly in the testimony of Maj. Gen. Sir Hugh Sandham Jeudwine, who proudly listed the traits the British brought to the war as "courage, devotion to duty, determination, and endurance."[13] Gen. Sir Henry Rawlinson believed victory was the result of the invincible will to conquer in every officer, noncommissioned officer (NCO), and man.[14] One gunner, W. H. F. Weber, observed that technology might achieve temporary success but victory depended upon national character.[15] J. F. C. Fuller described the officer corps as being composed of "men of honour, men who could be trusted, who were loyal to King, country, their men and to their caste."[16] Last, the *Field Service Regulations* (FSR) concluded that "skill could not compensate for the want of courage, energy, and determination."[17]

During the prewar debate about doctrine, the army's stated rationale for rejecting doctrine also helps to reveal the nature of the army's ethos. At a conference of staff officers in 1911, Capt. C. A. L. Yates suggested that the army should produce an officers' manual of applied tactics. The guide would provide a series of situations and solutions to tactical problems for the benefit of junior officers. Many officers at the conference loudly condemned the proposal as the first step toward creating an officer corps imbued with standardized responses to potential situations. Maj. Gen. F. S. May believed that the idea was dangerous because officers would study it to the exclusion of works of a more general interest. He believed that it would lead to stereotypical responses, which he considered a liability since Britain might have to fight anywhere in the world under greatly differing circumstances. Another officer, Brigadier General Davies, objected as well. He feared officers would become tempted to seek answers to tactical problems in a book rather than using their intelligence. After brief consideration, the general staff directors opposed the suggestion, supporting the arguments of Davies and May and citing the additional difficulty of keeping the FSR current with other manuals and their additional concern that it could not possibly be sufficiently comprehensive to cover all potential situations.[18] An article in the *Army Review* announcing the publication of a new edition of *Infantry Training* reinforced this viewpoint. It stated that "considerable latitude in applying principles and instructions to local conditions has been left to commanders," and that due to differences of training programs throughout the empire, strict adherence to one method would be impossible.[19] Finally, while this insistence upon geography provides one explanation, another author simplified the issue with the suggestion that all an officer needed to solve any situation was common sense.[20] J. F. C. Fuller, certainly among the most erudite of British officers, made the same observation. Writing in the *Journal of the Royal United Service Institution* in 1914, he concluded: "I have no doctrine, for I believe in none. Every concrete case demands its own particular solution, and . . . all that we require is skill and knowledge, skill in the use of our weapons, knowledge of our enemy's formations." He continued, "if there is a doctrine at all then it is common sense, that is[,] action adapted to circumstances."[21] A leading proponent of professionalism, Fuller did not belong to the school of thought that advocated an amateur army. He strongly believed that success in war required practice and study, yet he, too, saw no need for doctrine and preferred to let commanders, properly trained, find their own solutions to local situations.

In part, the rejection of doctrine was a continuation of the debate between advocates of a professional versus an amateur army that Tim Travers and others have described.[22] However, such a rejection also represents the recognition of structural realities that made ethos a more viable intellectual structure to follow. As an imperial army with widely different theaters of responsibility and an organization structure based upon the regiment, the British army's emphasis was on unit commanders making their own decisions with reference to the local environment. John Terraine noted that the British forces were not so much a single army as a reservoir of imperial garrisons, lacking the organizational unity and common doctrine to bind the regiments into a whole. John Keegan describes membership in the army not in terms of a military organization but rather as a large Victorian family, complete with ornate silverware in the mess and photograph-laden histories. The regiment contained all the components of upper-middle-class society, including an ancient lineage, connections to the gentry through an emphasis upon country life, and associations with the court through the practice of naming members of the Royal family as honorary colonels.[23]

For ethos to be effectively followed, however, an institution must disseminate its values widely, a requirement that the British readily achieved. Facilitating the dissemination and integration of the army's code was the fact that the officer corps recruits were traditionally drawn from a narrow, cohesive layer of society.[24] Class stratified the nation into a series of well-defined groups, and the army drew its officers from strata that shared its values and assumptions on the nature of society and their role in the military. Originally the preserve of the nobility, military families, and some clergy, the officer corps extended itself, over the course of the nineteenth century, to include the gentry and professionals. This relatively narrow pool of candidates encouraged a similarity of outlook and station.

Class barriers, however, while critical to one's acceptance as an officer were not totally impermeable, and it was possible for outsiders to cross the divide that separated the officers from the other ranks (witness William Robertson's rise from private to field marshal). During the war the permeability of the caste system became critical, as the army's rapid expansion and high number of officer casualties greatly increased the need to draw leaders from beyond the traditional sources of supply. When pressed by the needs of war, the army broadened the acceptable criteria of membership. The most important trait that determined a candidate's acceptance into "the circle" then became whether or not the individual was "a gentleman." Throughout the war the British strove to maintain the social exclusiveness of the officer corps. While they resorted to a number of expedients, such as shortening training periods and speeding up the process of commissioning, the army consistently made "gentlemanly qualities" a prerequisite for obtaining a commission. Initially the universities and public schools provided a ready source of suitable material, but after casualties forced the army to promote from the ranks it selected first from soldiers belonging to the professional and managerial classes and not the working class.[25]

Officer training battalions served not only to teach potential subalterns leadership but also to measure a candidate's gentlemanly qualities. Henry Ogle, promoted from the ranks, wrote a journal of his experiences at officer training school in 1917. The unit's commander, according to Ogle, believed it his duty to make his students into "officers and gentlemen." Commenting on mess practices, Ogle observed that the commanding officer had a "rota for cadets to dine at the officers' table, so many every day, so that he [the commanding officer] could note how we shaped at table talk and eating peas."[26] Social class was a potential indicator of a candidate's worth, but what really unified the officer corps into a monolithic institution was its adherence to the idea that all its members had to epitomize the ideals of a gentleman and possess a willingness to adhere to the values of the majority.

While one would expect an officer corps composed of individuals with similar backgrounds, educational experiences, and social attitudes

to develop or adhere to a common ethos, would the rest of the army—
the NCOs and other ranks—also share these values? In a society in
which class played such a dominant role, one might assume that each
group of people would develop its own ethos, derived from the unique
experiences of the middle class, the working class, or the various na-
tionalities that composed the United Kingdom. However, this was not
the case. The top echelons of British society were responsible not only
for the running of government but also for the setting of a national ideology. Moreover, the non–public school world recognized the supremacy of the upper class's cultural ideas and they filtered downward and
permeated all of society. Before the war anyone who could afford servants had at least one, a reflection of the divisions in society between
those who led and those who obeyed. After the war began, this distinction continued. Capt. Arthur Gibbs, a young officer in the Welsh
Guards who had attended Eton, reported that his new batman was "a
very nice boy who promises well. An ex-footman, he has quite the correct manner."[27] By providing junior officers with servants the army
was not merely preserving a tradition but deliberately attempting to
perpetuate the supremacy of the upper class; as the officer class expanded the army symbolically issued all the temporary officers their
own batmen. The class system worked in both directions. It required
the deference of the lower classes, not only in appearance or demeanor
but also in ideas. Volunteers responded by the tens of thousands to
Field Marsh. Lord H. H. Kitchener's call to arms and grown men
readily accepted in the trenches, with little resentment or reluctance,
the leadership of officers who were little more than boys but who were
also public school men.[28]

As the war progressed the army had to rely heavily upon the youth
of the upper classes to provide it with the necessary numbers of officers. Fortunately for the army, it was virtually impossible for a boy to
pass through the cultural system of elite society and not absorb the
qualities and attitudes expected of an officer. Before the war the majority of the army's officers had attended public school and university, a
pattern that was to play an important role as the army expanded. The
schools emphasized education "in a gentlemanly tradition of loyalty,
honour, chivalry, Christianity, patriotism, sportsmanship and leadership," which assured that their graduates met the army's educational
and social requirements.[29] Furthermore, private schools fostered devoted allegiance to one's house, school, and country, sentiments that
the army could easily adapt into devotion to one's regiment. Reinforc-

ing these tendencies were the schools' nearly maniacal emphasis upon sport, which not only developed the physical body but also instilled moral virtues, developed team spirit, and integrated the concept of striving for the common weal over the individual. The widespread use of sporting metaphors to describe the war is no accident. Every officer understood the need to "play the game." Boys were not merely graduates of these institutions but rather the products of a deliberate molding process, and throughout the British public school system the mold was the same. With such focus upon character-building in the schools, the staff at the army's schools at Sandhurst and Woolwich did not include leadership training in their curriculum but assumed that their candidates came equipped with the necessary social and moral qualities to be future officers.[30]

The military instruction of public school boys had existed in British society for some time, but for most of the nineteenth century it was a rather minor affair and most of the schools did not sponsor a cadet corps. At schools that did have their own corps, they tended to be small, poorly run, and little-respected activities. However, after the Boer War the environment quickly changed as the debate over military efficiency and fears of German invasion swept the public schools along with the rest of society. More schools founded cadet corps, participation increased, and the schools' administrations, as well as the boys, showed more enthusiasm for the program. Lord Haldane's establishment of the Officer Training Corps in 1908, as part of his military reforms, introduced the routine training of boys in the military arts. Haldane saw the Officer Training Corps as a potential source for officers for the regular army, the auxiliary, and the territorials. The War Office issued regulations for this training and undertook the examination process, thereby providing the army with an opportunity to expose cadets to its military values at an early age. Thus, while at school the boys not only acquired the gentlemanly character expected of an officer but also received exposure to basic military training and the idea that their future role was to be leaders of men. By 1914 over 100 public schools and 22 universities had officer training programs.[31]

Haldane's Officer Training Corps scheme helped to provide the army with a pool of candidates who could not only be quickly commissioned in case of national emergency but who also had already incorporated the army's ethos into their beliefs. On the day Britain declared war, the War Office sent out 2,000 invitations to university and public school men to apply for commissions. The War Office believed that these men had the background and Officer Training Corps experience to take up leadership positions with minimal additional training. Reliance upon the Officer Training Corps for a ready supply of officers quickly accelerated, particularly candidates from the universities. By the end of the first year Oxford had supplied 2,500 officers, Cambridge 2,300, and the Inns of Court 2,500, with smaller amounts contributed by the lesser centers of education.[32]

Other older boys who rallied to Kitchener's call but who wanted to serve with their friends instead of accepting commissions in a host of units, formed their own "pals battalions." The 18th through 21st Battalions of the Royal Fusiliers were organized into the University and Public School Brigade, while another battalion became the 16th Middlesex Regiment. However, these men came under pressure to take up their proper roles and the units became depots for officers. By 1917 the University and Public School Brigade had given off over 7,000 officers while the Middlesex a further 1,400. Instead of serving as ordinary soldiers, these older boys had to fulfill the responsibility for which their training and breeding had intended them: the leadership of men.[33]

While the need to be gentlemen helped make the officer corps into an exclusive club, the expenses of membership further contributed to the creation of a homogeneous institution. Not only was a public school or university education a major drain on a family's resources, but even after commissioning considerable private resources were necessary to support a young officer determined to pursue an army career. A subaltern's salary fell far short of the amount needed for the purchase of uniforms, mess bills, cases, servant's outfit, annual maintenance, the costs of field sports, and social events. In addition, officers in cavalry units had to provide their own charger and several ponies for hunting and polo. The regimental system helped to stratify the officer corps even more, as the costs of joining a regiment varied greatly, with the more prestigious units generally being more expensive. Financial resources helped to assure that one served with comrades who were from similar economic and social backgrounds and further strengthened the trend toward a uniform ethos.[34]

Kitchener's call to the colors might easily have resulted in the creation of new armies that were detached from the ethos and values of the Old Contemptibles. However, the army took advantage of the regimental system to instill a sense of tradition and familial association within newly raised units. Instead of inventing names or assigning arbitrary numbers to the new battalions, the War Office appended these units to existing regiments. Thus the four battalions raised from the city of Hull became the 10th to 13th Battalions, East Yorkshire Regiment, while the units enrolled in the Newcastle area became part of the Northumberland Fusiliers, and those from Glasgow joined the Highland Light Infantry. The raw recruits to the Sherwood Foresters inherited the regiment's glory gained by the winning of Canada, the victories of Wellington, and service in India and Egypt, while the volunteers of Tyneside became part of the Northumberland Fusiliers' record of service in the Peninsula, India, Afghanistan, and South Africa. Henry Ogle, a war-time volunteer, provides an example of the success the army had in inculcating regimental loyalty in the members of the expanded army. After receiving his commission in the King's Own Royal Lancaster Regiment, upon his arrival in France he protested his assignment to the rival Loyal North Lancashire Regiment. A staff officer brushed aside his protests, but in due course he made it to the King's Own. Kitchener's decision for the naming of new units linked these units to the victories of the past, created loyalties, and helped to ensure a continuity of ethos between the regular army and the new army.[35]

If this was the nature of the British ethos, did it matter that the army lacked a doctrine? Many historians have emphatically maintained that doctrine is an essential prerequisite for military effectiveness. It would be tempting to dismiss these scholars with the observation that, after all, the British were among the victors, which is surely the epitome of "effectiveness." But flippancy will not do justice to the full examination of this difficult issue. What these scholars have failed to note is that doctrine conforms to ethos, and it is ethos that provides the system through which an army interprets the problems of combat and tests the feasibility of solutions. The ability of a military institution to place the combat environment within its intellectual framework is a vital prerequisite if that army is to respond fully to the need for adaptation and innovation. In order to change an army must have the ability to adequately examine new ideas and situations. Ethos provided the British with this ability. Doctrine is important, but ethos is essential.

Decisive Victory—The Goal of Battle

Written under Sir Douglas Haig's direction, the FSR of 1909 established the principles by which the British army would wage battle in the coming war. At the core of the principles was a belief in the necessity for decisive battle. The FSR stated that "decisive success in battle can be gained only by a vigorous offensive."[36] Ten years later Haig would write that "it is an axiom that decisive success in battle can be gained only by a vigorous offensive," and that decisiveness in war has "long been recognized as being fundamental, and is based on the universal teaching of military history in all ages." After four years of carnage Haig not only remained convinced of the fundamental soundness of the army's conception of war but had elevated it to the status of self-evident truth.[37] The British believed that they had founded their way of war-making on basic, universal, and timeless principles, which explains why they never faltered from their quest and why Haig could claim after the conflict that it was all "one great and continuous engagement."[38]

For the British army, decisive success (or decisive victory as it will be called henceforth) meant a victory of such magnitude that the enemy was unable to continue to resist—Britain could then impose its will upon its beaten foe. The destruction of the enemy's army was central to the British interpretation of this concept, and when hostilities began the British objective was to seek out the opponent's main body and achieve "the quickest and most complete destruction of the enemy's forces."[39] The British were not alone in their belief in decisive victory, as all combatants of the Great War had to face the reality of modern weapons. Unlike the French, who sought the solution in terms of morale, or the Germans, who looked to mass, the British saw the possession of superior firepower as the key. The British believed it was necessary to develop the offensive power of modern weapons so as to counter the advantages those weapons conferred on the defense. Unfortunately, the development of such power would take time and be further complicated by the fact that the British had principally designed its army for imperial expeditions and, in 1914, was not prepared for a war against a major European power. However, by 1917 they understood what was required, and in 1918 they achieved success.

At Camberley, Haig studied the composition of a decisive battle which, he believed, could naturally be divided into four well-defined phases. Victory, he believed, would unfold like the plot of a play, each act building upon its predecessor, until, at the climax of the last act, the battle reached its crescendo and the army routed the enemy from the field and destroyed its broken foe with a vigorous pursuit. The first stage focused upon the advance as the British sought out their opponent, maneuvered for advantage, and fixed the enemy to the field of combat. The second phase was the fire position, the gradual buildup of British fire superiority and the diminution of the enemy's fire strength, thereby overcoming the ability of the enemy to interdict the battlefield. Next came the assault, in which the infantry would advance upon the enemy's position and force them from the field of battle. Once the attackers had pierced the enemy's position, the commander would order forward the general reserve which would break through the enemy's lines and strike the decisive blow. Finally, by pushing forward the cavalry and fresh troops as rapidly as possible, the British would annihilate the enemy in the pursuit.[40] Later, Haig referred to these phases as the guiding principles on which he had based his planning and declared that they "had proved successful in war from time immemorial."[41] When he oversaw the writing of the FSR Haig made sure that it incorporated these phases of battle and that they became an essential component of the British army's principle of decisive victory.

Once the war began the British largely remained true to these phases of battle, the only exception being that their orders and instructions tended to omit the first phase (for obvious reasons); since the onset of trench warfare there was no need to locate and engage the opponent. Even after the war British officers retained their faith in battle phases. Haig created a model for the war by correlating the theoretical stages of battle with stages in the conflict as it unfolded. He compared the first stage of battle, the maneuver for position and fixing of the enemy, with the state of the war at the beginning of trench warfare in late 1914. He identified the years 1916–1917 as the struggle for fire supremacy as the British morally and physically wore down the Germans. Finally, Haig interpreted the climactic blow as the final 100 days of 1918, when the British forced the now-beaten Germans back toward Germany.[42]

The British army published a lengthy series of manuals that laid out the steps a commander had to follow to achieve decisive victory. As the FSR explained: "The general principle is that the enemy must be engaged in sufficient strength to pin him to his ground, and to wear down his power of resistance, while the force allotted to the decisive attack must be as strong as possible."[43] The 1914 infantry training manual reiterated this point. It instructed commanders to divide their force into two parts. The first needed to develop the attack, wear down the enemy's resistance, and force him to commit his reserves to his firing line. Then, when the enemy no longer had any reserves, the commander would release the second part of his force—the general reserve—which would strike a decisive blow against the opposition's position.[44] Commanders were further instructed to refuse any requests for reinforcements from the general reserve, which had to be held in its entirety, and only committed at the decisive moment.[45]

Once the engagement had begun the initial objective was to develop a superiority of fire over the enemy in preparation for delivering the decisive blow. The infantry would not be able to begin the assault until the defender's firepower had been overcome.[46] The infantry training manual expanded on this point and explained that "the object of fire in the attack, whether of artillery, machine guns, or infantry, is to bring such a superiority of fire to bear on the enemy as to make the advance to close quarters possible."[47] As the war evolved there was a commensurate and crucial change in the nature of the struggle for superiority. At Loos and at the Somme the intention was to destroy the defenders, at Arras, Messines, and the opening of Passchendaele the emphasis was on suppressing the enemy, then during the final months of the war neutralization became the objective. However, despite tactical modifications in the application and intention of fire, the fire supremacy phase remained an integral sequence in the British battle plan. Until the war's end the advancing infantry's survival depended on the success the British had in achieving this dominance. If it were obtained, one brigadier suggested, then the infantry would have little difficulty in securing the enemy's position.[48] When the infantry closed with the enemy, the crisis of the battle had arrived; if they were successful the shock of their blow was to dislodge their opponent from its positions and create the opportunity for pursuit. During the pursuit, while the enemy was demoralized and disorganized, the greatest opportunity for its annihilation existed. As Haig noted, "The object of giving battle is to destroy the enemy's forces which are in our front. This result can only be obtained in the pursuit which must immediately follow the struggle. The annihilation . . . of the enemy's army can only be produced during his retreat."[49]

At Loos, in expectation of success, Haig instructed his subordinates that a "vigorous pursuit, regardless of losses, [was] essential."[50] The training manuals reinforced this point by claiming that the battle was only half won if the enemy had merely been driven from its position. Rather, a rapid advance was essential for the enemy's complete destruction.[51] The FSR instructed officers to press the pursuit "by day and night without regard to the exhaustion of the men and horses so long as the enemy's troops remain in the field."[52] And, it continued, "all pursuing troops should act with the greatest boldness and be prepared to accept risks which would not be justifiable at other times."[53]

The other combat arms also had roles to play in the battle's succes-
sive acts. Although the phases of battle defined the artillery's role in
terms of superiority, its ultimate objective was to assist the infantry's
advance by denying the enemy the ability to sweep the battlefield with
defensive fire. The field artillery's training manual identified several
specific tasks by which the guns would support the attack. When the
assault commenced, the artillery was to subdue the enemy's batteries to
protect the infantry from interdicting fire. As the infantry came within
range of defensive rifle fire the artillery was to provide covering fire
while also continuing to suppress the enemy's guns.[54] As the assault
progressed the artillery was to intensify its fire so as to demoralize the
enemy and lower its resistance.[55] The manual cautioned that it was impossible for the artillery to ensure decisive success by its own destructive action. Rather, "it is the advance of the infantry that alone is capable of producing this result."[56] It concluded that the underlying
principle of artillery tactics was the maintenance of the mobility and offensive power of the infantry.[57]

The experience of war led merely to a refinement, not a revision, of
these ideas. A 1917 publication stressed that, while the artillery was in-
dispensable for success, it functioned as support to the infantry. In the
"wearing down" phase of the battle the artillery was to prepare the way
for the infantry by overpowering the enemy's batteries, destroying
physical obstacles to the infantry's advance, lowering the enemy's morale, and lessening their numbers. When the attack commenced the artillery would assist the advance by beating down the enemy's resistance
from the front or flank and preventing the assembly and approach of
counterattacks.[58]

Though it was of a more limited nature, the cavalry also had a part to
play in orchestrating a decisive victory. The horse had to locate the enemy's forces, protect the infantry during the advance, and assist in the
pursuit.[59] Despite the difficulties of maneuvering horsemen on the
modern battlefield, the anticipated role they were to play in the exploitation phase insured their retention, even if at reduced levels. Haig was
reluctant to concede that horse and rider no longer had a role to play.
On many occasions throughout the war he ordered the cavalry to prepare for the breakthrough and pursuit phases of battle.[60]

Although not given over to a separate branch of the army, gas would
flourish within the British system as its practitioners were able to incorporate it—both intellectually and practically—within the scheme of the
phases of battle. There were, however, no prewar manuals to dictate its

use, for, as Ludwig Haber wrote in *The Poisonous Cloud*, "it sprang, as it were, in its final form, on an unprepared enemy."[61] The gas troops, therefore, had to discover the methods by which to wage chemical warfare in the midst of the conflict. Although this work will discuss the use of gas in greater detail in subsequent chapters; however, a brief mention of its place within the British conception of war is warranted here.

The British would divide their gas attacks into two principal components: operations conducted by the artillery and operations undertaken by the Special Brigade, a unique unit created by the Royal Engineers. Other branches participated in the gas war as well, but in minor ways. Gas shell evolved into an accepted munition, and the gunners incorporated its use into their prewar principles of infantry support, including the wearing down of the defender and the struggle to gain fire superiority. As the battle reached the decisive moment the gunners employed gas to assist the infantry as they crossed no man's land and assaulted the enemy's position. Although the Special Brigade employed different delivery systems than the artillery had, it too participated in the phases of battle and in the support of the infantry. Gas proved to be a highly effective weapon in reducing the enemy's morale, inflicting casualties and, most important, in helping the attacker overcome the advantages inherent in the defender's firepower.

To increase the possibility of success, training manuals provided principles by which leaders could multiply the offensive potential of their forces. The *FSR* instructed commanders to be flexible in how they determined the point for launching the decisive assault. It explained that during the course of battle unexpected opportunities might arise, such as a weakening of a section of the enemy's line, which, if exploited immediately, might force the enemy to fall back.[62] Manuals also instructed commanders on the benefits of surprise and envelopment. The *FSR* explained that an envelopment always affected morale greatly and that achieving fire superiority was facilitated by trying, from the outset, to turn one or both of the enemy's flanks.[63] Lt. Gen. Sir G. M. Harper, during the planning for the Battle of Arras, echoed these sentiments. One of his main principles of offensive operations was the envelopment of the enemy: "hold him in front and attack him in flank."[64]

Although following these principles could not guarantee victory, the British believed they were the only methods that provided the possibility of success. Any radical departure from following the phases of battle would assure defeat. When the British adopted this method, however, they had had no experience with warfare on the scale of the Great War. Even the Boer War, despite its difficulties and duration, did not compare with the intensity of conflict on the western front. Many prewar manuals give a sense that the authors envisaged war on a more Napoleonic scale. The army's commander, presumably watching from a hilltop with a clear view of the field, exerted complete control over the battle and directed it through its phases.

This suggestion—that the British developed their concept of battle on a Napoleonic or Boer War scale—raises an obvious question. In the face of total war, how could the British remain committed to these principles? Wasn't the nature of the western front enough to have forced the British to scrap their prewar ideas in order to develop new parameters for the conduct of battle? On the contrary, since the principles were believed to be timeless they did not require any change or modification. Instead it was simply the scale of the engagement that had to be adjusted so that the implementation of these principles came to reflect the vast realities of World War I. As the war approached one officer noted that "the principles of tactics are timeless. However, it is the application of the principles that need to be modified to meet modern conditions."[65] The British did expect war to bring change. A theorist wrote in 1910 that "It is perfectly true that circumstances change, that machinery changes, that weapons change; but it is also true that in the essence of war there is much more that remains constant, that does not change, than can be challenged by fresh inventions."[66] Additionally, there was no guarantee that radical modifications in the principles by which a nation waged war would result in success. Timothy L. Lupfer enthusiastically praises the German army for its ability to change its doctrine radically in the middle of the war. However, even though the Germans retrained their army, victory proved elusive and the new offensive tactics of 1918 actually assured their defeat.[67]

Even late in the war the British still believed that their methods remained valid. Writing in 1918 they asserted:

> The general principles laid down in the Field Service Regulations . . . hold good to-day provided due allowance is made for the time and space conditions of the present war. To understand the principles thoroughly and to apply them correctly under existing conditions, it must be realized that where in the Field Service Regulations periods of hours and days are specified or implied, periods of weeks and months must now be substituted; while in considering distances it is

necessary to calculate in hundreds of miles where formerly the problem was one of tens of miles.

These differences do not alter principles, but merely modify their
application.[68]

Haig appreciated how immensely greater was the scale of the western front when compared to prewar expectations and he accordingly
modified the program of the phases of battle. Decisive victory, Haig realized, could no longer be won in an afternoon but would require
lengthy preparation commensurate with the ability of industrialized
nations to sustain prolonged operations. At a conference on 8 January
1916, Haig gave his initial instructions to his army commanders regarding the summer offensive that was to become the Somme. He "directed
each army to work out schemes for (a) preliminary operations to wear
out the enemy and exhaust his reserves and (b) for a decisive attack in
the hopes of piercing the enemy's line of defence."[69] Haig envisaged a
buildup of activity, commencing in the winter and continuing until the
start of the offensive, through which the British would wear down the
Germans with a series of raids and minor operations. Gen. Sir William
Robertson agreed with Haig and argued for the advisability of employing wearing down attacks, slowly building to a crescendo, to prepare
the enemy for the decisive battle.[70] Instead of having the battle for fire
superiority last only a few hours, however, it would rage for months.

Haig's faith in the principles of the phases of battle did not limit the
army's ability to address the challenges of the western front. Nor
would the prewar conservatism of some sections of the army seriously
hinder the ability of the British to adapt their operations during the
war. Admittedly, before the onset of the conflict the army contained
powerful factions, particularly within the cavalry and the Royal Field
Artillery, which strongly advocated the retention of traditional tactics
and who resisted the abandonment of known weapons and methods.
The determination of some cavalry officers (Haig included) to retain,
for example, the lance, provides just one example of this pressure.[71]
However, despite this legacy, once they were exposed to the realities of
modern weapons in France and Belgium the British proved themselves
to be extraordinary inventors who constantly tinkered with existing
ways of warfare or sought out entirely new ones. Therefore, the image
of stalemate as the defining characteristic of the western front is a myth
and even though during the years of trench warfare the combatants'
lines did not move appreciably, within those trenches a dynamic, experimental, and innovative war was taking place. Although the British re-

mained steadfast to their underlying principles, there was no prohibition against developing new tactics or weapons that would lead to the restoration of mobility and the conditions necessary for decisive victory. Consequently, as the war progressed they showed great imagination in inventing novel methods, especially in the areas of battlefield survey, aerial reconnaissance, the use of tanks, and the employment of gas.

Yet to present a change of scale as the explanation for why the British adhered to their principles does not in itself adequately address the issue. First it should be noted that merely raising this question implies that the army's leadership should have changed its methods, and the officer corps is thus condemned by its failure to conceive new principles. The "donkey" school of British army historiography suggests that the officers' allegiance to their principles in the face of horrific casualties was due to their excessive stubbornness and mental dullness. In fact, however, this allegiance was one of the key, and positive, determinants of the British army and, instead of condemning it, historians should seek further reasons for the leadership's loyalty.[72]

Like many institutions that have faced a difficult problem, the British army assumed that its failure to achieve a decisive result was due largely to inadequate materials, a not unreasonable assumption given the small size and resources of the British forces when compared to the German army. As the war progressed the British, along with the other combatants, instinctively applied ever-increasing quantities of men, munitions, and materials to the pursuit of victory. As early as January 1915 Gen. John French declared that "if the attempt fails, it shows, providing that the work of the infantry and artillery has been properly coordinated, that insufficient ammunition has been expended."[73] Adding evidence to this argument were Britain's pitiful preparations for war when compared to those of the continental powers. The shell crisis of 1915 was not merely a shortage of munitions but a reflection of Britain's inadequate stockpiles of all tools of war. Throughout the war Britain struggled to gain parity with France and Germany in the quantity of materials. Furthermore, since Britain's lack of preparations forced them to play catch-up, it made it harder to determine the exact volume of materials needed for the job. Finally, the combatants may merely have been responding to a cultural imperative of modern industrial society. C. R. M. F. Crutwell has suggested that advanced technological societies, if they have access to raw materials, have the ability to create a virtually limitless supply of war resources which reinforce the practice of using brute force to secure a decision.[74]

A further explanation for the army's unwillingness to rethink its principles lies in the nature of its relationship with the government's political establishment. Civil-military relations in Britain during the years preceding the war were often quite strained and involved a long-standing pattern of misunderstanding.[75] Lord Kitchener's rejection of Lord Haldane's reserve system after Britain's entry into the war, and the even more extreme Curragh Mutiny, were symptoms of a professional officer corps that distrusted the judgments of its civilian masters. The running battle between Prime Minister Lloyd George and his senior officers during the second half of the war suggests that politicians also had doubts about their military experts. Furthermore, the British tradition of Treasury interference in even the most minuscule military expenditures promoted an environment of confrontation and mistrust between military experts and their amateur opposites in Parliament. Given all these factors it is easy to imagine the reluctance of the officer corps to admit any failings that might lead to a strengthening of government control over the internal workings of the army. For officers to have suggested that their prewar principles were in need of reassessment, particularly in light of heavy human casualties, would have risked an incursion of civilian participation into the intellectual and operational domains of the army.

Finally, the culture of the army itself inhibited any major changes in operational principles. The British army did not encourage self-criticism, and it lacked a formal mechanism for its members to perceive and debate flaws, except at the price of their careers. In his guidelines for contributors to the *Army Review*, French asked rhetorically the extent to which submissions should conform to the army's principles. His answer was that a great aid to military efficiency was an officer corps that guided itself by identical principles, and that the army should be a band of brothers united together by a community of ideas. French went on to admit that contrary ideas were welcome in the journal, but he also provided a series of restrictive tests that articles had to pass. Finally, he concluded that until the regulations incorporated new ideas, the existing principles must be the guide for everyone.[76] Thus, though he allowed for limited criticism of established ideas, it was not a process he encouraged, clearly signaling that conformity was the accepted route to publication.

Why did the British refuse to change their principles? Ultimately, as the above-mentioned reasons suggest, they maintained the status quo simply because they believed their methods were valid and that those methods would eventually bring victory. Although it took much longer than the army had anticipated, in the end they were right. The solution to the defender's ability to use firepower to subvert the attacker's attempts at decisive victory was the correct application of the phases of battle, although a version reinterpreted for the conditions of the western front. The German methods eventually proved less fruitful and the British were able to push on to victory in the final months of the war. The cost to the British was high, but the casualties that the French and Germans incurred were no less considerable, and no army during the war possessed the ability to secure victory cheaply. For example, while the German spring offenses of 1918 did achieve dramatic gains of territory, they did not bring victory and cost Germany nearly 1 million irreplaceable soldiers. Nor is it clear that had the British modified their principles their casualties would have been any less.[77]

Having established that the British army went to war in 1914 with a clearly defined and broadly accepted method of how it would fight, it is now important to show how the army put these principles into effect. What preconditions on the western front did the British perceive as necessary for the launching of the decisive attack, and how did they determine the moment for releasing the general reserve that subsequently led to the breakthrough of the enemy's lines and victory?

Superiority: The Means of Decisive Victory

According to British principles it was axiomatic that one could only achieve victory through the attack.[78] The conflict that existed in World War I between the vigor of the offense and the supremacy of the defense therefore posed a dilemma for British theorists. If the defense was superior, how could a combatant achieve victory? Would the war become trapped in a cycle of perpetual stalemate as the defense consistently rebuffed the offense? This fear, of course, was realized in the trenches of the western front and in the long struggle to counter the defender's advantages and establish the prerequisites that would make decisive victory possible. As one historian has stated in a not unreasonable summarization of the nature of the war, "from 1914 until the end of the war the history of the various offenses in the west is one long account of the different attempts to place the power of the offensive on [equal] terms with that of the defense."[79]

The British army used the term "superiority" to describe its efforts to establish the potential of the offense over the defense. They employed the term throughout their prewar and wartime literature, as Carl von Clausewitz does in his *On War*. However, superiority represented much more than simple quantifiable comparisons, such as the number of troops and guns or the relative technological development of each side's weaponry. Instead, the British asserted a much wider definition of superiority so that the term also conveyed the complexity of the power balance between the offense and the defense, and the idea that the relationship between the two can fluctuate rapidly in either direction.

Superiority can be defined as a condition in which a combatant has secured an advantage over its enemy in the pursuit of a victory. As with the contemporary concept of combat multipliers, a superiority advantage allows commanders to enhance the fighting strength of their army. More important, it is an indicator of the relative strength of two opponents, and a commander can gain an advantage not only by increasing the potential of his own force but also by decreasing the potential of his enemy's. Hence, superiority, although it does include a mere comparison of numbers, is a much broader concept that requires commanders to heed the intangible aspects of war—such as morale and fighting spirit—when assessing the threat posed by the enemy and the potential for victory or defeat.

The kinds of superiority that combatants pursue can be extremely complex, and the struggle for ascendancy in the relative balance of strength can occur on a strategic, operational, or tactical level. Some forms of superiority, such as surprise, are readily understandable and have effects that come into play only on the battlefield. Others, such as the integration of arms, require considerable training and preplanning. However, whatever its nature, gaining superiority rarely occurs by chance. Instead it is usually the result of careful and long-term analysis and study, and requires not only an understanding of the enemy's strengths and weaknesses but also an honest assessment of one's own capabilities.

The desire to achieve a superiority over one's opponent was not an innovation of the Great War. Perhaps the oldest known example is the Theban general Epaminondas who crushed the Spartans at Leuctra (371 BC) and Mantua (362 BC). Instead of distributing his soldiers evenly throughout his phalanx, as was customary, Epaminondas heavily reinforced one flank while leaving the rest of the line considerably thinner. When his troops collided with the Spartans, the increased combat power of the reinforced wing burst through the enemy's line. With their formation shattered the Spartans were helpless and the Thebans quickly overwhelmed their opponent while suffering virtually no losses themselves. In the age of firepower, Frederick the Great rediscovered this tactic as the "oblique order of battle" and employed it to defeat the Austrians at Hohenfriedberg in 1745.[80]

Some examples might be useful to further explain the concept of superiority. The Schlieffen Plan was an attempt by the Germans to secure strategic superiority. By screening the Russian forces with minimal troops, the Germans planned to concentrate their strength against the French and crush them in a giant pincer, one arm sweeping across Belgium and northern France and the other holding the enemy in Alsace and Lorraine. Schlieffen intended to bypass France's border fortresses and maneuver his army into the enemy's rear, capture Paris, and place the French at a terrible disadvantage.

The British invention of the tank is an example of the use of a new weapon to secure operational superiority. Even though the surprise factor was lost owing to its hasty introduction during the Somme, the tank continued to confound, terrify, and overrun German defenders, and its presence was a factor in every British success. German counteradaptation—the use of field guns in an antitank role—partially compensated for but failed to fully negate the advantage the British had established.

The British employment of the Livens projector to discharge phosgene onto enemy positions is an example of an attempt to achieve tactical superiority. The gas bombs arrived with little warning and established a high concentration of lethal vapors in the target area. A defender had only a few seconds to adjust his respirator because phosgene, when inhaled, could cause mortal respiratory wounds after only one or two breaths. However, even if well trained in anti-gas procedures, German soldiers were still at risk because the projector created clouds of such density that the phosgene could overwhelm the respirator's protective agents and enter the wearer's lungs, resulting in injury or death. The British use of the projector is also an example of an adaptation that combined surprise with a deadly substance to provide the attack with a superiority over the defensive capability of the enemy's anti-gas equipment.

The potential fields in which to establish a superiority relationship are numerous but not, in practice, infinite, as their selection must necessarily conform to the prevailing operational situation and to a military institution's preferences as defined by its method of waging war. For most of World War I the central factor that prohibited the attacker from gaining a decisive victory was the advantage that modern weapons conferred upon the defender. If they were to achieve victory, the British knew they would have to develop the means to overcome the resulting firepower-induced stalemate that existed on the western front. Therefore the critical question the British faced was determining which areas would they attempt to gain a superiority advantage in so that they could then counter the defender's ability to preclude a decision and thereby provide themselves, as attackers, with the opportunity to resolve the conflict favorably through battle.

The British addressed the problem of defender's firepower advantage through a number of approaches. The most obvious and direct means was that of mass. Britain started the war with a terrible disadvantage in numbers of artillery pieces, a situation further worsened by the army's inferiority in heavy calibers when compared to the quantities possessed by the enemy. The French army did possess a substantial number of guns, but it had overly specialized its force structure with the light 75mm field gun which exacerbated the enemy's lead in artillery mass. Further complicating the situation was that to compete with Germany solely on the basis of production would be a slow and uncertain path to take, especially when the enemy possessed the dominant industrial infrastructure in Europe. The Ministry of Munitions did tremendously increase the scale of the British army's artillery, but mass alone could not provide them with a superiority sufficient for victory. Instead of achieving a quantitative advantage, the British had to look elsewhere for the means to overcome the defender's firepower and thereby create the superiority that would end the equilibrium and allow their troops to wage a decisive battle.

The British concentrated on three areas in the struggle to wrest from the defender the ability to control the outcome of battle. Their effort took the form of an emphasis on morale, a determination to employ maneuver, and a pursuit of technical superiority in the application of firepower. Through a combination of these factors the British gradually built up the advantages necessary for ending the stalemate on the western front.

The selection of morale as one area in which to pursue a superiority is not surprising, since the knowledge of morale's primacy as a factor in shaping the efficiency of soldiers and its part in determining battlefield success are among the most ancient features of the conduct of war.

However, the British army did not perceive the contest for superior morale in the same way as theorists such as the Frenchman Colonel de Grandmaison did. Grandmaison wrote that, "it is more important to develop a conquering state of mind than to cavil about tactics."[81] Instead of massed, unreasoning assaults, Britain had trained its prewar regulars in fire and movement tactics and in the use of ground. The British goal was not to enable the infantry to advance into the face of withering defensive fire, as the French and Germans had attempted in 1914, but rather to obtain a reduction in the enemy's firepower that would allow the attackers to move forward in relative safety.[82]

While the Edwardian interest in Social Darwinism might have been an influence, it would be an exaggeration to identify this movement as a major factor in the decision to select morale as an element for superiority competition. Rather, the emphasis on morale must be interpreted within the broader parameters of the British conception of combat. By reducing the morale of the enemy's troops the British hoped to decrease their foe's ability to control the battlefield through the accurate and determined employment of their weapons. Broken or morally inferior troops lack the dedication to stand and fight and are more likely to surrender, retreat, or resign themselves to their own defeat; the result of the attainment of superior morale by the attacker is the degradation of the defender's firepower and fighting efficiency and a commensurate increase in the offensive strength of attacking troops. The British targeting of morale did indeed have an effect on the German army's defensive capability, and it helps to account for Germany's collapse in mid-1918.

The British pursuit of a superiority advantage in morale found expression in what Haig termed the "wearing down" process. While one aspect of this effort was the infliction of casualties and the consequent reduction of the enemy's manpower resources, another equally important element was a deliberate and concerted attack upon the enemy soldier's morale. Historians, however, have frequently dismissed Haig's wearing down plans as merely attritional. This is an unfortunate label as it does not fully appreciate the complexity of his objectives. Interpreted simply, British plans were indeed attritional because general headquarters (GHQ) perceived the struggle as a contest between two titans, and the winner would be the one left standing. Haig's "Back to the War Order of the Day" of 11 April 1918 certainly supports such a conclusion: "Many amongst us are now tired, to those I would say that victory will belong to the side which holds out the longest."[83] However, there was more to Haig's ideas than simply a preference for attrition. The wearing down process was a key component in the phases of battle and it played an important part in the struggle for fire supremacy. At a meeting with his staff in January 1916, Haig outlined his preliminary plans for the Somme which illustrate the connection between the wearing down of the enemy and the idea of superiority. He ordered:

1. Employ sufficient force to wear down the enemy and cause him to use up his reserves.
2. Then, and not till then, throw in a mass of troops (at some point where the enemy shows himself to be weak) to break through and win victory.[84]

The key is to recognize the relationship that existed between the weakening of the enemy and the attainment of a superiority that the British could exploit. The pinpointing of the onset of this transition was an extremely difficult task, requiring a precise assessment not only of one's own army but, more important, of the condition of the enemy's forces as well. The ability of World War I intelligence officers to make such estimates accurately were limited, and the exaggerated reports of the decline of the enemy partially accounts for Haig's misplaced enthusiasm during the first few days of the battles of the Somme and Arras, as well as on other occasions. However, wearing down remained an integral part of the British offensive mentality and their persistency contributed to the collapse of the enemy in 1918.

Gas played a critical role in the wearing down process, both as a method of inflicting casualties and as a means of increasing the misery of war and thereby contributing to the lowering of the enemy's morale. The British targeted German morale through the use of chemical agents in harassment missions and exhaustion bombardments. During the night British gunners fired gas on the trenches and on the tracks over which the enemy's work parties, reliefs, and supplies moved. Cutting off the enemy from their lines of communication or forcing enemy soldiers to perform their duties while wearing their masks were prime objectives of the artillery. The British correctly deduced that the isolation and extra hardship these tactics caused would have a detrimental effect upon the German soldier's morale.

Another debilitating tactic of the artillery was the use of bombardment programs that maintained gas clouds on enemy positions for prolonged periods. The British knew, as the German soldiers did, that the German respirator was inferior to the British equivalent and that it could keep out the dangerous vapors for only a relatively short period of time (approximately four hours). In this environment the British placed the German soldier in the position of dependency on his respirator though he would not have known if its protective capacity would outlast the toxicity of the environment. The heavier-than-air characteristic of gas also meant that it would seep down into the enemy's dugouts. These fortifications were all but invulnerable to high explosives but, despite the use of gas screens, could become death traps in the face of gas. Finally, the British employed gas in ways that exploited weaknesses in the German anti-gas appliances. As the British gained ascendancy in the chemical war, the effect of these methods upon the enemy's morale became more pronounced and is reflected in the enemy's increasingly strident orders and growing concern regarding the protection of their troops from gas.

The second area in which the British focused on achieving a superiority was that of maneuver. As with morale, the combat enhancement effect of falling upon an opponent's flank or rear was well understood by the combatants of World War I. However, freedom of maneuver was of particularly critical importance for the British, for they believed that only by directing the assault upon the enemy's weak point and following up a successful attack with a pursuit could they obtain a decisive victory. Russell Weigley highlighted this point in *The Age of Battle* when he wrote that "the military commander in quest of decisiveness needs an effective arm of mobile war."[85] While Weigley is referring to the cavalry of an earlier age, his comments are still pertinent for the Great War. Between the Boer War and the outbreak of World War I, the British intensely debated the future role of the cavalry.[86] Although traditionalists existed, most officers—the mounted arm included—accepted the reality that the cavalry could no longer act in the romantic image of the Napoleonic wars and still survive. Opportunities that influenced the course of battle continued to occur, but reformers recognized that the principal roles for the cavalry were reconnaissance and pursuit. It therefore fell to the infantry to provide the necessary shock to expel the enemy from their positions and precipitate a retreat that the cavalry could turn into a rout. By World War I it was the infantry who were responsible for penetrating the enemy's lines, turning their flank, appearing in their rear, and threatening their lines of communication, thereby creating an enormous superiority.[87]

To deprive the infantry of the power to maneuver was to rob them of the means to achieve a decisive victory. Yet when the western front settled down into its stalemate phase this was precisely what happened. However, it was not the continuous trench lines that created the stagnation, but rather the firepower that swept the approaches to the defender's positions. Although during the war the German army reinterpreted its conception of defense, each new creation relied on the use of firepower as the core of its defensive doctrine. For the first part of the war the Germans had denied the attacker's penetrative power by massing troops in the front lines who would use their personal weapons to challenge any attempt to assault their position. In 1917 the Germans revised their tactics, in time to thwart the Nivelle offensive, to a reliance on a defense-in-depth. In a defense-in-depth arrangement the defender became stronger as the attacker penetrated further into their lines. Though the Germans held their front line lightly, they supported it with interlocking zones of fire from concrete pill-boxes that gradually absorbed the assault's force until it ground to a halt. Despite the appearance of greater permeability, in reality the firepower advantage continued to create a solid barrier to the infantry's ability to advance and only late in the war did the British gain the ability to maneuver against these defenses.

Chemical agents also played a role in the army's quest to gain a superiority in maneuver, and the British devised a number of tactics that featured gas in this aspect of the conflict. The British frequently discharged gas against enemy strong points and battery positions so as to silence their defensive fire. As early as the battle of Messines, in June 1917, the British had gained a high degree of skill at this task, and by the war's final months they could virtually guarantee the silence of the German defenders. In battles such as Hamel and Amiens gas featured heavily in the British plans, and its use helps explain the infantry's success at crossing no man's land, at penetrating the German defenses, and at reaching their objectives. The British also used gas to deny the enemy its ability to maneuver. Beginning in 1917, gas troops established chemical barriers across likely German approach routes after an attack. These barriers helped to break up enemy formations before they could begin a counterattack and provided the British infantry with the time they needed to dig in and consolidate their new positions.

The key to unlocking the western front, and to providing the infantry with the means to maneuver, was found within the third area in which the British intended to obtain an advantage: the pursuit of technical superiority in the application of firepower. Whereas the defender's use of firepower was responsible for preventing the attacker from attaining the conditions necessary for a decisive victory, it was also true that the attacker could negate the advantages that modern weapons gave the defender by employing firepower to advance its own interests. Over the course of the war the British use of offensive firepower evolved from using firepower to destroy the enemy to suppressing the enemy's weapons and finally to neutralizing the enemy's defensive fire capability. Once the British developed the sophistication necessary to accomplish the latter task they consequently also gained the ability to deny the defender its advantages. At that point the British had achieved the superiority in firepower that their conception of war required for the waging of the decisive battle.

The British, however, needed to counter German firepower at every level in order to create a battlefield upon which the infantry could survive. The wearing down process contributed to this state, as spiritually weakened defenders were less able to fire their weapons efficiently and determinedly. However, due to the high rate of fire of modern rifles, machine guns, and artillery, and because of the dense concentration of weapons, if only a mere handful of defenders remained combat capable they could still repulse an assault. Therefore the British needed to develop additional techniques and technologies that they could employ to eliminate the defender's firepower from battle altogether.

These advances can be briefly summarized here. The British employment of the creeping barrage, behind which the infantry advanced, was aimed at preventing the enemy from manning the parapet and using their small arms to fire upon the advancing troops. With a similar goal in mind they used tanks to destroy enemy machine gun nests that had survived the attack's preparations. The British also employed smoke to screen their assaults from interdicting fire from the flanks of the attack zone, and discharged gas to force the enemy to don their masks, thereby impeding the defender's ability to fire their weapons.

However, while all these features were important, the most powerful source of the defender's firepower was their artillery, whose shells could rain down upon assaulting infantry and crush an attack. Until the Somme the British had attempted to use counter-battery fire to physically destroy the enemy's batteries. The tragedy of the first day of the battle revealed the failure of that goal and led to a revolution in both the British application of the counter-battery mission and in the means to control the defender's firepower. It is often assumed that the Germans were the pioneers in this art of war, especially as a result of the work of their most famous gunner—and postwar self-promoter—Col. Georg

Bruchmüller. Though Bruchmüller was undoubtedly a skilled practitioner, there was no shortage of excellent gunners in the British army; indeed, while the British were sometimes behind the Germans in the evolution of artillery tactics, in other areas they were actually well ahead. Scholars such as David T. Zabecki in *Steel Wind* have exaggerated the accomplishments of Bruchmüller.[88] Zabecki goes so far as to praise him for forcing the German army to adopt calibration and meteorological reporting, but fails to observe that the British had incorporated both of these adaptations more than a year earlier. Nor does Zabecki note the superior British achievements in sound ranging and flash spotting. Furthermore, the Germans failed to implement the most critical artillery advancement of the war, the development of the counter-battery staff office (cbso). The cbso was a corps-level operations center responsible for the integration of artillery intelligence with gunnery programs. Through the efforts of the center, the British developed the means to locate enemy batteries with a high degree of accuracy, and then neutralize them whenever necessary. Finally, the British were at the cutting edge of developing the technique of predicted fire, which they demonstrated to such effect at the attack at Cambrai.

The British adaptation to chemical warfare also reflected their desire to achieve technical superiority in the application of firepower. The most effective shell in counter-battery fire was gas, as it had the greatest ability of any munition to almost immediately silence a firing battery. The British also used devices such as the Livens projector to deliver highly concentrated clouds of lethal agents onto enemy strong points and other installations that were impervious to different forms of fire. Finally, they developed new tactics and dispersal systems that progressively extended the reach of gas deeper into the enemy's defensive zone, thereby increasing their ability to counter the defender's employment of firepower.

The result of these achievements was a revolution in the application of firepower. Before the war, theorists had feared that modern weapons would prevent the attainment of victory. During the course of the war the British realized that while modern weapons had the ability to prevent the attainment of decisive battle, firepower also had the ability, when used in a proper offensive manner, to advance the interests of the attacker. The problem facing the British, therefore, was the need to adapt their technical application of firepower so that when attacking they derived the advantages latent to firepower in support of offensive objectives. Technological and tactical advances in the use of firepower thus became a key component of the British method of waging war.

It remains necessary to refine the concept of superiority further in order to fully explain how its attributes affected British decision making on the western front.

Despite one side's attempt to achieve superiority, it is not axiomatic that the other side will try to counter its opponent's efforts. Furthermore, a response to a superiority challenge need not be reflective to succeed. In fact, it is more likely that the countering mechanism will be only indirectly related to the enemy's area of advantage. The German failure to detect, for nearly two years, the enormous tunneling activities under Messines Ridge allowed the British to achieve a major superiority imbalance that resulted in Britain's dramatic and relatively cheap victory in June 1917. Had the Germans discovered the tunnels, they could have closed the superiority gap there and averted the disaster by exploding camouflets, by shelling the enemy's densely packed trenches as their troops prepared for the assault, or by simply withdrawing their garrison on the eve of the attack. Each of these possible responses caused the British considerable anxiety; they initially feared that the German gas shelling of 3rd Australian Division positions, which resulted in over 1,000 casualties, was a sign that the enemy had caught on and that the battle was going to fail.[89] GHQ's concern demonstrates the transitory nature of superiority: once the enemy has acted to equalize the relationship the advantage is lost. The German submarine campaign against the British Isles is an example of this temporary advantage, and of the nonreflective nature of a successful response. Initially the British dedicated their resources to offensive techniques such as hunter-killer patrols of antisubmarine vessels. However, the ability of a surface vessel to locate and destroy a submarine was at best ineffective prior to the invention of underwater detection equipment, and Britain continued to incur severe merchantmen losses. When the British switched their emphasis to protecting shipping by introducing the convoy system they succeeded in negating the submarines' destruction advantage and won the battle for the western approaches.

The British also understood that the process of gaining superiority was a gradual one. A previous British success could lower the enemy's resistance and thereby make a positive contribution to a future contest. After the commencement of Arras, Robertson congratulated Haig on the battle's prosperous beginning (because its failure was not yet apparent). Robertson went on to confess that he had been afraid that the effects of the Somme might have worn off. He concluded, however, that the large numbers of prisoners indicated that the British possessed an advantage in morale over the enemy.[90] A few days later Robertson again commented on the incremental nature of superiority. He wrote optimistically: "Apart from the improvement in general fighting efficiency, tactics, administration, and training it seems to me that your success is largely due to superiority in morale and in artillery. As regards morale you are now reaping the fruits of the hard fighting on the Somme while as to artillery you have now not only practically unlimited ammunition but a far larger number of guns than you had last year."[91]

Though the British had failed to win a decisive victory during the Somme, Robertson believed that the campaign had still made a contribution to the gradual gaining of a superiority advantage. Although success would prove elusive at Arras, and for the rest of 1917 as well, Robertson's assertion was fundamentally correct as the cumulative effect of the British method of waging war gradually destroyed the integrity of the German army.

British officers also recognized that the relative strength of two forces did not remain constant. One had to press one's opportunities while they existed, as any advantage could evaporate. The FSR intoned: "Time is an essential consideration in deciding whether an opportunity is favourable or not for the decisive action. A commander who has gained a strategical advantage may have to act at once in order to prevent the enemy [from] bringing about conditions more favourable to himself."[92]

Haig's comments on the Somme suggest the unstable nature of superiority. In August he wrote enthusiastically to the chief of the imperial general staff that little doubt existed that the enemy was in a weakened state and that the "maintenance of a steady offensive pressure on the enemy's main fronts will result in his complete overthrow." His comments concluded with the opinion that the British must continue to pursue the attack well into autumn.[93] While asking for support from the commander of the French forces, Gen. Joseph Joffre, Haig pointed to the great losses and falling morale of the enemy and expressed his belief that the time was approaching when a determined effort might cause the enemy to collapse.[94] In September the troops received an order announcing that "For the last two and a half months we have been gradually wearing down the enemy. His morale is shaken, he has few (if any) reserves available, and there is every probability that a combined and determined effort will result in a decisive victory."[95] Two months later the tone changed and a dejected Haig reported that "the moment for decisive action was rapidly passing away."[96]

Haig's optimism would reappear during the war's final campaigns. Writing to the commanders of his five armies on August 22, he noted that the enemy's ability to defend itself after its recent defeats had diminished. The German troops were disorganized and worn out. Haig concluded that the British should keep up the pressure and increase the scope of their attacks. He told his army commanders to assign distant objectives to their units and to instruct their subordinates to press on without worrying about maintaining contact with adjacent units.[97] Haig rightly perceived that the enemy was on its last legs, and the following day he wrote again to his army commanders and suggested that they reinforce their successes and press the enemy relentlessly. Anticipating the pursuit phase, Haig went on to say that advances should be directed at points of strategic importance such as roads and rail centers. He believed their capture and the effect upon the enemy's line of communication would further demoralize the Germans and increase the superiority of the British.[98]

The British understood that they had to deny the Germans any opportunity to restore the equilibrium between the combatants and thereby negate Britain's superiority. Commenting on the 100 Day Campaign, Maj. Gen. Archibald Montgomery theorized that the Germans could have prevented their collapse if they had succeeded in withdrawing behind a defensive line they could have held for the winter. Such a withdrawal would have given them time to reorganize and close the superiority gap that the British enjoyed. However, he believed that Haig and Foch were determined to prevent the Germans from consolidating, and the Allies continued to attack relentlessly.[99]

The British approached the Great War with a well-thought-out and institutionally accepted concept of how to wage war. The codifying of the phases of battle, the recognition of the need to overcome the enemy's firepower advantages, and a commitment to pursuing the stated goal of achieving superiority before the decisive attack all indicate an institutional desire to think through the problems of modern war. Despite this, however, the conditions of the western front presented huge impediments to victory. The defender's ability to use firepower to overwhelm the attacker's offensive power locked war into a cycle of stalemate. Nevertheless, the British rejected the limitations of the situation and instead of accepting it as a new and ongoing reality of war continued to maintain that it was an aberration, an unnatural condition that they could overcome through adaptation. The opinions of Robertson and Haig on the definition of the "normal" nature of war gained codification with the publication of *Notes for Infantry Officers on Trench Warfare* in 1916. Intended as a training manual on how to conduct trench warfare, its first paragraphs contained the following disclaimer: "It must, nevertheless, be clearly understood that trench fighting is only a phase of operations, and that instruction in their subject, essential as it is, is only one branch of the training of troops. To gain a decisive success, the enemy must be driven out of his defenses and his armies crushed in the open. The aim of trench fighting is, therefore, to create a favorable situation for field operations, which the troops must be capable of turning to account."[100] While Haig correctly observed that the war was one continuous struggle, it was not a struggle without direction. Instead, the British sought the means by which they could create the necessary favorable superiority relationship that would restore decisiveness to battle and bring victory.

The central theme guiding their efforts to achieve decisiveness was the emphasis upon morale, maneuver, and firepower application. British operations, tactics, inventions, and technical improvements all contributed to reversing the defender's ability to use firepower to maintain the stalemate of the western front. During most of the war it was the inability of the attacker to master the defender's firepower that allowed the stalemate to continue. The British army's gradual buildup of a favorable superiority over the German army created the imbalance in the offense/defense power struggle that was necessary for the defeat of the enemy.

The British adaptation to chemical warfare occurred within the parameters of their desire to secure an advantage in morale, maneuver, and firepower application. The practical evolution of gas tactics occurred within the theoretical construct that underpinned the British conception of battle and to which they remained loyal throughout the entire war.

CHAPTER 2

Introduction and Reaction

As regards the gas question. I cannot see where the difficulty lies in deciding! . . . with the *very extensive* gas and smoke arrangements which have been prepared, decisive results are almost certain to be obtained. – Douglas Haig

The Arrival of Gas

In the early evening of 22 April 1915, at the Battle of 2nd Ypres, a new age in warfare made its debut.[1] At 5:00 P.M. German pioneers opened the valves on their cylinders and released deadly chlorine gas into the atmosphere. For five minutes the concentrated gas poured forth, spread into a cloud of yellowish green haze, and drifted toward the 87th Territorial and 45th Algerian Divisions (the French troops that guarded the northern face of the Ypres Salient). The French soldiers, engulfed by asphyxiating vapor, broke and ran, some not stopping for over five miles. The men of the 1st Canadian Division, stationed to the right of the French, quickly surmised that something was up. The increase in the enemy's bombardment and the rattle of musketry suggested a German attack, but it was the fleeing Algerians, ashen purple of face, gasping for breath, and reeking of chlorine, that signaled something unusual and terrifying had occurred.[2]

The Allied position rapidly became grave. The Germans had blasted a hole in the Allied lines and their advance threatened to trap the defenders of the salient. The Germans had seemingly restored a mobility that had not been seen since the war's opening campaign. The Allied position was saved by only the narrowest of margins. The Canadians extended and echeloned their left to the southwest, while local reserves moved up to close the gap created by the French rout. The Germans had not anticipated the scale of the superiority created by their innovation. They failed to allocate strategic reserves for the attack, and although there would be further discharges of gas and additional assaults they had spent the impetus of the offensive. 2nd Ypres continued until nearly the end of May, as the Germans tried to renew their drive and the Allies attempted to regain lost ground, but combat had once again become a positional struggle. The Germans had demonstrated the ability to restore the traditional balance between the offense and the defense, but as soon as their troops overreached the protection of the gas, the enemy's fire brought them to a halt and re-exerted the dominance of the defender.[3]

The French cracked not only because they did not have any means of defense against the gas but also because the psychological nature of chemical warfare was extremely debilitating, particularly against a surprised opponent. The Canadian official historian commented that gas increased the level of incalculability in warfare. Missiles followed a consistent and predictable trajectory, whereas gas was a weapon of variable speed, intensity, and range. Furthermore, when a soldier perceived the arrival of a missile he could escape its danger by seeking the cover of the trench. Gas, however, followed him down into the previously safe hollows and attacked by striking at a basic physiological imperative: breathing. The poison guaranteed a slow choking death to anyone who inhaled the deadly vapors.[4]

A number of British soldiers left memoirs of their initial exposure to this new form of warfare. Gas engulfed Lieut. V. F. S. Hawkins and his battalion of Lancaster Fusiliers on 2 May 1915. He wrote: "I don't know how long this asphyxiating horror went on. While it lasted it was practically impossible to breathe. Men were going down all about and struggling for air as if they were drowning, at the bottom of our so-called trench."[5] Sgt. Elmer W. Cotton recorded a similar impression on 24 May as he went into battle with the Northumberland Fusiliers. Moving forward he passed a dressing station and "propped up against a wall were a dozen men—all gassed—their colour was black, green & blue, tongues hanging out & eyes staring—one or two were dead and others beyond human aid, some were coughing up green froth from their lungs. As we advanced we passed many more gassed men lying in the ditches and gutterways."[6] Exposed to gas himself, Cotton had to fall out and was left in a trench with some other gassed men, the wounded, and the dead. However, he recovered and left a moving portrayal of what it was like to watch someone die from gas. It was, he said, a "fiendish death to die."[7]

Response

The reaction of the British to the events of 22 April was almost immediate. Recommendations on how to defeat chlorine poured into the salient almost as quickly as reinforcements did. The Oxford chemist John Scott Haldane designed the Black Veil respirator from materials used to manufacture women's veils, while millions of cotton waste pads hastily assembled by volunteers in Britain soon arrived. The pads, used to cover one's mouth and made by civilians across England from a pattern published in the *Daily Mail*, actually proved quite dangerous. When dry they did nothing to prevent the passage of chlorine, and when moistened they became an impermeable barrier to air. The army soon ordered them replaced. Local officers also seized the initiative and found their own solutions. Lieut. Col. L. J. Barley, a future chemical warfare officer, designed a respirator and had 80,000 manufactured in local French villages for his III Corps after dispatching couriers to Paris to buy raw materials and goggles. Scientists identified the gas as chlorine, and the War Office quickly issued soldiers with bottles of hyposulphite solution which, when applied to the respirator, acted as a neutralizing agent. In May another officer, Maj. Cluny McPherson of the Newfoundland Medical Corps, devised a helmet consisting of a flannel bag with celluloid window, impregnated with glycerine, hyposulphite, and bicarbonate of soda. It provided effective protection and proved superior to pads. The War Office authorized mass production of McPherson's helmet, the first in a series of helmets that were superseded only by the small box respirator in the summer of 1916.[8]

Simultaneously with these physical improvisations the British underwent a psychological adjustment. The initial response was not surprising. British soldiers and civilians castigated the enemy for its violation of the rules of war as defined by the Hague Convention, of which Germany was a signatory.[9] The British commander-in-chief, Gen. John French, wrote in an address to the 28th Division that the Germans "had recourse to the mean and dastardly practice, hitherto unheard of in civilized warfare, namely the use of asphyxiating gases," while Robertson described the German use of gas as the employment of an illegitimate means of warfare.[10] Kitchener believed that the employment of gas showed "to what depths of infamy our enemies will go, in order to supplement their want of courage in facing our troops."[11] Sir Henry Rawlinson expected his men to refuse to take prisoners as revenge for this latest act of villainy by the enemy.[12] For others the response was a lowering of the enemy's worth as an opponent. A junior officer in the 6th Duke of Wellington's Regiment concluded that "we now know that they must be destroyed like the spawn of some venomous insect and not just kindly [put] to sleep like a dog which we loved before it went mad."[13]

General French wrote to London on 23 April demanding retaliation.

He proposed to the War Office "that immediate steps be taken to supply similar means of most effective kind for the use by our troops." Kitchener replied tentatively, "before we fall to the level of the degraded Germans, I must submit the matter to the government."[14] However, French did not have to wait long, as the cabinet shortly endorsed retaliation and ordered the specialists to prepare a response, while a report issued in June called for the production of a lethal gas.[15] Robertson, meanwhile, announced the appointment of Maj. Charles H. Foulkes, R.E. (Royal Engineers) to coordinate the chemical offensive, and the War Office sent a letter to universities and public schools soliciting officers and men who had educational backgrounds in chemistry. These men were soon to become the nucleus of the Special Brigade, the Royal Engineers chemical warfare unit.[16] Robertson also wrote to Maj. Gen. S. von Donop, the master-general of the ordnance, that he expected gas to develop into a big thing and that it might become the army's fifth arm.[17] In late June the War Office authorized the creation of the first two companies dedicated to chemical warfare. Designated Special Companies, R.E., the two companies would be joined by a third in July and a fourth in early September.[18] That the British should quickly move beyond their initial reaction of moral outrage is not surprising—they could hardly let German superiority in chemical warfare remain unchallenged. The support of the troops demanded a response; left unattended British morale would inevitably decline if the Germans exploited their chemical advantage.

While Foulkes settled in to provide chemical warfare with a sound and proper basis, the army entered a short-lived period termed "the annoyers" phase, during which the War Office enthusiastically dispatched to France any substance that might have the slightest deleterious affect upon the enemy. The British filled grenades with small quantities of sulphur chloride, bromine, calcium arsenide, and even capsicine, an extract of hot peppers. Within a few days they had designed and filled 10,000 glass bulbs with similar compounds and some contained even more exotic compounds such as veratrin (a sneezing agent). By 20 June they had also shipped to France 26,000 one-pound tins of either bisulphide of carbon or sulphur dioxide, with a pinch of capsicine added to both. The artillery investigated the use of calcium arsenide, hydrocyanic jelly, phosphorus, and capsicine, and in mid-May the first ordnance had arrived in France. By August they had started to put into shells SK, a lachrymatory substance that would become one of the army's primary chemical warfare agents. All of these amateurish efforts, however, proved almost comically futile and did not even minimally approach the efficiency of the German chlorine. French reported that the gas hand bombs were innocuous and far less effective than grenades filled with high explosives. Furthermore, the tins had defective soldering so that all the gas had leaked out before the troops could employ them. Attempts to use these weapons during the struggles for Festubert and Aubers Ridge were total failures and only generated bitter complaints from the infantry. By the end of June, French had had enough and formally requested the War Office to halt the production of these materials.[19]

While the annoyers apparently had no affect on the enemy, the phase of the war when they were used did establish the future basis of chemical warfare. The British envisaged a three-tiered response: the Royal Engineers would man the Special Brigade and be responsible for the release of, at first, cylinder clouds and later projector drums, mortar bombs, and flame throwers; the artillery would employ gas-filled shells; and the army would develop personal chemical weapons, in the form of grenades, for the infantry. At first the engineers dominated, but as the British resolved the production and technical problems associated with shell gases, the artillery emerged as the most important arm of chemical warfare. Britain had clearly taken up the chemical gauntlet thrown down by Germany, and throughout the war British chemists fought hard to catch up to, and eventually surpass, their German competitors.

The British army's first serious attempt to use gas was its attack at Loos in late September 1915, though their reading of the lessons of 2nd Ypres and their experiences at the battles of Neuve Chapelle through Givenchy shaped their understanding of the efficacy of gas and its role in their plans for Loos.

The most important and perhaps most obvious conclusion derived from 2nd Ypres was the image of those poor Algerians and Territorials fleeing from the cloud of chlorine. Panic struck a highly sensitive nerve within the British hierarchy because of its fundamental association with morale. Victory required the destruction of Germany's ability to resist, and the most efficient means of achieving that objective was to cause the enemy to rout so that British cavalry and other advancing troops could destroy them in the pursuit. Inducing panic also suggested a means to overcome the defender's firepower, cut through their trenches, and break into the enemy's rear, while at the same time returning mobility to its proper role in warfare.

Another German adaptation reinforced the suggestion that novel or terrifying weapons could rapidly break down the defender's resistance and help the attacker gain its objectives. During the night of 29 July 1915 near Hooge, some pickets of the King's Royal Rifles noticed parties of enemy troops carrying heavy, bulky objects, working their way into no man's land. Suddenly they detected a loud hiss of escaping air and the smell of petroleum. Long fierce jets of flame swept over the trench and men fell back with burned hands and faces and their clothes on fire. This new horror, for which there seemed to be no defense, utterly disorganized the British and caused them to flee as the enemy rushed the trench. Although the defenders had sustained few casualties they had broken and abandoned their position. Upon hearing of the incident from Robertson, Haig concluded that the weapon's value lay largely in its effect on morale, its ability to terrify.[20]

British documents published in the aftermath of 2nd Ypres clearly highlighted panic as one of the potential effects of gas. A memorandum from general headquarters outlining what to do if caught in a chemical attack cautioned that gas was only effective in the offense when it resulted in panic among the defenders, and that good training and anti-gas discipline would eliminate the tendency to rout. The memorandum directed troops in the affected areas to seek higher ground or move back to the support line, but warned that the adjustment should not be so great as to leave the path of the gas uncovered by fire power.[21] Another memorandum noted that if British soldiers followed the recommendations regarding anti-gas drill, respirators, and wind measurements, they would be able to overcome the psychological threat of gas and remain in their positions unharmed. Finally, it warned: "The natural inclination on meeting poison gas is to run away from it; to do so is fatal. The gas travels as fast as a man can run, and he remains in the cloud instead of it passing over him. Moreover, when running the man finds he cannot breathe through the pad and so removes it, with fatal results."[22]

To panic and run meant death, if not physically then certainly in essence, since a broken soldier had no military value. *Defensive Measures Against Gas* acknowledged this point. It stressed an officer's responsibility to inspire his men's confidence in their ability to resist a gas attack. It declared that if the men understood the nature of the advancing cloud and if their training enabled them to immediately protect themselves, then the "moral effect of the gas becomes very small."[23] The nature of the struggle for superiority in the British response to gas is clear: they recognized that it was essential to provide the troops not only with physical protection from the vapors but also with a psychological buffer from any potential adverse affects to morale.

The dramatic German advance at the beginning of 2nd Ypres also affected the British interpretation of that battle and their hopes for Loos. While it was in actuality a gain of only a few miles, it was nonetheless the most successful movement forward in France, by either side, since the start of trench warfare. After the war Montgomery commented that the Germans had succeeded in pushing the French back so far that they had made the Canadians' position untenable, forcing the Canadians to either retire or face encirclement. He also noted that a subsequent and heavier German gas attack along Bellewaarde Ridge on the east side of the salient on 24 May pierced the front in 4th Division's sector, forcing another withdrawal. Gas had achieved two of the forms of superiority that the British most favored: it altered the relative relationship of morale and it restored maneuver to the battlefield. Against both the Canadians and the 4th Division gas breached the front, opened flanks, panicked defenders, and established the preconditions that the British believed essential for decisive victory.[24]

The Experience of 1915

The British keenly recognized gas's potential for creating superiority in morale and maneuver, but an additional factor in their decision to let gas dominate the plans for Loos was the lessons they learned from their attacks at Neuve Chapelle, Festubert, Givenchy, and Aubers Ridge from March to June 1915. By the standards of the time and of the British army, each of these battles was a major offensive, and each sought to alter the strategic situation on the western front sufficiently, it was hoped, to gain a decisive advantage for Britain and France and bring the war to an early conclusion. Each battle failed to achieve its objective, and thereby prodded the British toward the use of gas in circumstances where men, guns, and shells had failed.

French's plan for First Army's attack on 10 March 1915 was to seize the town of Neuve Chapelle and Aubers Ridge, which lay just to the east, then push through the cavalry to roll up the German flanks, press into the enemy's rear, and threaten their communication lines to Lille, upon which the Germans depended for supplies. The ultimate objective was nothing less than the general collapse of the German line as British horsemen wrought havoc in the enemy's administrative and support zones.[25] Haig, who was then the commander of First Army, planned to surprise the enemy with a brief 35-minute bombardment, lasting only long enough to blast holes in the wire and suppress the enemy's batteries. The British planned to then advance quickly onto Aubers Ridge in one big push, and, once the situation became fluid, exploit the success with mounted troops. Haig outlined his ideas at a conference on 3 March: "The advance to be made is not a minor operation. It must be understood that we are embarking on a serious offensive movement with the object of breaking the German line . . . Very likely an operation of considerable magnitude may result."[26]

The attack initially went quite well as the 8th and Meerut Divisions captured Neuve Chapelle; Haig then requested that French move forward at least one cavalry brigade from the general reserve to provide mobile support. The British failed to press boldly forward, however, and command control problems resulted in a lengthy pause. The delay gave the Germans nearly five hours to reestablish their defense, strengthen their second line, and move up local reserves. When the British renewed their attack it was nearly dark and they faced a fully alert opponent that was able to repulse the attempt. Haig continued the battle for two more days, but Aubers Ridge and the open country beyond remained an impossible goal; the attack had spent itself and the growing German strength made further efforts futile.

While the British had occupied Neuve Chapelle and captured 4,000 yards of enemy line, the troops had only penetrated to a maximum depth of 1,200 yards, far short of the open fields beyond. After the battle the British examined their failure and decided that material shortages were the principle reason for the lack of success—not a surprising interpretation since they had already identified the artillery as the key requirement in their plans. In his description of the offensive, Rawlinson commented: "An undertaking such as that which is under consideration depends for its success almost entirely on the correct and efficient employment of the artillery. It is primarily an artillery operation and if the artillery cannot crush and demoralize the enemy's infantry by their fire effect the enterprise will not succeed."[27] French wrote to Kitchener that, "cessation of the forward movement is necessitated today by the fatigue of the troops, and above all, by the want of ammunition."[28] During the three-day battle the British used up one-third of their available gun ordnance, and it would take 17 days to replace the expended rounds at the then-current production rate. French planned to renew the attack on 22 March, but on the 15 March he changed his mind due to the risk of depleting the supply of shells beyond the limits of safety.[29] Rawlinson, the commander of IV Corps, also blamed the insufficiency of ammunition and hoped that for the next attack the guns would be well supplied.[30] Units that attacked on the flanks in support of the main effort also experienced acute shortages of ammunition. I Corps, to the left of Indian Corps, reported that the lack of success was due to a relative shortage of artillery for the attack's frontage, the inability of the guns to clear the wire sufficiently, the absence of surprise, and the enemy's well-sited machine guns. Its commander concluded that without more heavy artillery the objectives were beyond reach.[31]

Rawlinson did propose a temporary expedient that he anticipated would enable the British to continue to attack despite inadequate resources. His idea, which he termed "bite and hold," would overcome enemy superiority through tactical innovation; he hoped to get the Germans to use their resources against themselves. To Clive Wigram, the assistant private secretary and equerry to George V, Rawlinson pointed out that most of the British casualties at Neuve Chapelle had occurred during the second and third days and that instead of continuing the attack the British should have consolidated their newly won positions and met the German counterattack. He expected the enemy to lose twice as many troops as the British when they tried to regain the lost ground. The following month he wrote again and reiterated the two-for-one ratio, suggesting that these tactics could prove to be a useful means for wearing down the enemy.[32] He explained to Kitchener that with proper preparations the British could seize any trench they desired and, upping the ante, also claimed they could inflict four times as many casualties as they lost. Rawlinson thought these tactics would be useful only for the next two months, however, because by then the British would have sufficient stockpiles of shells for a major attack and the Germans would have been weakened by the minor operations. He concluded that "bite and hold" was useful, but only as a means to advance the wearing down of the enemy. It would not result in decisive battle.[33]

After a pause to recover from the German offensive in Flanders, the British returned to the attack on 9 May at Aubers Ridge. French planned to break through the enemy's lines, sever the road linking La Bassée and Lille, and press on to Bauvin to strategically dislocate the German position in the sector while also trapping the defender's troops along the La Bassée Canal. French assigned the attack to First Army, and Haig conceived a two-phase assault. In the first part, I, IV, and Indian Corps were to breach the enemy's lines and by rapid advance gain a footing on the ridge. Having secured their positions the army would then press on to its ultimate objectives along the line Bauvin-Don, a distance of a further five to six miles.[34] First Army would rely on surprise, allowing only a 40-minute bombardment for destroying the enemy's wire and parapet, annihilating their strong points that might contain machine guns, and suppressing the German artillery. The British anticipated success due to the ease with which the artillery had paved the way for the advance at Neuve Chapelle. General headquarters optimistically believed that "by means of careful preparation as regards details and through previous registration of the enemy's trenches by our artillery, it appears that a sector of the enemy's front line defence can be captured with comparatively little loss."[35]

British preparations, however, failed to consider that the Germans had also studied the lessons of Neuve Chapelle and had increased the strength of their fortifications to such an extent that only heavy shells could breach them. The British bombardment began at 5:00 in the evening and the infantry attacked 40 minutes later. The defenders met their charge with devastatingly accurate rifle and machine gun fire as the shelling had failed in its principle task, the neutralization of the enemy's firepower. Furthermore, the guns had blasted few holes into the Germans' six-foot high breastworks and had left the wire largely intact so that it still formed a continuous obstacle. Few attackers made it into the enemy's trenches, most being cut down as they crossed no man's land, and the Germans bloodily repulsed a second attempt in the afternoon. That evening, Haig canceled the attack.[36]

Haig blamed the battle's failure on the quantity and quality of his artillery and ammunition. He complained of defective shells that failed to grip the gun's rifling and were therefore impossible to fire accurately. Haig also noted a report from the general staff that at current rates of consumption his army would soon run out of ammunition. Supplies on hand for 18-pounders, 4.5-inch howitzers, 6-inch howitzers, and 9.2-inch howitzers were good for only three days or less.[37] After the war Edmonds concurred with Haig and identified three reasons for the attack's failure: the strength of the German defenses and the clever concealment of machine guns; the British lack of sufficient shells of large enough caliber to deal with these positions; and the inferior quality of the British munitions so that gunners were unable to either suppress the enemy's batteries or silence the machine guns. In particular, he continued, many fuses were defective and shells failed to burst on striking the ground. Edmonds concluded that the bombardment did no appreciable damage to the enemy, but instead alerted them to the immediacy of the attack which allowed them to man their positions in anticipation.[38]

Yet the question remains as to what effect these deficiencies in artillery had on senior commanders' conception of the parameters of combat on the western front. At a conference at Lieut. Gen. Hubert Gough's I Corps headquarters in the aftermath of the battle, Haig discussed the requirements of breakthrough. He believed the enemy's defenses were so strong and so carefully sited with mutually supporting machine gun fields of fire that a methodical bombardment was necessary. Furthermore, to annihilate the strong points it was essential to have observed shooting by heavy guns. Finally, to destroy the defensive power of the enemy and shatter the nerves of the machine gunners the bombardment had to continue through the night.[39] Maj. Gen. Richard Butler, Haig's deputy chief of staff, formally disseminated these ideas to the First Army's corps commanders and wrote that the next attack would have recourse to more deliberate methods.[40] Rawlinson, in command of IV Corps on the left of the attack, reached a similar conclusion: "the hostile fortifications were such that our artillery preparation, well directed as it was, had not the desired effect on the enemy . . . he [the enemy] was able to man his parapets before the infantry could deliver their assault."[41] Rawlinson continued that the enemy had converted basements into fortified strong points and the artillery could not penetrate these defenses.[42]

These deficiencies, however, did not prevent French, under considerable pressure from Gen. F. Foch, from immediately ordering another attempt in conjunction with an attack by his ally. He hoped to gain the ridge and threaten German communications through Lille, even though his stockpiles of artillery and even small arms ordnance were at critically low levels. French identified the objective of the Battle of Festubert as the general retirement of the enemy. "The idea was to employ the whole force at the First Army commander's disposal and to fight a decisive battle."[43] Once again the task fell to Haig. Instead of a surprise attack following a brief bombardment, Haig intended a more systematic approach. He proposed a multiday barrage of heavy guns against the enemy's strong points, both to destroy the positions and to shake the morale of the defenders. General headquarters sanctioned the new method and wrote: "The Commander-in-Chief [French] considers that you should be prepared to prosecute a deliberate and persistent attack. The enemy should never be given a complete rest either by day or night, but be gradually and relentlessly worn down by exhaustion and loss until his defenses collapse."[44]

The bombardment began on the morning of 13 May and the infantry attacked two days later. General headquarters conceived the battle in greatness but with only limited means, especially compared to German resources. The battle continued spasmodically for 11 days and resulted in over 16,600 British casualties, but realistically First Army never had the strength for the task. Heavy guns and high explosives remained too scarce. Later, the historian of the Highland Division blamed the inadequacy of the artillery preparation for the attack's failure.[45] Stocks of shells reached such low levels that by 26 May the amount of ammunition under First Army's control had been practically exhausted. The number of rounds per caliber, per gun, was 13-pounder, 2; 15-pounder, 4; 18-pounder, 40; 4.5-inch howitzer, 12; 5-inch howitzer, 13; 6-inch howitzer, 27; 6-inch gun, 0; 9.2-inch howitzer, 36; and 15-inch howitzer, 7. The army had not had enough for its defense, let alone a successful attack.[46]

Another effort on 18 June at Givenchy resulted in a repetition of what had already become a distressingly familiar pattern. The attack was again unsuccessful and Haig once more identified the villain as insufficient ammunition. Robertson visited First Army but all he could suggest was for Haig to economize on shells. The attack at Givenchy, however, also clarified one further tactical observation: the inadvisability of attacking on a narrow front. The Germans subjected the British jump-off positions to a concentric ring of fire as batteries from positions on either side of the assault were free to fire upon the attackers. To prevent such an assault the British would have to broaden their frontage so that the enemy's guns in supporting sectors would lack the range to interfere.[47]

In retrospect, the problem the British faced at these battles was considerable. How were they to launch attacks leading to a breakthrough when they had inadequate artillery resources to make the effort? Their principles of the phases of battle required a period of wearing down, during which they would reduce the enemy's effectiveness, both materially and morally, and thereby gain a firepower superiority, as a preliminary step to launching the decisive blow that would lead to the opponent's collapse and their destruction during pursuit. However, the British could not compete against the German advantage in guns and shells, especially in 1915 when these materials were in such short supply. Eventually British industry would produce munitions in abundance, but in the meantime the British needed to explore short-term steps that might correct the tactical imbalance, or even shift it to their favor.

Rawlinson's idea of bite and hold tactics suggested another option but it was scarcely a viable choice. To nibble away at the enemy's lines might slowly regain France, although it was questionable whether the British could have achieved an adequate attrition rate. But even Rawlinson recognized that such a move would not create the opportunity for a decisive battle. Furthermore, the Germans, with their abundance of materials, could certainly "bite" harder and "hold" stronger if the British pushed tactics in that direction. If the Allies were to win in 1915, or at least set the stage for the war's successful conclusion the following year, breakthrough and exploitation remained their only options.[48] During the summer Haig began to consider another means to achieve a local superiority that would enable his army to blast a hole through the German lines and release the cavalry into the enemy's line of communications. Instead of the guns, he turned to gas.

In July, while planning another effort against Aubers Ridge, Haig met with Major Foulkes, his gas adviser, regarding the use of asphyxiating gas. Haig wanted to discharge it on a five-mile front, but Foulkes thought supplies were inadequate for such a scale and advised that it would be better to wait and preserve the element of surprise. Two weeks later Haig saw Robertson and, while reiterating the strength of the enemy's defenses on his front, also claimed that with gas he believed it would be possible to seize the ridge. At a general headquarters conference held shortly thereafter to discuss these plans, he expressed his hope that gas would be available.[49] Rawlinson shared Haig's optimism about gas. On the failure of 10 May he wrote: "If we had some 1000s of gas cylinders we could get a move on them, for our trenches are close enough together to enable us to use gas on quite a wide front but it must be heavy and poisonous the better to reach the deep dug-outs—are you not going to send us out some proper gas?" Rawlinson then complained about the poor quality of the infantry gas bombs that London had provided for the battle of Aubers Ridge. He declared that "the stink bombs that have arrived are perfectly useless. . . . Until we get something effective in this direction we shall not get the Germans out of France.[50]

Haig and Rawlinson would soon have their wish.

The Battle of Loos

The Battle of Loos of 25 September 1915 has engendered a great deal of controversy, both during and since the war. Edmonds describes the attack as the result of France's intractability winning out over extreme British reluctance, a none-too-subtle attempt to lay the blame for the battle on Britain's Gallic ally. Historians also typically have focused their attention on the conflict between French and Haig over the employment of the general reserve, the reserve force's failure to intercede at the critical point on the first day, and its rout on the second day when it attempted to breach the German lines. French lost the argument, resulting in his dismissal and Haig's arrival at general headquarters. Those who fought the battle remember it because it was Britain's first use of gas, an unpleasant experience for those poisoned by their own side. However, all these points obscure the most important aspect of the battle: the use of a new weapon to overwhelm the enemy in an attempt to gain a decisive success.

Edmonds is correct to a point. Loos did evolve from the strategic plans of Joffre and Joffre's hope of ending the war in 1915. Joffre's conception was truly grand, nothing less than the nipping off of the great German salient, a 150-mile bulge of occupied territory that stretched from Verdun in the east to Loos in the west with Noyon at its apex. Joffre envisioned a two-pronged attack. The Second and Fourth French Armies would strike northward from Champagne while the Tenth French and First British Armies would attack eastward from Artois. The objective of all four armies was the dislocation of the enemy's logistical system. The Champagne wing's target was the rail center at Mezieres, while troops from Artois would sever the German supply connections leading to Lille on the Douai Plain. If isolated, the three German armies in the salient would then have no choice but to retreat or face encirclement. Ultimately Joffre hoped that in the ensuing crisis British and French troops could push into Belgium, liberate most of northern France and compel the Germans to retreat beyond the Meuse River, possibly ending the war.

Joffre and other senior French officers strongly pushed their plan on a reluctant British Expeditionary Force throughout the summer. Foch, who would command France's effort in Artois, believed that if the British gained command of the hills around Loos and if his own troops seized Vimy Ridge then they would control the Douai Plain and force the enemy to retreat.[51] At the Boulogne Conference of 20 July and the Frévent Conference of 27 July, French attempted to cool his ally's ardor for the attack, or at least substitute a more limited role for his own army, but Joffre remained committed to the battle and insistent upon the necessity of British assistance. In early August Joffre explained to French that, "the experience of this war constantly shows the importance of attacks on wide fronts as the only means of preventing the enemy from concentrating his artillery fire from both flanks."[52] The following week he reminded French that for the British support to be effective it had to take the form of a large and powerful blow, delivered by all available forces and carried through to the end.[53] Joffre's implications are clear: he required and expected a major effort from his ally.

British hesitancy was present from the beginning and was only overcome, and then not completely, in the final weeks before the battle. Haig, whose First Army would launch the attack, concluded that following such a plan would be extremely hazardous. The terrain featured numerous clusters of villages as well as several fosses (mine pit–heads) and crassiers (large piles of mine waste). The Germans had a strongly wired position and excellent observation posts for their artillery. Haig recognized the great defensive fire power the German position possessed and noted that "the ground above is so swept by gun and machine gun and rifle fire that an advance in the open, except at night, is impossible."[54] In a report to French, Haig attempted to dissuade his associate from the attack. Haig believed that an advance beyond the German front line was improbable because the terrain blocked fire beyond that point. As he explained, "It is believed to be impossible to bring observed artillery fire to bear on the second line, or to cut the wire in front of it, from our present position; and it is doubtful if observation stations could be got for the purpose even if we occupied the German front line trenches."[55]

Butler reported that the supply of shells was insufficient to support an attack in the heavily defended sector.[56] Haig therefore asked Gough and Rawlinson if they thought it possible to carry out the proposed scheme with the ammunition available. If they did not, he wanted them to prepare a plan for what they believed they could do.[57] Haig raised the issue of munitions directly with French at their meeting on 23 June, suggesting that it would be most unwise to wage a battle without several weeks' supply of shells and that general headquarters should postpone an attack if the ammunition was inadequate.[58]

By July Haig was still objecting to the plan; he complained that the resources were insufficient to permit an offensive on a scale large enough to lead to freedom of maneuver. Instead he insisted that only a limited attack was viable.[59] Material shortages certainly still plagued the British Expeditionary Force. The deficiency in heavy guns and shells that was identified during the battles earlier in 1915 still existed.

The War Office had accomplished much, but shell availability for most calibers remained less than half of authorization, and daily production of shells stood at 22,000 (compared to 100,000 for the French and 250,000 for the Germans). British authorities had concluded that a major offensive, if it was to have a reasonable chance of success, required 1,150 heavy guns. In June the entire British Expeditionary Force had only 71 howitzers or guns of 6-inch caliber or greater, and by the battle at Loos the number had risen to only 147.[60]

The British intentions, as conceived in early August, only served to annoy Joffre and push the alliance into a crisis. General headquarters had instructed Haig not to risk British infantry; he was directed to draw up a plan in support of the Tenth French Army that would limit itself to an artillery bombardment. Haig's role was to neutralize the enemy's guns and to hold their reserves on his front. First Army was to advance only if the opportunity presented itself.[61] At a conference with his corps commanders on 13 August, Haig reiterated the same limited operational objectives, along with the possibility of an advance as far as Hill 70 several miles to the east. However, orders received from Butler on the same day authorized a minor assault to secure the German front-line trenches west of Loos and capture the Hohenzollern Redoubt. The seizure of Hulluch, Loos, and Hill 70 was contingent upon French success. As late as 22 August Rawlinson proposed a IV Corps advance in two stages that aimed in the initial drive to seize only the German front line. After a pause of somewhere between seven and ten days, his command would drive on Loos and possibly press on to the enemy's second line. None of these exchanges called for the British to break through.[62]

However, British policy soon changed dramatically. As Rawlinson was submitting his limited objective proposal to Haig, French and Joffre were agreeing that the attack would be "pushed through to the utmost of our power."[63] By the beginning of September, at a First Army conference, Haig declared that, "it is not enough to gain a tactical success," and that "regardless of fatigue and losses all must press forward in a great combined and continuous effort, until the enemy's strength is broken."[64] The "General Principles for the Attack"—the document describing the proposal—outlined the objectives and means in greater detail. It required that: "The enemy is to be beaten on a certain length of front and driven out of it, and must not be allowed time to reform in rear of the captured trenches. For this a violent and continuous action is required. Commanders must bear in mind that, once the enemy's line is broken, it is the intention to follow up such actions as will cause a general retirement of a great part of the enemy's line. Thus the operations will be continued during a considerable period."[65] Haig concluded that the British must strike into the enemy's rear to cut communications and force a retreat.[66]

Edmonds accounts for this sudden reversal by pointing to the tremendous pressure put upon general headquarters by Joffre, Kitchener, and the British government. On the 19 August Kitchener agreed that, as the French commander-in-chief, Joffre had the power to set objectives and dates for operations by the British Expeditionary Force, while the British commander retained the choice of means of execution. The war minister's concession to the French was apparently dictated by the worsening situation on the eastern front. The Russians had suffered a series of defeats during the summer and seemed powerless to prevent the loss of Poland. Compounding the situation was the failure of the Italians to make any progress on the Isonzo, and the British lack of success at Gallipoli. Kitchener and Herbert H. Asquith's cabinet had favored a policy of defense on the western front until 1916, when the new armies would be ready. However, the poor strategic situation and the need to relieve the pressure on Russia forced a political crisis that led to the decision to support Joffre's plan. News of Russia's loss of its last foothold on the Vistula tipped the balance, and Kitchener telegraphed French to confirm his conversation with Joffre and tell him to "take the offensive and act vigorously."[67]

Edmonds's recognition of the political context of the decision making does reflect the pressures the Allies were under that summer. However, the implication that the politicians foisted the offensive on a completely reluctant general headquarters is not nearly as convincing. British field commanders eagerly awaited the arrival of large quantities of deadly gas so that they could not only pay back the Germans for 2nd Ypres but also use it to break through the enemy's lines. Coincidentally, on 22 August—the same day that French conceded to Joffre's demands—20 to 30 senior generals attended the chemical specialists' first gas demonstration at their depot at Helfaut. Foulkes recalled that Haig, Rawlinson, Gough, Pulteney, and Willcocks, among others, left the trial most impressed.[68]

British interest in the offensive employment of gas had accelerated as the summer progressed. The first cloud gas experiment occurred on 4 June near Manchester at the Castner Kellner chemical works, when workers released chlorine from cylinders. Foulkes witnessed it in the company of observers from the War Office and military attachés from

Japan, Russia, Italy, and Belgium, then reported his satisfaction to general headquarters. He thereupon received a free hand in organizing personnel, the nucleus of the Special Brigade. Later that month French drew upon Foulkes's report, and announced his conclusion to the War Office regarding the use of gas against the enemy. His proposals stressed the need for surprise, a wide frontage, a large quantity of gas, and a discharge of at least 30 minutes, as well as the need to supplement cylinder gas with more poisonous materials and a means of deployment (such as shells from guns and mortars, and bombs dropped from aircraft).

French's ideas represented the first theoretical statement of how the British would employ the new weapon, and his outline of principles was later used at Loos.[69] B. B. Cubbitt, at the Ministry of Munitions, replied to French's proposal by stating that they hoped to send over 1,600 cylinders (40 tons of chlorine gas) by 17 July, enough for a half-hour attack on a 5,000-yard front. Cubbitt went on to say that they aimed to produce 150 tons a week by the end of July, enough for two half-hour attacks per week.[70] French next discussed the likelihood that the Germans had issued respirators that could shield against chlorine and that it would be necessary for the British to produce gases from which the enemy did not have protection.[71] Gas was also on the agenda at the Boulogne Conference of 19 June, and topics discussed included the procedures necessary to make a cloud gas attack, the anticipated effectiveness of artillery gas shells, and the need to replace chlorine with a more lethal substance. Foulkes, who attended the conference, presented information about the value of phosgene and recommended its production. Much more deadly than chlorine, phosgene eventually became the principal killing agent of the British army's chemical warfare establishment, and its adoption reflected a British awareness of the transitory nature of any advantage as well as a willingness to raise the stakes in the chemical war.[72]

Gas also figured in the ideas of a widening circle of general headquarters and First Army planners. In late June Rawlinson complained to Maj. Gen. W. P. Braithwaite, of the inability of the artillery's guns, even the 9.2-inch howitzers, to destroy the enemy in their dugouts. He concluded that "what we want is a favourable wind and plenty of good strong chlorine and bromine gas which will sink right down into the deep trenches."[73] In early August, Haig met with Foulkes to discuss the arrangements for the use of gas on his front and then requested that his gas adviser provide an estimate of requirements.[74] Foulkes replied shortly thereafter that First Army needed at least 3,000 cylinders to launch a proper gas assault.[75] Later in the month they met again, and this time Haig requested even more gas, enough for 6,300 yards of front by 15 September. Foulkes believed that there would be no difficulty in providing the materials.[76] Haig and Rawlinson, who were supposed to be planning a limited attack, were in actuality also considering a bigger operation with the aid of gas. Clearly First Army and general headquarters were playing a double game. On the one hand they strongly protested their inability to support Joffre with a major push, while on the other they were quietly ascertaining the availability of gas and considering its use to enable a broad, aggressive thrust at the enemy.

Gas next crept into the official instructions for the battle. Most significant were orders issued to First Army on 7 August by Brig. Gen. Frederick Maurice, the director of military operations. While largely concerned with authorizing Haig to draw up plans for a limited, principally artillery-led attack in support of the assault by Tenth French Army, Maurice also included a curious clause which noted that, "it is anticipated that an ample supply of asphyxiating gas will be available should you think desirable to make use of it on this occasion."[77] Haig shared the hint with his corps commanders at their meeting on 13 August, and Butler, in orders to I and IV Corps, reminded them of its availability and suggested that they consider its employment in their attacks.[78]

The use of gas in what was still intended to be a limited attack is rather strange because its suggestion contradicts the intent of the main part of Maurice's instructions: the reliance upon the artillery to hold the enemy's reserves on the British front. How could gas, released from cylinders in the British front line and carried by the wind over to the German lines, possibly have any effect on the status of the enemy's reserves? The gas would have to travel over several lines of enemy entrenchments, all the while dissipating and gradually losing its toxicity. While chemists had not yet determined the specifics of gas cloud dispersal, the British must have surmised, based upon their experimental discharges of chlorine and experience gained at 2nd Ypres, that gas diminished in strength the further it traveled and that the effects upon the enemy's reserves would be, at best, minimal.

One could still conclude that the British hoped to fulfill their mission of keeping the Germans occupied by using gas as a diversion, dealing the enemy a quick, deadly blow that would cause them to keep their reserves nearby in case the British infantry started to advance. This ar-

gument also fails, however, on two counts. First, general headquarters
had already decided that they wanted their first use of gas to be a surprise and thereby gain the full benefit of the adaptation. The British
certainly understood that to waste the weapon on a mere diversion
would cost them a major advantage if and when they seriously employed gas later on.[79] When they did use it at Loos they went to extraordinary lengths to hide its arrival. Second, the use of gas in support of a
limited attack also violated their intellectual understanding of the
weapon's role. As explained above, the primary lesson they had learned
from 2nd Ypres concerned the ability of poisonous vapors to instill
panic. They themselves had made strenuous efforts to equip and train
their troops with anti-gas devices and to imbue their men with the confidence necessary to resist the terror induced by gas. If the British believed that gas would cause the defenders to break and abandon their
positions, thereby creating the opportunity for an advance, even possibly into the open, there would be no benefit to using it in a supporting
attack for which they anticipated little or no forward movement. The
inclusion of the announcement of the availability of gas in an instruction that otherwise mandated minimal assistance to the French suggests that general headquarters was making a subtle point, one that did
not escape Haig's attention. Joffre and the others may have succeeded in
pressuring the British field leadership to increase British army participation in their great plan, but the British Expeditionary Force was on
the verge of making that same decision on its own.

The speed with which the British incorporated gas into their plans
for Loos offers further evidence that general headquarters had been
considering the gas option for some time. On 22 August Haig received
French's order to support Joffre with a bold breakthrough. The next
day First Army announced that it had "decided that gas will be employed to assist the offensive on the first day of the infantry attack."[80] A
circular by Butler worded the decision more strongly. He reported that
Haig had decided to employ all the resources of gas and smoke at all
points simultaneously along the whole line prior to the first assault of
the infantry.[81] At a conference on the twenty-fourth Haig told his corps
commanders that he aimed "to use gas lavishly and to attack to the utmost of his resources." Both Gough and Rawlinson replied that they
would have their infantry follow the cloud and push on as far as they
could go.[82] The next day, Haig reported to Foulkes at general headquarters that he intended "to make the fullest use of gas and smoke on the
first day of the infantry attack," and requested over 7,000 cylinders of

of chlorine. He explained that he wanted "a gas cloud . . . sufficiently strong and of sufficient duration to make absolutely sure of knocking out the Germans for a depth of 800 yards."[83] Haig explained to his subordinates on 6 September that the conditions of the attack were different from any other. He argued that "in view of the great moral effect which the gas may have on the enemy, it is absolutely essential that the attacks be everywhere pushed forward to gain as much ground as possible in the first advance."[84] Haig reinforced his point by reminding his officers of what Henderson had taught at Camberley: the necessity of cutting the enemy's line of communications and forcing them to retreat.[85] Haig could change gears so quickly only if he had already been considering the subject for some time. The deciding factor was not pressure from outsiders but availability. Once it became clear that sufficient cylinders of chlorine would be ready, there was no longer any rationale to insist upon limited participation in Joffre's plans. Gas would permit the British to bid for decisive victory.

On 18 September general headquarters issued the "General Instructions for Commander of Armies and G. H. Q. Reserve," which identified the objectives of the battle as: (1) breaking the enemy's front, (2) preventing him from reestablishing his line, and (3) defeating decisively his divided forces.[86] The instructions went on to conclude that: "Once the enemy's defenses have been pierced a situation must be created in which maneuver will become possible, and to do this the offensive must be continued with the utmost determination directly to the front in the first instance. . . . The advance must be made in depth so that rapid maneuver may be possible."[87] Thus French had committed the British to a breakthrough attack, but it fell to Haig to deal with the specifics of the offensive. First Army planned to begin the battle with a preliminary bombardment on day x-4 with the intention of cutting the wire along their opponent's entire front, destroying the enemy's observation stations, and shelling the Germans defenses and communications. The bombardment would continue deliberately up to the infantry assault. During days x-2 and x-1, gunners north of the La Bassée Canal would secretly move their pieces to prepared positions to assist the attack south of the waterway. On x day the infantry assault would take place, immediately preceded by a half-hour gas discharge. The infantry would advance as soon as the gas ceased, and smoke bombs would cover their flanks. Significantly, Haig made no provisions to cut the wire around Loos or in front of the enemy's second line as these defenses were either beyond the range of the field artillery or lay in ground that the British could not observe.[88]

Once the decision was made, gas became the central, controlling feature of British planning. Preeminently, Haig hoped to outdo the German success at 2nd Ypres, with the rupture of the enemy's front and a swift advance onto its lines of communication leading to the collapse of the enemy's position on the western front. However, Haig did not plan a lengthy battle for fire supremacy as a prelude to the launching of the decisive blow that would lead to victory. Instead, gas would strike at the enemy's morale and create panic within their ranks. First Army headquarters suggested that "Corps commanders should remind their subordinates of the great moral effect which attended the use of gas by the enemy on the first occasion near Ypres."[89] At a subsequent conference with his corps commanders, Haig identified morale as the heart of the British attack. He went on: "In view of the great moral effect which the gas may have on the enemy, it is absolutely essential that the attack be everywhere continuously fed from the rear and rapidly pushed forward to gain as much ground as possible in the first advance."[90] The 47th Division headquarters instructed its units to avoid communication trenches and other sheltered features, and stressed that "success will depend upon the infantry following up the gas at a rapid pace over the open."[91] Gough added his own suggestion that they discharge the gas at or just before dawn, a time when the enemy would likely be tired and more susceptible to panic. He also recommended that the British discharge the gas along the entire First Army front and not just on the I and IV Corps' positions responsible for the attack. He believed that the preliminary artillery preparations might alert the Germans to the threat and they would probably concentrate their reserves opposite the I and IV Corps' sectors, thereby denuding their defenses along the rest of their line.[92]

The critical issue for British plans was the availability of Red Star, the code name they gave to chlorine cylinder gas. Haig had called for over 7,000 cylinders of chlorine, but production difficulties made getting that amount impossible. Last minute arrivals meant that the British would rush gas to the sector and install cylinders into the front line right up to the eve of the battle. Haig complained on 26 August that the number of cylinders on hand was far less than promised and warned that if the situation did not improve he would have to either postpone the attack or modify his plans.[93] On the twentieth the Ministry of Munitions promised between 4,000 and 5,200 cylinders by 6 September and an additional 1,500 by 11 September, but by 1 September only 3,337 had arrived. By the fifteenth another 900 had arrived but it was clear that Foulkes had to reduce the allocation of cylinders. III Corps would have none and Indian Corps only 160 for their diversionary attacks. The final shipments began to arrive on 17 September. Special trains rushed the gas to the front, and the engineers installed the final lot on the night of the twenty-fourth. In the end, the special companies had only 5,500 cylinders containing 150 tons of chlorine to open, and the British had to rely on a ruse to convince the enemy of the deadliness of their cloud. Foulkes arranged for smoke candles to supplement the chlorine emission.[94] The gas adviser provided his men, who were manning the cylinders in the British front line, with the following instructions:

0 (Zero Hour)	Start the gas and run six cylinders one after the other at full blast until all are exhausted.
0.12 to 0.20	Start the smoke. The smoke is to run concurrently with the gas if the gas is not exhausted at 0.12.
0.20	Start the gas again and run six cylinders one after the other at full blast until all are exhausted.
0.32 to 0.40	Start the smoke again. The smoke is to run concurrently with the gas, if the gas is not exhausted by 0.32.
0.38	Turn all gas off punctually. Thicken up smoke with triple candles. Prepare for assault.
0.40	ASSAULT.[95]

To increase the density of the cloud, the special companies were also ordered to fire smoke bombs from the newly arrived 4-inch Stokes mortar.[96]

Haig realized that technical or meteorological problems might prevent the discharge of the gas and, since it played the key role in the attack, had his corps commanders draw up plans for a modified attack that proceeded without the assistance of chemical agents. There was no denying Haig's keenness to use gas. On 16 September he wrote to Robertson at general headquarters that he believed there was no question regarding the use of gas and that he anticipated decisive results with its assistance. However, if conditions prevented the use of gas he intended to revert to an attack similar to the one planned for the limited offensive he had proposed earlier in the summer and which had so annoyed Joffre. Haig concluded to Robertson that, "under no circumstances should our forthcoming attack be launched without the aid of gas."[97]

In essence, the British had recognized one of the inherent problems of gas when it is released as a cloud: the impossibility of controlling the weapon. Haig understood that cylinder gas was dependent upon the direction and force of the wind, and chemical warfare would soon be responsible for the creation of a front line weather reporting network and the training of company-level gas officers in the art of measuring wind velocity and direction. However, the question remained as to what to do if the wind was nonexistent or if it was blowing from the wrong quarter. Having designed an attack dependent upon gas and linked to two French attacks, Haig faced a quandary: could he still launch his own attack without the weapon upon which his success depended?

Haig corresponded with general headquarters on 13 September, strongly advising the postponement of the attack, deciding on going ahead from day to day if necessary, in order to gain a favorable wind. He also expressed his belief that without gas it would only be possible to secure the enemy's front system of trenches.[98] Three days later he met with Rawlinson and Gough and formally asked which modifications they would have to make if they had to attack without gas. Both corps commanders believed they could only seize part of the enemy's front line.[99] Rawlinson, who had at his disposal only four 9.2-inch and eight 8-inch howitzers, believed that he did not have enough heavy artillery to assure the destruction of the enemy; without gas he could not contemplate attacking on a wide front. He believed it would be necessary to cut back the scale of the offensive.[100] The commander of the 7th Division, Gen. T. Capper, also opposed attacking without gas, particularly since he needed it to neutralize the powerful Hohenzollern Redoubt on the left flank of his attack.[101] Haig then reported to French that without gas he would have to limit his attack to a two-, not six-, division assault and again urged the necessity of postponement if the weather was unfavorable. Alternatively, Haig requested from his superior a three-day window of opportunity, believing it improbable that not one of the days would prove suitable.[102] Having spent all summer mentally moving from a limited to a breakthrough attack, the British had come full circle on the eve of the battle. Their reliance upon gas was complete. The attack depended on the fickleness of the wind to carry their essential weapon to the enemy, and the weather would determine if the British would have their chance at decisive victory.

An important factor in the battle's planning was the British understanding of the enemy's anti-gas arrangements. The British naturally assumed that the Germans had made defensive adjustments after the arrival of chemical warfare, but they needed to know whether the equipment was effective and whether the soldiers were well-trained in its use. Experience from 2nd Ypres showed that subsequent gas discharges, even with the primitive protection then available, were not as successful as the initial discharge. The British, therefore, had a great incentive to determine the efficacy of German anti-gas measures. From late August into September, British intelligence officers interviewed a series of prisoners to determine the status of the enemy's gas protection. A prisoner from the 16th Bavarian Reserve Regiment possessed a makeshift respirator but was ignorant in its use (and in any case it was not proof against asphyxiating gas). An Alsatian prisoner reported that a bullet pierced a bottle of lethal gas in his trench and killed eleven soldiers, an indication of poor anti-gas discipline. An unidentified prisoner possessed a new model respirator that did protect against chlorine, but his captain considered it inferior to the British helmets. Another prisoner believed that he could not rely on his equipment. Others stated that they had received cotton wool respirators and bottles of solution, equipment that was certainly inferior to British standards at the time. Finally, one prisoner reported that the regiment had issued respirators but they were kept with the trench stores and were only to be passed out in case of a gas attack.[103] Based upon information gathered from sources such as these, as well as an examination of the enemy's protective devices, Haig concluded that the enemy had inefficient respirators.[104] Just before the battle Butler reiterated this position and advised "there is reason [to believe] that the Germans have not got an effective smoke helmet and, as we have not yet made use of gas in our attacks, it is likely that its use by us may come as a complete surprise to the enemy."[105]

Even if the enemy had improved its equipment, the British had another reason to believe that their gas might still prove effective. At 2nd Ypres on 1 May the Germans attacked the 15th Infantry Brigade on Hill 60 with chlorine. The troops did have respirators but suffered heavy gas casualties nonetheless. An investigation concluded that the men were not adequately trained in the use of their equipment and recommended that commanders needed to give special attention to the hasty adjustment of respirators by their men. It also noted the need to keep cotton pad devices moist throughout the day since during an attack there would not be time to apply the protecting chemicals.[106] Butler, in his circular, wrote: "experience has shown that, if men are not prepared for a gas attack, and if they are not wearing their gas helmets or have not time to put them on properly, the effect of a sudden cloud of gas may be

Table 1. Comparison of Shell Expenditure between Loos and Messines

Artillery Caliber	Battle of Loos	Battle of Messines
18-pounder	203,124	1,977,499
4.5″ howitzer	30,568	642,246
60-pounder	4,937	175,479
6″ howitzer	11,241	540,541
6″ gun	340	13,647
8″ howitzer	3,218	120,934
9.2″ howitzer	2,239	83,664
12″ howitzer	—	6,717
15″ howitzer	216	803
Total	*255,883*	*3,561,530*

Source: Edmonds, *Military Operations, France and Belgium, 1915,* 2:177.

very great indeed, not only in the front trenches but also in the support and reserve trenches for some considerable distance in rear."[107] As the scheduled battle at Loos approached, the British had some reason to hope that the Germans had not yet institutionalized thorough anti-gas training. Furthermore, prisoner interrogation had demonstrated that some Germans still possessed the inferior cotton pad devices that the wearer needed to keep moist, a liability if the owner was not well trained. The course of the battle would prove the British gamble correct. The Germans had neglected to issue all their troops with effective equipment, and had not seriously addressed the importance of defensive gas training. The Germans would have to experience the harshness of chemical warfare themselves before they could absorb the lessons that they had taught the British at 2nd Ypres.

The British still envisioned an important role for the artillery but they limited its objectives, both due to resources and design. The guns would facilitate the attack, but it was gas that would make victory possible. The artillery's role fell into several basic categories. The guns were to destroy the enemy's defenses (such as the wire and parapets) and were to fire counter-battery missions to neutralize the enemy's artillery. Additionally, the British expected the four-day bombardment to lower German morale and planned to exacerbate the enemy's panic by having the gunners fire into any fleeing troops.[108] The British did not expect great things from their guns, principally because of the limited number of heavy pieces and the paucity of rounds. Table 1 illustrates this point by comparing shell expenditure at Loos in September 1915 with the Battle of Messines in June 1917.

Further complicating the difficulties for the British artillery were German defenses which, even at this early stage, were largely proof against all but a direct hit from the heaviest shell. Therefore it fell to gas to sink silently into German strongholds and destroy their occupants.[109]

The British did plan a modest shell gas contribution for the artillery. The Germans had first used this ammunition against the British at Neuve Chapelle in 1914 and had subsequently fired large quantities during the Battle of 2nd Ypres. Shortly after Ypres the British began a program to produce their own chemical shells, though technical problems and the need to address the critical shortage of high-explosive shells first would postpone large-scale production until 1917. On 16 August the British conducted tests of chlorine-filled shells for the 4.5-inch howitzer and, while they were generally pleased with the results, they experienced some difficulties with excessive upward dispersion due to the presence of too much high-explosive in the bursting charge. Still, at the end of the month general headquarters promised to send to Haig 1,000 4.5-inch chlorine howitzer rounds, and possibly a second 1,000 filled with the lachrymatory agent SK.[110] However, by 24 September only a partial consignment had arrived and I Corps had barely 250 rounds to divide among the howitzer batteries of the 2nd and 9th Scottish Divisions. Their targets were the village of Auchy, located between the German lines, and the village of Haisnes, located just beyond the enemy's second line.[111] Rawlinson noted the arrival of some lachrymatory shells but IV Corps records do not identify the quantity.[112] Haig also received a small amount of chlorine-filled lethal shells (CP or CPS) for his 32 4.7-inch guns. Again, the exact number of shells is difficult to determine but it may have been as many as 27 rounds per gun for a total of 864.[113] At a minimum, each 4.7 inch gun had a combined total of 158 gas and high-explosive rounds.[114] As with their role during the battle, the artillery's employment of chemical rounds was not overly significant. However, the new shells were a harbinger of the future and a representation of British determination to try to exploit all possible avenues for chemical warfare.

At First Army's advanced headquarters, Haig spent an anxious night watching the weather. Every hour 40 gas officers, positioned along the assault zone, reported the estimated wind velocity and direction to Foulkes, while Capt. E. Gold, the army's meteorologist, received bulletins from weather stations in London, Spain, and other locations.

Foulkes plotted the reports on his map while Gold analyzed the data and developed his forecast. Haig still had to decide whether to use the gas and, if so, when to begin the attack. The weather for most of the twenty-fourth and the preceding days had been poor, but at 6:00 P.M. there was a slight improvement. Gold estimated that the wind was on the borderline between favorable and unfavorable. By 9:00 P.M. he reported that conditions were improving and he anticipated a shift of direction to the desired west by the morning. At 9:45 P.M. Haig sent the message confirming the use of gas;[115] at 3 A.M. there followed the announcement to open the cylinders at 5:50 A.M.[116] The wind, however, proved fickle, and prevented the release of much of the gas.

At 5:50 A.M. on 25 September the men of the special companies opened the cocks on their cylinders, releasing Red Star in Britain's first chemical attack, while the Stokes mortarmen fired 10,000 smoke bombs. Members of the special companies, with assistance from the infantry, had cut over 400 gas emplacements into the front line parapet, with those on the main front containing 11 to 13 cylinders each.[117] Working in their gas helmets and hampered by leaky pipes and frozen valves, they followed Foulkes's program and released the chlorine, interspersed with smoke, generating a cloud that obscured the entire battlefield. However it proved more difficult to release the gas in the crowded, muddy trenches while under an enemy barrage, than it had on the practice field. Cpl. Charles Ashley of 186 Special Company explained that time was lost because the chlorine was terribly cold when released, which caused the connector nuts to contract and thus made it virtually impossible to reattach the pipe to the next cylinder.[118] This difficulty, combined with the problems with the wind, caused them to release only about 80 tons of gas or slightly more than half of the expected amount.[119] Forty minutes later the infantry clambered out of their trenches and advanced toward the German lines.

The support provided by the gas was mixed. The right flank received its full benefit, the center had some assistance, and for the left flank it was a painful liability. The wind blew most favorably on the fronts of the 47th London and 15th Scottish Divisions and consequently their advance was the easiest. Maj. Gen. C. St. L. Barter's Londoners left their trenches on time and within a few minutes had entered the enemy's front line. By 7:30 they had reached their final objectives on the outskirts of Loos and the embankment of the Double Crassier, where they were to prepare a defensive flank for the 15th Scottish Division. The division reported that immediately after the discharge the

Germans opened with heavy artillery, rifle, and machine gun fire, but as the cloud reached the enemy's positions their aim became high and wild and then ceased. At 6:38 A.M. the division's war diary recorded that the German rifle fire was dying down, and by 6:59 it had become faint. In this sector gas had succeeded in counteracting the enemy's defensive fire.[120]

The Scots also set out quickly, but their final objectives—the villages of Loison and Annay—lay a mile and a half beyond the Germans' last prepared defensive line, a distance of nearly six miles. The 15th Division's attack was critical, and it had to rapidly advance straight through the enemy's defenses in order to open the way for the general reserve. Emerging from Russian Saps, only 200 yards from the enemy, the 15th's troops plunged into the German positions. By 7:00 A.M. they had reached the Loos line, and although its defenders had fled, some partially cut wire held up the British. As they forced their way through the wire several German machine guns opened fire, but once bombers had silenced them the 15th again swept forward. Elements of the 44th and 46th Brigades then stormed up and over Hill 70 and rushed down the rear slope towards the Germans' final line. However, during this final push their direction pulled toward the south and the village of St. Laurent instead of heading east toward the village of St. Auguste. In the end it did not matter. The 800 to 900 men of the spearhead got within 80 yards of the German line, but, caught by heavy rifle fire on an exposed slope, enfiladed by machine guns, and confronted by virtually intact wire, most were then cut down. A few desperate parties attempted to work their way through the wire but they were either killed or taken prisoner. A subsequent counterattack by the Germans forced the British off Hill 70 and the Scots dug in on its slope. Units that had reached the final German defenses suffered grievous casualties in their attempt to break through. When relieved from Hill 70 during the night, Capt. Duncan Stang, the senior officer of the 8th Seaforth Highlanders, withdrew with one other officer and 35 men.[121]

The advance of Rawlinson's third division, the 1st, was less successful, and the troops found that gas could be a two-edged sword. The 1st Division's distant objective was the village of Hulluch on the far side of the Germans' last defensive line. At 5:50 A.M. the wind was light and variable but generally blowing in the correct direction. However, 10 minutes later the wind shifted and gas poured back over the British positions, causing heavy casualties in the 2nd King's Rifle Regiment. The assault was delayed a few minutes to allow time for the gas to drift away; the 1st Division went over the top at 6:34 A.M., four minutes late. The men had to advance through the gas, and as they did so they came under enemy machine-gun fire. When they reached the German line they then discovered that the artillery had done a poor job and the wire was mostly still intact. The Germans thus had time to emerge from their dugouts and man their positions. The division took heavy casualties but it succeeded in breaching the German line and pushed on to the outskirts of Hulluch. There, once again, they faced intact wire and only a few British soldiers temporarily penetrated the position.[122]

The situation further north, in I Corps's sector, proved more problematic. As for IV Corps, Gough's final objectives lay more than a mile east of the German's last defensive position. The troops of the 7th and 9th (Scottish) Divisions were intending to press forward in one great rush in order to clear the way for XI Corps in the general reserve. The 2nd Division, the northernmost, was to straddle the La Bassée Canal and form a defensive shield to protect the flank of the other attackers. The 7th Division, along with the 26th Brigade of the 9th (Scottish) Division, succeeded in overrunning the Hohenzollern Redoubt, got as far as the German final line, and even occupied parts of it for a short time, but the rest of the attackers, to the north, were unable to penetrate the enemy's front line, a failure that allowed the Germans to enfilade and heavily punish the advancing British. The contributing culprit was gas. The chlorine in front of the 28th Brigade, the leftmost brigade of the 9th (Scottish) Division, at first appeared to move into no man's land, but it then blew back and tumbled into the packed British trench, then continued on to the west. Seriously depleted, the battalions emerged from the trenches promptly at 6:30 A.M., but had to traverse the intervening ground between their lines and the enemy's lines fully exposed, without the cover of the cloud. Immediately raked by machine guns the Scots suffered heavily, the German fire virtually annihilated the 10 Highland Light Infantry within 20 yards, and the 6th Kings Own Scottish Borderers lost 605 of the 650 men they sent forward. Those who managed to reach the German position found it protected by broad belts of heavy uncut wire. To the far left of I Corps was the 2nd Division, the northernmost unit to participate in the attack. Though it had been assigned the relatively minor task of securing the offensive's flank, the division failed in that task and, at day's end, its battalions were back in their jump-off positions. The officer of the special companies in charge of the gas on 2nd Division's front refused to open his cylinders due to the unfavorable wind. However, the 2nd Division HQ insisted on the discharge. Upon release the chlorine created a cloud of such density in the British trench that even soldiers wearing their respirator helmets became casualties. The troops then advanced but the Germans mowed down the attackers, even before they reached the virtually intact German wire.[123]

Encouraged by the swift advance of IV Corps, and sensing the possibility of breakthrough, Haig asked for the transfer of control of the general reserve from general headquarters to First Army, a request French agreed to at 9:41 A.M. Haig ordered the 21st and 24th Divisions forward to attack between the 1st and 15th Divisions, aiming to break the German line between Hulluch and Cité St. Auguste. Meanwhile, in preparation for the pursuit, he instructed other units to prepare crossing points for the cavalry and field artillery to pass over the captured German trenches. However, French had positioned the reserves too far away and the new army troops, only recently arrived in France and already exhausted from almost a full night of marching, could not get through the choked roads quickly enough. Haig had to postpone the attack until the twenty-sixth when the new troops advanced into their maiden combat experience and attempted to smash their way through the Germans' final line while the 15th and 1st Divisions tried to retake Hill 70 and Hulluch. Their task was impossible. The reinforced Germans, still protected by intact wire, wrought havoc on the advancing lines. The men of these "green" divisions wavered and then broke under the pressure. Only the advance of the Guards Division stabilized the British line and prevented disaster.[124]

On the twenty-seventh the Guards Division renewed the attack but it too was repulsed, while variable winds forced the British to abort a gas discharge on the 2nd Division's front near Cuinchy. The reinforced Germans launched a series of local counterattacks and retook the Hohenzollern Redoubt, which diverted British attention to this critical position. Hohenzollern's loss, along with the increasing strength of the enemy, forced Haig to change his approach. For the attack on 13 October he set limited objectives, including the regaining of the redoubt along with the tactically important locations of Fosse 8, the Quarries, and the Dump. The plan called for a gas discharge at 1:00 P.M., and the special companies opened 1,217 of the 3,170 Red Star cylinders they had prepared. An uncooperative wind prevented the opening of the other cylinders. The infantry assaulted an hour later but the Germans repulsed them. Haig next proposed a night-time gas discharge for the sixteenth, followed by a broad surprise assault, but the worsening autumn weather forced its cancellation and the battle effectively came to an end. The French offenses, for which the British fought in support, also ended in failure. General d'Urbal's Tenth Army moved forward on the afternoon of 25 September but stalled after occupying parts of the enemy's front line, and Joffre's other thrust from Champagne also failed to secure its objectives. The French renewed their attacks the next day but there was no longer any sense of coordinated purpose. Instead, the battle had become a series of limited attacks and the opportunity for a decisive outcome had passed.[125]

At the battle's conclusion the commanders began the process of learning its lessons. While gas had been the battle's primary focus prior to the assault, the artillery had important issues to consider. Brig. Gen. C. E. D. Budworth, Rawlinson's gunner, noted that the objectives of a preliminary bombardment were:

1. [To] Demoralize the enemy.
2. To subjugate the hostile artillery.
3. To destroy hostile personnel, material, and all kinds of obstacles to the infantry advance.[126]

These themes were codified in *Artillery Notes* in 1916 and eventually formed the basis for the employment of shell gas.[127] Budworth also recommended an increase in the assignment of artillery to counter-battery actions and suggested that artillery planners should allocate as many batteries as possible to this task. In addition he observed the inadequacy of siege batteries in dealing with the enemy's deep dugouts, and suggested that the benefit of these weapons when aimed at German infantry was primarily to affect morale. Finally, he believed that during future gas discharges it would be valuable to have the field artillery fire shrapnel upon the enemy's parapets and communication trenches, both to catch the defenders who manned their positions in anticipation of an assault and to eliminate those who had fled before the cloud.[128]

Another officer concluded that "the chief hope in future operations lies in greater development of artillery power rendered possible by an increased supply of guns and ammunition, and a greater experience in the handling of them."[129] He added that a truly crushing artillery bombardment had not yet been seen and furthermore it would require heavy howitzers, heavy guns, and enough ammunition to obliterate the opposition. At the moment of assault the guns should precede the infantry like a wave and overwhelm all in its path. While the British would build enormous quantities of materials to be able to compete directly with the

Germans in the struggle for artillery dominance, they would also reinforce their efforts by perfecting the techniques of air-ground control, indirect fire accuracy, the operation of gunnery intelligence command centers, and the use of shell gas. All of these approaches would play a role in the eventual supremacy of British artillery over the enemy.[130]

For those concerned with the effectiveness of gas the lessons were equally far-reaching. An analysis of the effects of gas published on 25 September stressed the primacy of the cloud's dependence upon the wind, which made coordination with an infantry assault extremely problematic. To achieve a safe and successful discharge the wind had to be perfect, a condition that the planners could not guarantee. Gas could therefore never be a dominant battlefield weapon. Never again would the British precede an attack with a discharge of gas from cylinders. They did continue to make use of chemical weapons, and in increasing volumes, but decided that if an attack's plans included an infantry advance they would use a different method of delivering the vapor to the enemy. The report also made other observations that were of a more practical nature. For future cylinder discharges they believed that the wind needed to be a steady four to 16 miles per hour, and that 30 minutes was an insufficient length of time for the discharge. While the gas did not kill many Germans directly, the enemy did suffer considerable shrapnel casualties when the gas forced them from their shelters into the open. Finally, the report noted the need for considerable training by the chemical warfare troops in order to perfect their art. Problems, such as leaky apparatus and outlet pipes damaged by the enemy's gunfire, required improvements in equipment, and the engineers would have to change the slow, labor-intensive one-by-one opening of cylinders to a multiple discharge system.[131]

Capt. P. R. Sanders, R.E., commander of 187 Special Company R.E., also submitted an analysis of his experiences before and during the discharge. He observed that the method of moving the cylinders, which each weighed over 100 pounds, from the supply head into the trenches was extremely arduous. On one night alone nearly 4,500 men were engaged in bringing some of the cylinders used on the IV Corps front into the trenches, and the work was so exhausting that a man could make only a single journey. The demands for labor required the special companies to seek assistance from the infantry, a task that did not endear the foot soldiers to cylinder attacks. Sanders also reported a need for improvement in quality control. A number of cylinders arrived either empty or leaking, and the filling plant had affixed the cylinder caps so tightly that the engineers had to loosen them with blow torches. He also complained of faulty valves and joints, leaky tubes, and the vent pipes being so long as to be practically immovable in the trenches.[132]

The reaction of officers varied according to their location and the success of the gas. Foulkes, the enthusiast, believed that the Germans were completely surprised by the gas and that it caused a panic. After the war he insisted that the gas attack had been a complete success and that without its help no ground would have been gained.[133] Foulkes's comments certainly applied to IV Corps's front, where Rawlinson also reported success. Rawlinson's troops, except for those affected by the blowback along 1st Division, moved forward quickly and experienced little resistance.[134] In his diary he recorded his impressions: "The morning of the 25th was far better than one could have possibly expected. . . . It was a wonderful sight—the cloud was 2[00] to 300 feet high and extended from La Bassée Canal down to our junction with the French."[135]

One final issue to be considered is an assessment of the role of gas in the battle's failure. The consensus was that gas had done its expected part where the wind had blown correctly, as it did in the IV Corps's sector, and though the blowback was painful on the I Corps's front, the chlorine was not solely responsible for the inability of the British to break through. The British attack plan was simply too ambitious for the resources available, and the Germans were too strong. The power of the defense to overwhelm the offensive remained unchanged, while the German army was still morally a match for the British and would require considerable wearing down before the British Expeditionary Force gained an essential advantage in the relationship. Furthermore, even if the wind had blown in the correct direction and at the right velocity, and even if general headquarters had properly controlled XI Corps so that it closely followed behind I and IV Corps and interceded at the crucial point, the potential for the British to have secured a breakthrough was, one can easily speculate, remote. Overshadowing the failure of the gas was an even more serious problem: the failure of the guns. Across the battle zone the advancing infantry had to work their way through intact German wire. Worsening the situation, areas in which poor conditions impeded the gas discharge also tended to have large belts of uncut wire. Astute observers realized that success was impossible without more artillery, as well as advances in firing procedures, reconnaissance, and coordination with the infantry, all innovations that would arrive later.[136]

Yet on the 47th London and 15th Scottish Divisions' fronts the gunners had done a good job in destroying the wire, and the defenders had panicked and bolted before the cloud, a combination that Rawlinson claimed had allowed his infantry to reach their objectives without undue losses.[137] Why then did these units fail to break through the Germans' final position? After a rapid advance through Loos and over Hill 70 the British troops were simply exhausted and their numbers too greatly reduced. Furthermore, the farther they advanced the weaker the chlorine became, due to its dispersion into the atmosphere. Then, as they came down the far slope of the hill they confronted an alert enemy who had not faced the full effects of the deadly vapor and who had a dense belt of wire to protect their position. British guns had not even attempted to destroy the wire systematically because it lay beyond the range of the field batteries and too few heavy pieces were available for the task. Even if the latter had existed the position lay far beyond the gunners' ability to observe and correct the shooting. Thus, in the end, it was British over-ambition and an acute shortage of guns that doomed Loos to failure, for its success unreasonably required virtually every German to flee before the cloud.

The failure at Loos revealed the difficulties of establishing a strategic superiority by using gas. However, there is little doubt that where the wind blew as desired it did achieve a tactical superiority. The British discussed the effectiveness of gas in some detail after the battle and decided that, while disappointing in its material effect, it had had a great effect on the enemy's morale. A report by the 47th London Division reached a similar conclusion.[138] While the gas discharge did not kill many Germans outright, the absence of German bodies in the captured positions suggested that the remainder retreated rapidly and that the demoralizing effect of the cloud had thoroughly cowed the enemy.[139] Foulkes also concluded that the gas attack had come as a surprise and that it had caused a panic on IV Corps's front.[140]

The Battle of Loos, initially presented as a limited attack to hold the German reserves on the front while the French sought a breakthrough elsewhere, soon evolved into the largest British undertaking of the war up to that point. While to some extent one can label it a political battle fought to appease the allied French, Loos was also Britain's last attempt to win the war quickly and cheaply. With its failure British commanders resigned themselves to a long war of relentless wearing down as they sought the superiority necessary for victory.

It might be convenient to regard the British use of gas as merely a necessary retaliation, or an effort to compensate for their lack of artillery. In fact it was neither. Haig's use of gas was an attempt to compress the "struggle for supremacy" phase of battle down to one instant. Instead of the extended battle for fire superiority codified in their prewar manuals, the British gambled in the hope that surprise and the enemy's poor anti-gas preparations would cause the toxic vapors to sweep the enemy from the field and allow the British to combine the advance of the fire line and the launch of the decisive blow into a single phase, leading to breakthrough, pursuit, and decisive success. The British were well aware of the potential of the weapon to provide a crushing superiority. One post-battle evaluation noted that the success they did enjoy was due not to the destructive value of gas, but rather to its novelty. It further recognized that "it is possible that a more destructive auxiliary means maybe found in the future; it is doubtful whether the total effect produced will be greater."[141] In reality Loos was a unique attempt to modify the British principles of war. Haig employed a novel weapon in a way that stretched the existing intellectual conception of the nature of war. To Haig and the British the belief in the sanctity of the principle of the phases of battle was axiomatic; yet, while they did not change the sequence of phases at Loos, they did attempt to eliminate one phase. The battle represented a willingness to experiment with the army's operational parameters. While the British stayed within the bounds of their prewar principles, they did display an ability to define these principles in the broadest possible way. Loos showed that the operational principles of the British army were not rigid or nonreactive. Rather, as the prewar theorists had believed, the institution's ethos permitted wide latitude and encouraged initiative and interpretation that readily allowed the incorporation of novelties and new ideas.

The British paid a heavy price for supporting their French ally. Including the subsidiary attacks on the Indian, III, and V Corps' fronts, Loos cost the British over 59,000 casualties, of whom 7,766 were dead and another 18,486 missing, a figure more than double Edmonds's estimate for the German "butcher's bill."[142] For their effort the British could claim the village of Loos, an assortment of mine works and pit towers, and about 8,000 yards of the enemy line. But they had fallen far short of their strategic goals: breakthrough and decisive victory. Despite the initial optimism created by the rapidity of the 15th (Scottish)

Division's advance, Loos was a costly failure. Yet the battle had great significance. Its lessons not only molded the future role of gas, but also confirmed the British faith in the veracity of their prewar conceptions and shaped their methods for the rest of the war. The battle's failure renewed Haig's belief that there could be no shortcuts. He accepted the fact that the war would have to be long and brutal in order to change Britain's position of inferiority into one of superiority. The use of gas had been a technological attempt to shortcut the methodical progress that modern war required and which the phases of battle demanded. Gas was simply not technically effective enough at Loos to gain the advantage necessary to garner success. Its failure meant that the British would need to return to the intellectually agreed-upon parameters that would produce both the Somme and eventual victory.

CHAPTER 3

Experimentation

I consider it of first importance that an immediate supply of lethal gas shell should be sent. – Sir Douglas Haig

Gas had failed to bring about decisive victory at Loos. Nevertheless, it was successful enough to suggest its potential as a useful adjunct in future attacks. Despite the problems with blowback, gas would eventually find a role in the British method of waging war. The officer corps had accepted it as a weapon that should be used at every opportunity, they had created specialized units charged with its employment and incorporated operational lessons on gas into training materials and courses, and they had committed resources to satisfy the growing demand for necessary gas materials. However, relative to other weapon systems, the importance of gas declined during 1916. At Loos the chlorine cloud was the battle's critical element, while at the Somme the various gases and their delivery systems represented a minor subtheme to the supremacy of the gun. Throughout 1916 British use of offensive chemical warfare was a small affair when compared to the commitment they made to other weapons. Yet this state of affairs was not the result of a lack of enthusiasm for the weapon but rather the result of material shortages. As the war progressed and Britain expanded its chemical infrastructure, the value of gas and the army's commitment to it greatly increased. Though gas would never again be the most vital weapon, it did evolve into one of the more important auxiliaries.

Over the course of the year the War Office and the Ministry of Munitions laid the basis for a vast expansion of gas production that would compensate for the nation's scandalous prewar neglect of its chemical industry. The results were dramatic. By 1917 the shortages eased, by 1918 the position relative to the Germans equalized, and by 1919, had the war lasted, Britain would have dominated the chemical battlefield. The year of the Somme also witnessed the creation of the Special Brigade and the acceptance of new dispersal systems particularly designed for the Royal Artillery, systems that the British would employ in their quest for a superiority. The chemical struggle against Germany was a constant one. First there was the need to find the means to dominate the enemy chemically, and second was the necessity of fitting gas within the British perception of how they had to fight the war. Throughout 1916 the British army sought effectiveness and accommodation on both levels.

Organization

The special companies ended 1915 with a number of independent Red Star and Blue Star attacks.[1] The objective of these discharges was to gain experience and use up the chlorine, which was soon to be replaced by White Star, a mixture containing the far more deadly phosgene.[2] In early January 1916 the chemical troops withdrew to their winter quarters at Helfault to train for the next summer's attempt to win the war and absorb reinforcements as the companies expanded to a brigade-size organization.

During February, Foulkes's command increased from four to 21 companies with a force of more than 5,000 officers and men. The War Office establishment provided four battalions of four companies each (companies A through Q, omitting I), a mortar battalion of four companies (1 through 4), and an independent company (Z Company) which was originally responsible for flamethrower operations but, after that weapon's discontinuance, instead carried out gas discharges or experimental work. Foulkes changed his command's structure as needed, but the company designations remained constant until the Armistice. Also attached to the brigade was the Special Factory Section, a company-size unit that took over a French phosgene plant at Coulogne near Calais. In an output-sharing arrangement with their ally, the British ran the factory nonstop, working three shifts around the clock every day until the war's end. The final components of the brigade were the gas advisers who served on the army- and corps-level staffs. These officers were responsible for coordinating with the local units all Special Brigade operations on their fronts and overseeing the command's anti-gas training. The leadership of the chemical warfare service also changed as Brig. Gen. H. F. Thuillier, R.E., became director of Gas Services, while the attack and defensive aspects of chemical warfare were split between two offices: Foulkes became assistant director–offensive and commanding officer Special Brigade, and Lieut. Col. S. L. Cummins assumed the position of assistant director–anti-gas. Foulkes continued to direct Special Brigade operations and also served at general headquarters as gas adviser to Haig.[3]

As the Special Brigade underwent its training, the primary difficulty lay in the inadequate provision of offensive materials. Throughout 1916 all gases were in acutely short supply, which hampered the participation of both the gas engineers and the artillery in the wearing down phase of battle. The greatest shortages involved the four-inch Stokes mortar, for which they had a supply of smoke bombs left over from Loos but would not receive any further ordnance for more than a year after that battle. The 1915 issue were 13-pound red phosphorus bombs which had performed poorly at Loos. The 13-pounders created an inadequate cloud, had a limited range with a maximum of 350 yards, and tended to fail to ignite upon impact. When they did explode, the bursting charge was excessive and blew the smoke skyward.[4] The 13-pound phosphorus bomb's replacement was the vastly improved 25-pound white phosphorus bomb, but it was not yet available. Except for the inferior red phosphorus shells, Foulkes's four mortar companies would have little to do for the first three months of the Somme, and even by the end of the year the availability of their ordnance remained inconsistent.[5]

This state of affairs regarding mortar ammunition was unfortunate, as Stokes's invention proved to be one of Britain's most effective inventions of the war. The four-inch mortar, like the two- and three-inch versions belonging to the infantry, enabled the user to target a specific position, such as a machine gun nest or an observation post. For the chemical troops it also had the advantage of permitting a much more discreet attack than a cylinder discharge could and was more reliable since it was less dependent upon the wind. Furthermore, when compared to other projectiles a mortar bomb contained a high percentage of gas relative to its weight. When filled with phosgene the four-inch Stokes shell contained 7.5 pounds of gas (as opposed to 4.27 pounds in a 4.7-inch shell, or the minuscule 1.32 pounds contained in a French 75mm shell). Although its maximum range of 840 yards could not compete with that of the artillery, the mortar did have a high rate of fire (20 rounds a minute) and could establish a dense, localized concentration of lethal gas with great rapidity.[6]

In December 1915, Lieut. Col. Arthur Crossley reported to the Ministry of Munitions the British Expeditionary Forces' (BEF) needs regarding chemical ordnance for the Stokes mortar. Crossley called for the production of a four-inch lachrymatory bomb, but if not enough tearing substances were available he recommended the substitution of an asphyxiate filling. Foulkes suggested a two-month deadline for the bomb's production. He also requested white phosphorus rounds for use as smoke bombs, although he did abandon the idea of an abrasion round filled with carborundum to jam the enemy's machine guns.

Crossley also noted Butler's support for a thermite bomb and a shell filled with an inflammable liquid.[7]

Foulkes's expectations of rapid production were unquestionably too optimistic, and repeated proddings from general headquarters failed to produce any ordnance at all. In late January general headquarters asked for 40,000 rounds of SK to arrive by mid-April. A month later it raised this figure to 200,000. In April general headquarters modified their priorities and requested 40,000 SK and 200,000 smoke bombs. On 16 May headquarters noted the lack of ammunition and reiterated the urgency of the appeal. On 23 August London received another requisition, which for the first time included the demand for a lethal filling while also requesting 6,000 lethal, 9,000 SK, and 15,000 smoke bombs per week. Finally, on about 20 September, 3,000 SK bombs arrived and on the twenty-fourth they were put into use against Thiepval. The initial batch of white phosphorus smoke shells did not arrive until mid-October.[8]

Brigadier General Thuillier went to London in late August to resolve an increasingly embarrassing situation: the virtual idleness of an entire battalion of specialized troops while the British army waged the greatest battle in its history. At a conference held at the War Office on the thirtieth, the Trench Warfare Department informed Thuillier that the inability to produce smoke bombs was due to shortages of phosphorus and that no steps had yet been taken to increase the nation's capacity to produce the compound. Nor was Thuillier given any satisfaction on when the gas service might expect a regular supply. In mid-September the Trench Warfare Department told Thuillier that he could expect, at best, 5,000 rounds of phosphorus bomb a week—only one-third of what he had requested. The supply of SK was also alarmingly low. The Trench Warfare Department estimated that supplies of this gas would allow for the production of only 3,000 bombs per week, which was, again, a third of the initial request, although London had not thought it necessary to alert general headquarters to the low stocks of SK prior to the inquiries from the director of Gas Services. The Trench Warfare Department did suggest that it would be possible to increase the production of lethal ordnance for the Stokes mortar, though no pattern for this variation had, as yet, passed inspection.[9]

As an interim solution Thuillier proposed re-arming the mortar companies with the two-inch Stokes, for which gas bombs were available. This munition was already in use by some divisional trench mortar batteries, and intelligence had credited them with some success. The

24th Division had fired 20 rounds into Guillemont on 3 September and investigators subsequently ascertained that the enemy had suffered numerous casualties; they discovered some Germans in the process of donning their respirators when they were overwhelmed by the gas. The Special Brigade did take up the weapon and employed it, firing White Star bombs on six occasions in September and October 1916. However, the Special Brigade's commitment to the smaller weapon was fleeting and the mortarmen continued to wait for their promised ammunition.[10]

Supplies were more plentiful for cylinder discharges, but Haig still received only a little over half of the gas materials he requested for the opening of the Battle of the Somme. The Ministry of Munitions managed to produce only 16,600 of the 35,000 White Star cylinders requested, and shipped 6,300 (less than a fourth) of the 26,600 pipe fittings required. To make up the shortage the Special Brigade still had approximately 10,000 Red Star cylinders as well as 2,100 Two Red Star containers waiting in France.[11] Despite the fact that chlorine was considerably less lethal than phosgene, as well as unable to penetrate German respirators, the British had to continue to employ it in alarmingly large quantities. The battlefield consequences of the Ministry of Munitions' inability to provide sufficient stocks of phosgene is, perhaps, best examined by comparing the relative lethality of the major war gases.

Table 2. Lethality of Major War Gases

Gas	Lethality Index
Chlorine	7500
Mustard Gas	1500
Chloropicrin	1000
Diphosgene	500
Phosgene	450

Note: The lower the figure the more deadly the gas. The figures represent the product of the concentration of parts per million and time in minutes required to cause death. These figures are based upon the research of Haber during the war and should be viewed in relative rather than exact terms. See Haber, *Poisonous Cloud*, 43–44, and Prentiss, *Chemicals in War*, 14.

In 1916, therefore, the British had to maintain in their arsenal a weapon that was nearly 17 times less deadly than the best available substance. To their credit, however, the Special Brigade did manage to make nearly 90 gas attacks, in addition to a large number of smoke discharges, over the months of the Somme.[12]

The final major gas dispersal system available to the British before the Somme were the guns. Shells had been the initial means to discharge gas, and the Germans had used them first against French troops at Neuve Chapelle on 27 October 1914. Since 2nd Ypres, gas's employment by the enemy, as well as by the French, had increased greatly, and during the Verdun battle the combatants made profligate use of the weapon. The British were once again behind the enemy in developing this weapon, but, along with the other players, they correctly anticipated a massive role for the artillery in chemical warfare. By the end of the war, the average amount of gas shells as a factor of total shells was approximately 50 percent for Germany, 35 percent for France, 25 percent for Britain, and 15 percent for the United States (and the British and Americans had planned further increases for 1919). However, Haig set the 1916 objective at 10 percent and then only for three weapons: the 4.5-inch howitzer, and the 60-pounder and 4.7-inch guns. Even these modest objectives were not reached.[13]

The usefulness of gas shell and its manifold superiority over cylinder discharges was readily apparent. The employment of shells made it easier to surprise the enemy, since the attacker delivered the gas directly to the objective with little warning. Surprise increased the potential of harming or killing enemy troops before they could don their respirators, as contrasted with the cloud method, where an observant defender might hear the release of the gas or see its approach. Artillery, although not free from constraints, could be used during a much wider range of wind conditions, and the use of shell also avoided the onerous task of carrying forward and positioning the heavy and awkward cylinders. Tactically shells allowed more flexibility and selectivity, and the artillery range permitted the gunners to fire upon distant targets, protect the infantry from enemy batteries, or help assaulting troops defend their objectives from hostile counterattacks. For some missions gas shell proved particularly useful, especially in counter-battery and counter-preparation, as well as for use in harassment and isolation fire. Finally, artillery permitted the establishment of a prolonged gas attack, an approach frequently used by the British with the objective of killing or wearing down the morale of the enemy by forcing them to wear their anti-gas equipment for lengthy periods of time. A long exposure to poisonous fumes would render the enemy's respirators useless by exhausting their neutralizing chemicals, while being forced to breathe through a gas mask was an effective method of lowering morale. However, cloud gas did have certain advantages that the artillery could not duplicate, especially the dense concentration of lethal agents that the Special Brigade obtained.[14]

Later on the gunners would usurp the Special Brigade's position as Britain's principal wagers of chemical warfare. During the Somme, however, the Royal Artillery felt the shortage of chemical munitions severely. Throughout 1916 the pressing need facing the Ministry of Munitions was to end the inadequate provisions of high explosives that had made conduct of the war so difficult the previous year. The allocation of resources for the production of chemicals for artillery shells and the building of specialized factories to fill these shells came in a poor second behind the need to assure a large supply of explosives. Gas had to wait, and the gunners had to make do with the chemical shells available.

Although the principal hindrance to the rapid production of chemical shell was the shortage of both the filling and the containers in which to put the limited amount of chemicals that did exist, the situation was further exacerbated by the army itself. General headquarters was unsure of exactly what they wanted and in what quantities, which led to a blizzard of requisitions and revisions. Initially Haig desired lachrymatory shells for the 4.7-inch and 60-pounder guns and the 4.5-inch howitzer, but his staff also made requests for designs for the 6-inch, 8-inch, 9.2-inch, and 12-inch howitzers and the 6-inch gun, along with asking for changes in the nature of the fillings. Even Haig admitted that his needs were uncertain because the whole affair was still of an experimental nature. The Chemical Advisory Committee recorded its despair over the army's varied requests for chemical shell, cylinder gas, and mortar bombs, and adopted a resolution at its 24 May 1916 meeting which noted testily: "The committee desires unanimously to record their opinion that, had the demands for chemicals now made known been put forward in the latter part of last year, those demands could have been, by this date, adequately met."[15] The committee's claim is dubious, as the problem they faced was not only one of defining needs but also of creating a whole new class of delivery systems. The designs of the shells and whether to use cast iron or steel for them were only two of a whole series of complex technological issues. Hence, the Ordnance Committee did not approve the specifications of an SK shell for the 60-pounder gun or the 4.5-inch howitzer until mid-February, nor a general purpose chemical shell for these calibers until a month later, and the 4.7-inch gun drawings only in April.[16] The army's planners, therefore, never had a clear idea of how many chemical shells they would have available, or for which guns, as they made their preparations for the Somme. Shell gas would be a part of the British arsenal but the quantity remained uncertain.

The Ministry of Munitions placed its first order for a gas-filled shell in October 1915 when it directed the Royal Arsenal at Woolwich to produce 10,000 cast iron lachrymatory shells for the 4.5-inch howitzer at a delivery rate of 500 per week, an order the arsenal did not complete until late April 1916. In mid-January general headquarters requested that the Ministry of Munitions attempt to provide a continuous supply of chemical shell for the 4.5-inch howitzer and 60-pounder gun at the rate of 10 percent of their total production, and up to 5 percent for the 12-inch howitzer. Butler reiterated this position at the end of February, although Maj. Gen. John Du Cane noted that the only shell actually being manufactured, and at a rather torpid rate at that, was the 4.5-inch cast iron one. However, in early March the War Office did prepare to place an order for 1,000 rounds a week for the 60-pounder, a figure it soon raised to 6,000. Organizational progress occurred on 10 March when the War Committee approved the construction of a factory for the filling of phosgene shells, a plant that would begin production in late summer; it passed a resolution calling for the accumulation of as large a supply of gas shells as possible in France.[17]

In April the demand clarified a little as the army made a request for weekly shipments of 34,610 chemical shells: 4.5-inch, 18,000; 60-pounder, 7,840; 4.7-inch, 930; and 6-inch howitzer, 7,840. The figures represented 10 percent of the supply of ordinary shell for these calibers, though the War Office delayed action on the 6-inch howitzer because its supply of high explosive shell took priority and did not meet requirements.[18] The Ministry of Munitions replied a few days later and estimated supply as:

4.5-inch cast iron—10,000 completed by 1 May, 500 per week thereafter.

4.5-inch steel—delivery to commence in May and working up to 10,000 per week by the second week in June with a considerable increase in July.

60-Pounder steel—delivery to commence in May and build up to a rate of 1,000 a week by mid-June and increasing to 2,500 in July.

6-inch Howitzer and 4.7-inch gun—available in summer.

The report went on to caution that filled shells actually existed for only the 4.5-inch cast iron and that the others were still in the experimental stage and were subject to delay.[19]

In early June general headquarters produced its own estimate of what it would have on hand for the Somme. By 15 June it expected to have 12,000 rounds for the 4.5-inch howitzer with possibly another 4,000 by the battle's beginning; for the 4.7-inch gun and the 60-pounder gun it anticipated 2,000 shells by the end of the month. However, a different report from the same period revised the figures downward and noted that there would be only 7,330 4.5-inch SK shells assigned to Fourth Army and a further 1,000 to Third Army. There would be none of the other calibers available. Haig's shortages forced him to ask Joffre for the loan of up to 20 batteries of 75mm guns equipped with as many gas shells as possible. The French came to Haig's assistance, and their batteries fired considerably more chemical shells than did those of the British on the first day of the Somme.[20]

Circumstances did improve as summer passed into autumn, but a report of 1 September showed that a considerable gap still existed between supply and demand. The army now wanted 30,000 lethal rounds a week but could only count on 2,500 Jellite, 6,700 CBR, and 11,000 PS, although its request for 5,000 SK was now being met. Mortar demand for lachrymatory shell stood at 9,000 but availability was 3,120, although a few days later this figure rose to 5,000 and the request for 6,000 lethal Stokes bombs remained unfilled as the shell's design was still unapproved. The problem, however, was no longer a shortage of chemicals but of shell in which to pour the chemicals, and of production lines to assemble the ammunition. Britain's expansion of its chemical infrastructure was starting to bear fruit, and though much remained to be done to close the gap with the Germans, the British had laid down the foundation for a massive expansion of the necessary industries.[21]

The Somme

The British army based its plans for 1916 on the agreements reached by the Allies at the Chantilly Conference of 6 December 1915 and renewed at the Paris meeting of 27 March 1916. Plans called for the French, British, Italian, and Russian armies to launch simultaneous offensives, as soon as possible, with the objective of seeking a decisive action. Further, until the event reached its decisive point the Allies were to continue to build up their own resources while wearing down the enemy's morale and using up its reserves.[22] The German success against the

Russians at Gorlice-Tarnow, the collapse of Serbia, and the attritional battle with the French at Verdun ruined the Chantilly plan of coordinated offenses. These setbacks, however, caused Britain's political leaders to recognize that the preservation of the coalition necessitated that their forces play a greater role in the land war against Germany. The Asquith government agreed that the time had arrived for Britain to release the "Kitchener Divisions" and to make a major effort in France in order to relieve the pressure on their allies. The main effort would fall on the western front, the theater that many factions—including the chief of the Imperial General Staff, the general staff, and Haig, the new commander of the British Expeditionary Force—all agreed was the decisive one.[23]

At a meeting with his army commanders on 8 January 1916, Haig explained the offensive's objectives and the means by which he planned to achieve victory. He directed his subordinates to "work out schemes for (a) preliminary operations to wear out the enemy and exhaust his reserves, and (b) for a decisive attack in the hopes of piercing the enemy's lines of defence."[24] A few days later Haig's offensive program for 1916 took a more structured form. He now broke his instructions into three parts, specifying that:

1. "Winter sports" continue into the spring, i. e. capturing lengths of enemy trenches at favourable points.
2. Wearing out fight similar to [item] one but on a larger scale at many points along the whole front. Will last about three weeks to draw in enemy reserves.
3. Decisive attacks at several points: object to breakthrough.[25]

The first point used the term "winter sports" as a euphemism for small unit attacks, including raids by the infantry, surprise bombardments by the artillery, and discharges of gas by the engineers, all with the intention not only of causing casualties but also of weakening the enemy's morale. Additionally, success would increase the morale of British troops and result in a superiority. In the second point, Haig's reference was to brigade- or division-size operations whose primary purpose was to force the enemy to commit his reserves, which would then be unavailable when the British struck the decisive blow. These medium-sized operations were to precede the principle attack by no more than two weeks. Haig's reference to the decisive blow at several points in his third section alluded to the need for the Allies to coordinate their efforts and for all of them to participate in the final struggle. Haig also left open the option for the British to launch an attack on one sector, and if such an attack did not achieve a breakthrough, to quickly switch the attack to another section of his front.[26] At this point in time Haig favored an attack in Flanders under the direction of Plumer's Second Army. Only later in his preparations, and at Joffre's suggestion, did his focus shift to the Somme and Rawlinson's Fourth Army.[27]

Haig expected the final struggle to come in June or July, and the army was to spend the intervening months in training and wearing down exercises. The armies were to stage raids from February to the beginning of April, then from the second half of April the scale of the operations was to increase to division-size battles.[28] The army commanders responded quickly to their assignments and at the end of January, at another conference, they reported the commencement of these operations and their initial success.[29] Haig held strong opinions on the efficacy of raids. He saw them as an essential ingredient of the wearing down process and as a means of cultivating the offensive spirit, and hence the morale, of his own men.[30]

Joffre did not fully agree with Haig's intentions and instead wanted to launch the large-scale preliminary attacks at an earlier date in the sequence. Haig, however, insisted on such attacks occurring no more than 10 to 14 days in advance of the decisive battle. He believed that their primary task was to force the enemy to commit his reserves; to begin these battles too early would allow the enemy to stabilize the situation and then transfer units back into the reserves. Instead, Haig preferred to keep the focus on minor operations to advance the wearing down process.[31] He reiterated his position in his "Plans for Future Operations," a position paper that correlated the success of the summer's offensive with the strength and efficiency of German reserves. Again he pointed out the need for minor operations to wear down the Germans, and argued that they should increase in scope as the main offensive approached. He scheduled the divisional operations for no more than two weeks prior to the decisive battle and re-emphasised their importance in engaging the enemy's reserves. However, by April Haig had lost his enthusiasm for the preparatory attacks and, in light of the German losses at Verdun, no longer believed them necessary.[32]

Haig conferred with his army commanders in late May and identified the Somme sector as the likely location for the assault. In support of Fourth Army he asked the commanders of First, Second, and Third Armies to provide plans for misleading the enemy as to the site of the real attack. He suggested a program of:

1. preliminary preparations such as advancing our trenches and saps, construction of dummy assembly trenches, gun emplacements, etc;

2. wire cutting at intervals along the entire front with a view to inducing the enemy to man his defences and causing fatigue;

3. gas discharges, where possible, at selected places along the whole British front, accompanied by the discharge of smoke, with a view to causing the enemy to wear his gas helmets and inducing fatigue and causing casualties;

4. artillery barrages on important communications with a view to rendering reinforcements, relief, and supply difficult;

5. bombardment of rest billets at night;

6. intermittent smoke discharges by day, accompanied by shrapnel fire on the enemy's front defences with a view to inflicting loss;

7. raids by night, of the strength of a company and upwards, on an extensive scale, into the enemy front system of defences. These to be prepared by intense artillery and trench mortar bombardments.[33]

Also distributed at the meeting was a paper on the Special Brigade and the use of gas and smoke. It outlined the composition of Foulkes's unit, its weapons, and its gases. The paper also included a 10-year history of wind direction in France, and Haig instructed the armies to take advantage of any winds from between west-southwest and south-southwest. On 12 June the army commanders received their orders to commence the subsidiary operations.[34]

Haig's paper also identified one of the fundamental problems of chemical warfare: the difficulty of effectively attacking an enemy equipped with adequate respirators. A technological solution, and one which the combatants pursued throughout the war, was to develop a vapor against which the enemy's mask afforded no barrier. However, in 1916 no such agent existed and the only chemical that had any penetrating ability was PS, and it had only partial penetration. The other solutions were tactical: either surprise the enemy's troops so that they took a few breaths of corrupted air before they realized their peril, or create either a dense concentration of gas or an exposure of such duration that the poison overwhelmed the respirator's protective capabilities.[35]

At the time of the report's presentation the British had lethal gases only for cylinder operations. The report recommended that in order to disable the enemy before they put on their masks it was necessary to have a brief discharge from a great number of cylinders. To eliminate them by wearing out their respirators it was necessary to open a series of cylinders gradually in order to sustain the discharge for at least two hours. It continued that:

1. For surprise effect, at least 4 cylinders simultaneously per bay, but it would probably suffice to discharge half the contents [and] only then turn [it] off.
2. For wearing effect, one cylinder per bay every 15 minutes, combined with smoke—possibly one cylinder in every second bay would suffice.[36]

As for the type of gas, the report recommended White Star for surprise effect and either Red Star or Two Red Star for a lengthy flotation. Finally, to increase the chances of surprise, the report proposed the policy of making cylinder discharges at night. These tactics became the basis of Special Brigade attacks, and the artillery also adopted them.[37]

While it fell to Haig to outline the offense's objectives, it was Rawlinson's task to develop the plan. From the available evidence, the two generals did not share the same perceptions about the nature of the operation. However, despite Haig's desire for a breakthrough battle and Rawlinson's preference for a "bite and hold" assault, it is clear that their ultimate goals were the same. They both envisioned the Somme as a decisive struggle. On 26 June Haig entered into his diary that he hoped to "(1) break enemy's front; (2) secure position about Bapaume and Givenchy; (3) enlarge breach; (4) advance on line Cambrai-Douai."[38] Had the British achieved these ambitions their advance would have severed the enemy's lines of communication and forced the Germans to abandon much of their conquered territory in northern France and western Belgium. Even Haig's designation of Gough's force as Reserve Army—not Fifth Army—showed his intention to use it as a breakthrough mass once Rawlinson had created a breach. As the battle progressed Haig maintained his optimism. He created a temporary Cavalry Corps to take advantage of the enemy's rout and continued to believe that normality was about to return to warfare.[39]

However, historians have exaggerated the controversy between senior officers that Edmonds discussed in the official history. While Rawlinson's initial plan did call for the seizing of the enemy's front line and the left parts of its second line, he nevertheless sought a decisive battle. Instead of a rapid breakthrough, Fourth Army was to grab parts of the German position and then bleed the enemy when they tried to recover their lost territory. Rawlinson explained his ideas in his paper on preparations for the battle. He wrote: "Our object rather seems to be to kill as many Germans as possible with the least loss to ourselves, and the best way to do this appears to me to be to seize points of tactical importance which will provide us with good observation and which we feel certain the Germans will counter-attack."[40] Rawlinson was reviving one of the observations he had made about the battles of 1915 but on a bigger scale.[41] He wanted to rely upon the superiority of the defense over the offense to destroy the German army. In effect Rawlinson wanted to attempt what Gen. Eric von Falkenhayn had failed to do to the French at Verdun. When the Germans had fought themselves into exhaustion and their morale had collapsed from the futility of their attacks, the time would have arrived for the British to resume the offense, smash through the enemy's lines, release the cavalry, and bring about the end of the war.

Haig, of course, had the final say in defining Fourth Army's objectives. On 22 June Rawlinson issued a memorandum explaining that if the enemy's resistance broke down sufficiently on the first day to permit the use of the cavalry their objective would be Bapaume, the principle railhead for the sector. A further notice sent just days before the attack recommended that if the enemy collapsed, the nearest infantry unit should immediately press forward so that no time would be lost in expanding on the initial success.[42] At a conference with his corps commanders, Rawlinson stressed the need for the assaulting troops to maintain a continuous forward movement and to press through to their objectives.[43] Lieut. Gen. Launcelot Kiggell, Haig's chief of staff, was extremely confident of success and told Rawlinson that if the attack went well then the cavalry had to move quickly on to Bapaume.[44] Haig's entreaties wore the Fourth Army commander down, and in his orders for 1 July, Rawlinson noted that a large part of the enemy's reserves had already been drawn into the battle and it was therefore essential to keep up the pressure to wear out the defense.[45] Rawlinson then entered in his diary: "I feel pretty confident of success . . . though only after heavy fighting."[46]

Ironically, after the debacle of 1 July, British operations tended to resemble Rawlinson's idea of bite and hold rather than Haig's single decisive stroke. Subsequent attacks looked for opportunities to kill the enemy and to seize limited chunks of territory. However, with every advance Haig remained hopeful that the enemy would break and his orders continued to remind his subordinates that they needed to be prepared to switch immediately to unlimited objectives if the Germans collapsed. At a meeting before the attack of 14 July he advised Rawlinson to make sure his divisions were ready to push forward if the enemy's defenses broke down. Haig's hopes for a breakthrough were revived in September with the introduction of tanks, and he again impressed upon his officers the need for bold action and the avoidance of unnecessary delay in moving forward. Finally, he always sought a role for the cavalry, who continued to prepare for their chance.[47]

Gas and the Somme

For a week the British had subjected the Germans to a relentless barrage in preparation for the assault. At 6:25 A.M. on the morning of 1 July the program intensified and at 7:22 A.M. the gunners unleashed a hurricane bombardment as shells and mortar bombs rained down upon the enemy. At 7:30 A.M. the infantry rose and, under the burden of 66 pounds of equipment, began their slow, lumbering walk toward the enemy lines. The results are well known. German machine gunners emerged from their deep dugouts, won the race to the parapet, and began to scythe through the British ranks while enemy guns concentrated their fire upon the exposed infantry caught in no man's land. The day's carnage would cost Britain nearly 60,000 men.

There were some small successes. On the far right the French Sixth Army, which attacked in support of the British, quickly and cheaply reached their day's goals. The British XIII Corps, also on the southern flank, did manage to get as far as some tertiary objectives but the next corps in line, the XV, was less fortunate and only its 7th Division reached its intermediary objectives, while the 21st and 34th Divisions barely achieved their first objectives. Further to the north the situation was worse. The assaults of the III, X, and VIII Corps were largely repulsed with little or no gain, while the diversionary attack at Gommecourt by Third Army's VII Corps also failed. Gough, who was at Fourth Army headquarters, waited in vain for the chance to advance the cavalry of the general headquarters reserve.

Rawlinson's plan had depended upon the effectiveness of the artillery to physically crush, or at least destroy the morale of the German defenders. The preliminary bombardment began on 24 June and continued with increasing ferocity up to the assault. Unfortunately for the attackers, the enemy's deep dugouts had provided a secure refuge which the artillery did not penetrate, a problem exacerbated by the high percentage of defective shells in the British ammunition and an inadequate number of heavy guns for an attack of such depth and breadth. The battle was far from over, however, and the British renewed their offensive the next day and made a series of fresh efforts into November. The catastrophe of the first day would not be repeated and the Somme settled into an attritional exchange with the combatants' casualties virtually the same (allowing for the exception of 1 July), so that the experience at the Somme became equally horrific for German and British soldiers alike.

What part did gas play in the preparations for the battle, and did British ideas on gas respond to problems revealed in the tactical environment once the battle began? Also, what role did the battle have in shaping the future use of gas? The supply situation had doomed gas to a minor role in the battle, and these material shortages—not a shortage of ideas—had stifled implementation. To the extent that gas was available, the British used it successfully to gain an advantage over the enemy and thereby establish the essential conditions for a decisive victory. Rawlinson saw gas as a means for reducing German morale and for assisting the maneuver of the infantry on the battlefield.

Morale remained crucial to Rawlinson's understanding of the nature of war. In his "Tactical Notes" of May 1916, he stressed the continued importance of the intangible aspects of war and expressed the conviction that "this war will be won by superior discipline and moral[e]."[48] The same month general headquarters issued a leaflet entitled "Training of Divisions for Offensive Action," which also emphasized the critical nature of morale, soldierly spirit, and the determination to succeed, along with the principle that "decisive success in battle can be gained only by a vigorous offensive."[49] General headquarters expected gas to contribute to this battle for morale. They believed that forcing the enemy to wear their suffocating masks for long periods would induce fatigue and thereby lower their efficiency. On 27 May Haig informed Rawlinson that he had instructed the other armies to implement a program to exhaust the enemy's morale. His orders included the extensive use of raids, the bombardment of rest billets, and the discharge of gas.[50]

Rawlinson knew that there were two key problems, the solutions to which would determine the success of the battle. The first was the enemy soldiers who manned the trenches and strong points. Hidden underground in their deep bunkers beneath sturdy layers of chalk, or in the basements of fortified villages, the enemy was invulnerable to all but a direct hit from a large-caliber howitzer.[51] Rawlinson understood the strength of these defenses, particularly the enemy's strong points, and how difficult it would be for the British gunners to subdue them. His "Tactical Notes" concede only two practical solutions: either screen the positions with smoke or neutralize the defenders by causing them to panic. The British attempted both methods during the battle.

The second threat was the enemy's batteries, which could bring devastating fire onto the assaulting troops or isolate the first wave from followup units by interdicting the battle zone. If the British counter-battery failed to suppress the enemy's guns, the attackers would suffer heavily.[52]

Rawlinson was initially reluctant to use chemical warfare at the Somme. In his operations plan of 3 April he wrote: "As regards gas, generally speaking, now that the enemy is provided with efficient masks, it appears to me that the disadvantages of using gas outweigh the advantages on account of its dependence on a suitable wind, its danger to our own troops, and the handicap to our men of wearing masks when assaulting."[53] Some of Rawlinson's subordinates also voiced their own concerns regarding the use of gas, particularly the potential that its release would alert the enemy to the commencement of the assault.[54]

However, Rawlinson's objection to using gas rested upon his fear of a repetition of Loos rather than any particular scepticism toward the weapon itself. Prior to the writing of the Somme plan he had signaled an interest in the use of poisonous vapors. In March he queried his corps commanders on their requirements for chemical warfare and demanded an estimate of their gas and smoke needs. In April he followed up with another inquiry, this time asking for information on their needs for a one-hour discharge. Even in his original battle plan, although he rejected gas he also made allowances for its use. The plan suggested the use of cloud attacks on the defensive fronts and went so far as to recommend the releasing of small quantities of gas mixed with smoke in order to compel the enemy to put on their respirators and thus be at a disadvantage when faced by nonmasked British troops. By mid-May he had provisionally scheduled two half-hour discharges, along with shrapnel barrages, along his entire front for the evening of x/y day.[55] General headquarters also made it known that it expected not only Fourth Army but all the armies to make gas discharges. In May Haig told his army commanders that they would each have at their disposal 3,000 White Star and 2,000 Red Star or Two Red Star cylinders along with a battalion of troops from the Special Brigade. In addition, he let them know that general headquarters held a reserve of cylinders that he would release as needed.[56]

1. Field Marshal Sir Douglas Haig.
Australian War Memorial negative
no. A03713.

2. Gas drill by Australian troops at Dier-El-Belah in early 1917 illustrating the gas helmet pattern respirator. Australian War Memorial negative no. J02257.

3. Studio photograph of Pvt. Cecil Ernest Bartlett, 32nd Battalion, Australian Imperial Force. Note that Bartlett chose to pose with his rifle in one hand and his gas mask in the other. Australian War Memorial negative no. P01781.001.

4. German troops caught in a gas bombardment on the Flanders coast in July 1917. Australian War Memorial negative no. H13183.

5. Livens projectors in a camouflaged position near Dernancourt on 14 June 1918. Australian War Memorial negative no. E04897.

6. Soldiers of the 45th Battalion, Australian Imperial Force, in the Ypres sector wearing their small box respirators, September 1917. Australian War Memorial negative no. E00825.

7. Australian soldiers blinded by
mustard gas rest in the open near
Bois De L'Abbe on 27 May 1918.
Australian War Memorial negative
no. E04851.

By the end of May Rawlinson had gone from being reluctant to use gas to being enthusiastic. Despite his allocation of only 5,000 cylinders, he advanced a program that required 11,400 cylinders, the preparation of 571 bays, and two battalions from the Special Brigade. The attack along 14,000 yards of front was planned to last two hours; he would authorize its launch at any time up to and including the day before the battle. By 6 June the program had expanded to include a heavy shrapnel bombardment of the front line, to destroy any Germans who manned their defenses in expectation of an attack, along with the shelling of communication trenches and reserve billets.[57] Additionally, the British infantry were to engage in rapid rifle and machine gun fire to help preserve surprise by covering the noise of the gas during its initial release. Ten to 15 minutes after the end of the discharge the artillery was to unleash a heavy concentration of fire to catch the German relief and medical parties.[58]

The gas program that Rawlinson authorized conformed to the discharge principles that Haig had outlined to his commanders at their conference. Fourth Army aimed to use a surprise release of a dense cloud of phosgene to kill the enemy before they had adjusted their masks, and then follow up with a prolonged discharge to wear out the protective elements of the German soldiers' respirators. Then, a final release of concentrated White Star would finish off those Germans whose masks no longer afforded adequate protection. His intentions were clear. Rawlinson wanted to cause massive casualties along the entire front along which he intended to attack, and thereby force the Germans to replace the depleted units with reserves. He also anticipated that the unexpected defeat would cause a sudden drop in the enemy's morale. Additionally, it is probable that Rawlinson was experimenting with a means to reach the enemy even while they were protected from the British artillery by their deep shelters, and that he hoped to devastate the enemy's rear area installations such as headquarters or batteries. There is no hard evidence to support such a claim, but later developments in mid-July suggest that the British had begun to apply gas for such a purpose.

The plan, if anything, was too ambitious, and its grand scope did not long survive. One problem was the size of the attack. At 14,275 yards the convoluted front was far too long. A simultaneous discharge of gas required the unlikely event of a suitable wind blowing along the front's entire length, and a wind that was acceptable along one sector might actually be quite dangerous to the British front line soldiers at another point. Additionally, Rawlinson's plan simply called for more gas than the army could provide.

As the battle time neared, Rawlinson remained uncertain as to how to schedule his gas. On 12 June he revised the cloud gas program and noted that "although the discharge will probably be of great value and inflict considerable casualties," he found it necessary to leave it to the discretion of his corps commanders as to when to discharge and in what quantity. However, he still recommended that they use up their more-lethal White Star first, followed by Red Star and Two Red Star. Yet two days later Rawlinson relieved the commanders of that responsibility and told his subordinates that army headquarters would set zero hour for the discharge by 5:00 P.M. on the afternoon prior to the attack.[59] The program for the preliminary bombardment authorized the release of gas on any night from U day forward if the wind was favorable, with the exception of the final evening before the assault (when he forbade any discharges). The prohibition was designed to prevent the gassing of British troops, and in the recognition that a discharge tended to cause an enemy retaliation against the point of flotation. On Y/Z night the trenches would be packed with assault troops, and inducing a barrage could result in severe casualties.[60]

On the twenty-seventh Rawlinson again reversed course and scheduled the evening of U day for a simultaneous discharge along his army's front. He forbade corps-level releases until the mass cloud attack had taken place. His instructions also reminded his subordinates that the ultimate decision to open the cylinders resided with the Special Brigade officers and was dependent upon the wind. On the twenty-fourth the weather forecast was favorable and Rawlinson ordered the attack for 10:00 P.M., U day. However, by evening the wind was nearly nonexistent and the gas officers canceled the discharge, except in front of 4th Division where the air speed was 3 MPH.[61]

Once again the weather proved to be the critical element in cloud gas attacks. Although the wind had ruined Rawlinson's plan for a synchronized release over the next several days, the Special Brigade launched a series of attacks along the entire British Expeditionary Force front, opening over 10,000 cylinders. For a summary of the operations during the preliminary bombardment see table 3.

After the commencement of the Somme, the chemical engineers continued to support the offensive with discharges on nonbattle fronts, to both cause casualties and reduce the enemy's morale, in fulfillment of Haig's orders for the other armies to hold the enemy to their sectors and

Table 3. Gas Discharges during the Preliminary Bombardment

Date	Army	Location	Ammunition
26 June	4th	N of Beaumont Hamel	150 White Star
26 June	4th	SE of Hebuterne	178 White Star
26 June	4th	SW of Beaumont Hamel	378 White Star
26 June	4th	Becourt–Mametz Road	1,043 White Star
26 June	4th	NW of Thiepval	436 White Star
26 June	4th	E of Authuille	302 White Star
26 June	4th	SE of La Boiselle	66 White Star
26 June	4th	W of Ovillers	163 White Star
27 June	4th	N of Ovillers	152 White Star
27 June	4th	N of La Boiselle	125 White Star
27 June	4th	SE of La Boiselle	200 White Star
27 June	4th	SW of Ovillers	439 White Star
27 June	3rd	Beaurains	968 White Star
27 June	3rd	E of Monchy	1,757 White Star
27 June	4th	W of Serre	178 White Star
27 June	4th	SW of Thiepval	346 White Star
27 June	1st	Angres & Lievin	1,055 White Star
28 June	1st	Hulluch Salient	815 White Star
28 June	3rd	Blairville/Ficheux	1,862 White Star and Red Star
28 June	2nd	NE Wulverghem	610 White Star
29 June	3rd	E of Monchy	185 White Star
29 June	2nd	Wulverghem	219 White Star
30 June	4th	W of Carnoy	51 White Star
30 June	4th	N of Carnoy	79 White Star
30 June	4th	NW of Carnoy	107 White Star
30 June	2nd	Le Ruage	210 White Star
30 June	2nd	Le Touquet	498 White Star and Red Star
1 July	2nd	Le Touquet	334 White Star and Red Star
1 July	2nd	NW of St. Yves	223 White Star
1 July	2nd	Bellewarde	119 White Star

Source: Data taken from, "SB Ops," WO142/266, PRO.

to cause them losses.[62] Due to local conditions, some targets became favorites of the Special Brigade, such as the Hulluch Salient on the First Army front. It received 1,037 White Star cylinders on 5 July, 927 more White Stars on 20 August, and another 2,537 White Stars and Red Stars on 5 October. The last date was a busy one for the chemists as they also released nearly 2,000 White Star cylinders at Nieuport in support of a French operation. Most operations, however, were much more modest and took the form of harassment or wasting assaults on small frontages. Foulkes's companies opened an additional 26,262 cylinders by the battle's end.[63]

Foulkes's mortarmen also played a role in the battle. Initially, due to the lack of gas ammunition they had to limit their participation to the creation of smoke screens. On 1 July, at 7:30 A.M., as the British infantry began their assault, the Special Brigade mortars opened fire along the line, targeting in particular the enemy's fortified villages and strong points such as Thiepval, Fricourt, Gommecourt, and Ovillers. Their objective was to obscure the advancing infantry from the machine guns hidden within these locations. Within minutes they had set off over 4,300 red phosphorus bombs. As the battle continued the planners repeatedly called upon the Special Brigade to provide smoke, such as for XIII Corps attacks against Guillemont on 16 and 21 August.[64]

The mortar companies eventually did get gas bombs and began using them in September. As a temporary expedient they employed the 2-inch Stokes mortar to fire phosgene into High Wood on 2 September and into Guillemont the following day; it was not until 24 September when they fired their first 4-inch lachrymatory gas ammunition against Flers and Thiepval. Over the next two months they shot over 2,000 rounds of SK, 1,100 of which were used against Beaumont Hamel on 28 October. In the final days of the battle the Special Brigade received its first lethal gas bombs and dispatched 15 CG rounds into enemy positions south of Beaumont Hamel.[65]

Smoke also acted as a ruse to compel the enemy to wear their masks and thus be at a disadvantage when the British infantry attacked. In May, Foulkes wrote that smoke had two purposes: to simulate gas and to cover the movement of infantry. Thus the Special Brigade released smoke and gas on the evening of 2 July to assist a raid by the 4th Australian Infantry Brigade, and general headquarters ordered the reserve army to assist Rawlinson's attack on 14 July with a release of gas and smoke.[66]

Also becoming a part of the infantry's routine issue at this time were gas grenades used to clear enemy dugouts. Because even the nonpersistent gases tended to linger underground, it was possible to quickly establish a dangerous concentration of gas that would rapidly kill a surprised defender or wear out the protective chemicals in the German respirator and force the enemy to the surface. Gas grenades came in a variety of fillings including Red Star, White Star, SK, and PS, and also a white phosphorus model called the P-grenade. Experiments had demonstrated that SK and PS were highly effective, and an unprotected observer could not remain in a contaminated dugout for more than a few seconds even 14 hours after the gas's release.[67]

On the first day of the Somme the Special Brigade's Z Company took the opportunity to demonstrate their new flamethrowers. They had installed the massive machines in a shallow mineshaft just in front of the enemy's position near the Canoy–Montauban Road. At zero hour the engineers pushed the flame pipes through the thin roof of their hidden installation, fired the weapon and incinerated the target. They subsequently used flamethrowers against Guillemont on 3 September and against High Wood on 8 September, but the flamethrower never became an efficient weapon and Foulkes soon discontinued its use. The weapon's enormous frame and storage tanks meant that the engineers required days, if not weeks, of secretive and hazardous digging to install it near its target. Its short range of less than 100 yards also limited its flexibility because to fire at a different target the engineers had to dig up the weapon and reinstall it elsewhere.[68]

After the Special Brigade, the Royal Artillery played the next most important role in the discharge of gas during the Somme. Early in 1916 gas officers undertook to disseminate policy regarding the use of gas. They identified the objectives of a chemical attack as two-fold: to incapacitate the enemy's infantry and possibly his artillery in order to facilitate the advance, and to wear down the opposition through its effect on morale.[69] Rawlinson built upon this and defined two principle missions for chemical shell at a Fourth Army conference in April. Rawlinson believed that the two critical missions for his guns were counter-battery and the neutralization of the defenses within the enemy's fortified villages. At the April meeting he pointed out the value of lachrymatory shell for counter-battery, although he admitted not knowing how much lachrymatory would be available.[70] He noted to his subordinates that "counter-battery work is becoming more and more important. For this, gas shells will be useful, they last a long time, and if thick will stop a battery firing."[71] The British believed that gas was "the most powerful weapon for neutralization. With it we can, if not entirely deny the Bosche access to his guns, at least ruin his morale and force him to wear his gas masks, which will seriously impair his accuracy and rapidity of fire."[72] As a consequence, Rawlinson authorized his gunners to use gas shells freely to suppress hostile batteries.[73]

At the time the only agent the British had was the highly persistent lachrymatory substance SK. Although not lethal, its effect upon the eyes was most dramatic. It forced the enemy gunners to wear their masks and could even cut a battery off from relief or resupply. Its persistence, however, did create a problem when it was used against strong points, as British troops could not then immediately occupy the position. Rawlinson therefore warned that they could only use SK against villages that they planned to surround and not immediately possess. He also recommended its use against isolated strong points to induce the defenders to surrender.[74] The British also had the lethal gas shells that the French had provided when they had loaned the 75mm guns. Haig assigned these to counter-battery, especially those using special shell no. 4, which required a high concentration to become effective and was therefore unsuitable for large targets. The French shell had an additional benefit to the advancing infantry of being highly volatile; the British believed it would be safe to traverse contaminated ground within 30 minutes of the last shell's arrival. Rawlinson's plan called for gas counter-battery bombardments to commence during the evening prior to the assault.[75]

Rawlinson's tactics suggest a concern with the need for his infantry to safely maneuver on the battlefield if they were to obtain a breakthrough. If the artillery succeeded in obliterating the enemy's trench defenders, the next threats to his troops were the interdicting fire of machine guns from the fortified villages and the enemy's ability to isolate the advancing infantry with its artillery. SK had the potential to neutralize the firepower of both of these obstacles, and if the attackers observed the prohibition of not occupying the contaminated ground they might be able to maneuver around the strong points and penetrate deeply into the enemy's position.

After the battle began it was virtually impossible to gain any direct proof of the effectiveness of gas shells. However, there is considerable circumstantial evidence that shell gas made a powerful impression upon senior planners after the assaults on 1 and 14 July. Haig corresponded with the War Office on 17 July and demanded an immediate supply of lethal gas shell. He wrote: "The valuable effect has been most marked, both for counter battery work and for the attack on villages, and it seems probable that not only has the use of this shell considerably assisted the progress of the operations, but some attacks on villages have failed when a liberal use of this shell, if available, would probably have led to the attack being successful."[76] Haig followed up by dispatching Thuillier to London to hasten the provision of gas shells, a matter the Ministry of Munitions took up immediately.[77] Haig's request for more gas shells was an attempt to solve one of the fundamental problems of the Great War: maneuver upon the battlefield. If the British were to break through the enemy's defenses then it was essential that they find some method to neutralize the defensive fire coming from the enemy's strong points, villages, and batteries.[78] Haig's appeal for lethal shell, instead of a demand for an increase in the lachrymatory ammunition that his gunners already had, also represented a realization that SK, while ideal for suppressing a position, was highly persistent and would prevent the British from following up a gas attack with an advance. Phosgene met this requirement but it would not be available in quantity until 1917.

Rawlinson, who had first suggested the use of gas against dugouts in 1915 in the aftermath of the failure of Aubers Ridge, had hinted at a similar policy for attacking woods and villages as described in his "Tactical Notes." He feared that without panic in the enemy ranks it would be extremely difficult to conquer the fortified positions. The ability to cause otherwise stalwart men to panic and lose their morale was, of course, one of the first capabilities the British had attributed to gas. Rawlinson went on to explain that the artillery could neutralize a defended locale by a heavy bombardment of high explosive, smoke, or gas shells. Furthermore, he suggested the establishment of a shrapnel barrage around the perimeter of the target so as to destroy any enemy who attempted to flee or reestablish in an adjacent position. Rawlinson indicated the importance of these tactics. By neutralizing the target the advancing infantry could turn the objective's flank or rear and thereby encourage its surrender. For example, Rawlinson ordered XIV Corps to use their 4.5-inch howitzers to fire gas into Bouleaux Wood in support of the successful attempt to capture Ginchy on 9 September. Germans positioned in the woods protected the village's flank which would make an attack on Ginchy expensive. This policy also explains why XV Corps fired 9,000 rounds of PS into Flers on the nights of 13–14 and 14–15 September in preparation for their attack on the stronghold. Essentially, Rawlinson saw the suppression of the hostile defending troops in woods and villages as a prerequisite to opening up the battlefield and restoring the infantry's ability to attack.[79]

In August general headquarters issued a circular, "Notes on the Em-

ployment of Gas Shells," that emphasized the usefulness of gas in counter-battery work and in attacks on villages, woods, and other enclosed
positions. The report identified the four gas shells that were now becoming available and summarized each's properties. It explained that if
the intention was to render a position uninhabitable for a long time then
SK was the best choice. To obtain a quick effect immediately prior to an
assault, the proper gas was Jellite. Where the British desired a temporary neutralization followed somewhat later by an attack, PS was appro-
priate. Finally, White Star was the most effective chemical for causing
casualties. A companion document, "Gas Shell Bombardments,"
made the point that a concentrated SK bombardment of a village would
make all the dugouts and cellars uninhabitable for at least 12 hours.
Thus, as the defender's masks wore out the gas would drive them to the
surface where the artillery could destroy them with shrapnel.[80]

The need to address fortified positions also became the driving force
behind determining the types of fillings for gas shells. The day after
Haig's demand for chemical shells the Ministry of Munitions took up
the question of whether or not to fill shells with Jellite, a lethal gas developed by the Royal Navy. By mid-July there were already over 50
tons of the substance in England with a production capacity of a further
four tons per week. The result was a reordering of priorities with the
lachrymatory substance SK being shifted from top to last priority, and
Jellite, Phosgene, and PS—Chloropicrin—moving to the fore. Since
Haig wanted lethal shell and Jellite was available, the Ministry of Munitions pressed it into service. Its role in the war was a brief one as its battlefield performance proved inferior to other lethal compounds and its
use was soon discontinued.[81]

The need to overcome fortified positions also determined the production ratio that the British settled upon in late July for the three calibers then approved for chemical munitions. The British estimated that
it was necessary to use between 5,000 and 8,000 shells to suppress a defended locale, depending upon type, caliber, and weather conditions.
However, the other part of the equation was time. How quickly could
the British get the shells to the target to build up an effective concentration of gas? In a study they performed, using the village of Guillemont
as an example, they found that gas-capable guns that the artillery could
typically bring to bear were 36—4.5-inch howitzers, 16—60 pounders,
and 4—4.7-inch guns. After factoring in the different rates of fire, the
report concluded that the production ratio should be 6:4:1 for the 4.5-

inch, 60-pounder, and 4.7-inch pieces. Haig subsequently submitted to London a request for 30,000 shells per week at the above ratios.[82]

On 23 July the Special Brigade presented its own method designed to obliterate the defenders of fortified locales: the Livens projector. Capt. William H. Livens, an inventive engineer and commander of Z company (the unit responsible for the flamethrowers), had rigged up an experimental version of what would evolve into the most-feared chemical weapon of the war. Livens's prototype was literally an old oil drum emplaced into the ground at a 45-degree angle and pointed at its target. (He determined range by varying the amount of propellant.) His first bombs were homemade three-gallon lubricating oil cans filled with a highly inflammable oil. While never a terribly refined device, the future model consisted of a smooth-bore 9.5-inch steel tube with a closed bottom, along with a base plate to prevent the recoil from sending the device further into the ground. The engineers dug the ensemble into the ground and left only the muzzle exposed. They placed the firing charges at the bottom with the detonator wires running up the side and connecting to a detonator that could fire up to 20 projectors at once. The drum was simply lowered into the muzzle until it rested upon the propellant at the base. The engineers could fire the weapon again as long as the blast did not shift the projector's alignment in the ground.[83]

The basis of the claim for the weapon's supremacy was its ability to deliver a large amount of gas onto a target with virtually no warning. The projector's drum contained 30 pounds of pure phosgene, an enormous amount, especially when compared to artillery shells. The projector quickly became the most devastating weapon possessed by the Special Brigade and would eventually rival and supplant the use of cylinders as their most important activity. By the war's end the Special Brigade received over 150,000 projectors, and discharged more gas through this method than all the other Special Brigade methods combined. Furthermore, projectors were less labor intensive to install than cylinders, and a special company could ready 1,200 in a single night without the help of the infantry.[84]

The projector was an area weapon, but due to its large capacity it could still envelop the target in a dense cloud of phosgene. Lieut. Col. Arthur Crossley, who witnessed Livens's work, was greatly impressed by the volume of gas that was simultaneously released in a hostile position. He wrote that "the *instantaneous* liberation . . . of gas . . . would be certain to find a number of the enemy engulfed in a high lethal concentration of gas without time to fix their masks before being overcome by it."[85] Even fitting a mask gave no guarantee of a soldier's survival, since the concentration of gas the Livens projector obtained was so high it could overwhelm the protective agents in the German respirator. After the battle Foulkes established the weapon's tactical principles. He recommended its use against "*areas* which are strongly held and which contain underground shelters designed to defy artillery bombardment."[86] For best results he preferred a night discharge to help preserve surprise, and the ideal wind was dead calm so that the gas saturated the area. The British always used lethal gas with the projector, and while there was some risk to discharging it at the time of an assault, they could safely fire it the evening before. Foulkes expected that a gas discharge would weaken the defenders and leave them without sufficient time to bring up replacements or to relieve the garrison.[87]

Livens repeated his experiments with incendiary rounds on 18 August and 3 September against High Wood but, on the 3rd the Special Brigade also increased the lethality of their attack by firing their first phosgene bombs into the stronghold of Thiepval. The objectives of the discharges on 3 and 15 September were probably attempts to cause casualties in support of the army's breakthrough attempt at Flers. However, the next barrage, at the end of September, was directly connected to the British seizure of Thiepval and the ridge it stood upon. At a conference on the 21st the Special Brigade received its orders to put gas into the village on the evening before the attack. They were also to have materials ready to employ against any outstanding strong points on the night after the attack.[88] Thus if the assaulting infantry ran into any positions that they could not handle they were to let the Special Brigade asphyxiate these positions with gas. On the evening of 24 September the Special Brigade's mortarmen dropped 517 rounds of SK onto the fortress, forcing the garrison to don their masks. The next evening 24 Livens drums exploded onto the target, releasing phosgene onto defenders whose masks had already been depleted by exposure to the long-lasting SK the night before. The next day, at 12:35 in the afternoon, the British attacked and swept the Germans from the position. After his capture the second in command of the garrison said that it was an extraordinary concentration of gas, the most he had ever encountered.[89]

Foulkes employed the same tactics against Beaumont Hamel on 28 October in an independent attack while the Battle of Ancre Heights was underway. At noon, 1,126 SK Stokes mortar bombs rained down on the ruins, followed that evening by 101 Livens drums of phosgene.

An additional 34 Livens, along with 30 2-inch White Star trench mortar bombs blanketed the nearby village of Serre. Again, Foulkes's intention was to first wear out the defenders' respirators and then kill them with phosgene. Beaumont Hamel received similar attention on 12 November followed by its capture on the 13th.[90]

As gas shells became more common they gained additional missions. To further wear down the enemy British gunners routinely fired harassment missions, which were sudden and brief bombardments of locations where personnel tended to congregate, such as trench junctions or positions where the enemy was making trench repairs. Much of this work was done at night, and the British therefore could not bring to bear observed fire from their batteries. As an area weapon, however, gas did not require the same degree of precision as high explosives or shrapnel to inflict casualties, and if wind conditions were acceptable the Royal Artillery would freely use chemical munitions at night. Gas also developed a role in counter-preparation fire. The British realized that they could inflict serious losses or disorganize the enemy troops by shelling locations where they anticipated an enemy counterattack might develop or traverse. Counter-prep built upon one of the lessons learned at Loos, in which an enemy counterattack succeeded in sweeping the British from the summit of Hill 70. The British frequently fired such missions after the completion of their attacks in order to give the infantry a chance to consolidate their newly won positions.[91]

After the commencement of the Somme, Haig continued his battle with the Ministry of Munitions for more gas shell, again asking for 30,000 a week, divided among the 4.5-inch, 60-pounder, and 4.7-inch in the ratio of 6:4:1. However, because he was anxious to get his hands on anything, he added the proviso that until supplies became regular he wanted them to fill any of these types whenever they were available and send them out as soon as possible. He also added that the fillings could be of the best substance that happened to be available. General headquarters increased its demands the following month when they asked for 35,000 shells per week, but this was broken down as 30,000 lethal and 5,000 SK, along with 6,000 lethal and 9,000 SK rounds for the Stokes mortar and 3,000 cylinders. Haig's memorandum again closed with a statement on the experimental nature of the request, but this time it explained that the figures were a minimum and that future revisions would be for increased amounts of chemical shell.[92]

Despite these constant and detailed requisitions, the greatest hand-

Table 4. Expenditure of British Gas Ammunition during the Somme

Caliber	23–31 June	1 July–31 Aug.	1–30 Sept.	1–31 Oct.
4.5" SK	3,772	842	6,605	4,144
4.5" lethal	—	—	25,706	3,898
4.7" SK	—	2,818	2,049	60
4.7" lethal	—	—	787	505
60-pounder SK	—	1,484	2,104	1,744
60-pounder lethal	—	909	8,341	2,145

Source: Data collected from "Ammunition Expenditure—23 June 1916 to 31 August 1916," Rawlinson's Fourth Army Records, vol. 2, IWM; and "Ammunition Expenditure—23 June to 1 October 1916, and "Summary of Special Ammunition Other than Shown in Daily Summaries—Expenditures during October," Rawlinson's Fourth Army Records, vol. 4, IWM.

icap facing the British use of gas continued to be the woefully inadequate supply of chemical munitions. During the Somme, gas shell represented a minuscule proportion of the ammunition consumed by the guns. The French initially supplied 100,000 rounds for their 75s but the capacity of each shell was considerably less than that of a British 4.5-inch shell.[93] Furthermore, the provision of gas shell for the 4.5-inch howitzer fell short of even the minimal estimates, and no gas shell was available, at first, for the 4.7-inch and 60-pounder guns. Table 4 outlines the expenditure of British gas ammunition from the beginning of the battle through the end of October.

Instructions issued by general headquarters illustrate the extent of the British shortfall in chemical munitions. General headquarters estimated the number of shells needed to bombard a village of 500,000 square yards so that the garrison was neutralized by the gas. The amount of shells required for a bombardment by 4.5-inch howitzers is outlined in table 5. The report also expressed the figures in shells per thousand square yards per minute. This formula allowed the gunners to determine the ammunition requirements for any target based upon its size. Table 6 outlines this information for the 4.5-inch howitzer.

The Effectiveness of Gas
The effectiveness of the British use of gas at the Somme was rather difficult to establish, and unless raiders gained the enemy's lines it was

Table 5. Number of Shells Required to Neutralize a Village

Gas	Number of Shells	Ratio
Lachrymatory SK	4,950	100
Lethal PS	6,200	125
Lethal White Star	7,425	150
Lethal Jellite	7,425	150
White Star in Damp conditions	8,650	175

Source: Data taken from "Gas Shell Bombardments," 23 August 1916, wo158/436, PRO.

Table 6. Shells Per 1,000 Square Yards Per Minute Required to Neutralize a Village

Gas	Opening Concentration of 5 Minutes	Continuation Bombardmant for Next 25 Minutes
Lachrymatory SK	.88	.22
Lethal PS	1.1	.27
Lethal White Star	1.32	.33
Lethal Jellite	1.32	.33
White Star in damp conditions	1.54	.38

Source: Data taken from "Gas Shell Bombardments," 23 August 1916, wo158/436, PRO.

practically impossible to collect any solid information on the results of the discharge. Frequently the British had to base their assessments on indirect evidence. In some case the proof was impressionistic, such as the comments of Maj. Gen. H. Hudson, commanding officer 8th Division, who noted after a nighttime discharge on his front that he was "inclined to think that the comparatively feeble retaliation directed against our lines was due to the casualties and confusion caused."[94] On another occasion it was the presence of six ambulances behind the enemy's position the next morning, and the sound of motors from additional ambulances during the night, that convinced the British that the enemy's casualties had been heavy.[95] The British also had to rely upon prisoner interrogation such as that taken from two soldiers of the 62 Bavarian Reserve Infantry Regiment, who told their examiners that their unit had sustained great losses in a recent gas attack, including 50 percent casualties in one battalion.[96]

Proof was easier to collect when the British coordinated the discharge with a trench raid. On the evening of 27 June, O Company, Special Brigade, R.E., launched a massive gas flotation on the front of the 47th (London) Division. They released White Star from 1,070 cylinders—approximately 30 tons of phosgene—over a two-hour period with heavy concentrations of gas at the beginning and end of the discharge. Lieut. Gen. Henry Wilson, IV Corps commander, concluded that the raid's success was due to the phosgene. He noted that:

1. We crossed "No Man's Land" and entered the enemy's trenches without being met by either machine gun or rifle fire.
2. The enemy's artillery was very slow in coming into action and were wild in their shooting when they did fire.[97]

Wilson decided that he would try gas again when the wind permitted. Maj. Gen. C. Barter, the Londoners' commanding officer, believed that the enemy had to have suffered considerable casualties and loss of morale because "it is difficult to suppose that our infantry could have penetrated into the German trenches with so little opposition without its assistance." He also suggested that the ineffectiveness of the German gunners was due to the necessity for them to wear their respirators, which hindered their performance.[98]

C Company, Special Brigade, R.E., conducted another major attack on the 8th Division front on the evening of 5 October. They released nearly 80 tons of gas from over 2,300 White Star and Red Star cylinders in three dense waves with smoke filling the intervals. The assault lasted two-and-one-half hours. Their intention was to both surprise the hostile troops and wear out the enemy's respirators. While the raiders failed to enter the enemy's lines, the indirect evidence suggested a major success. The weather conditions were perfect, the night dark, the retaliation weak, and with the field batteries and trench mortars soon dying down, the enemy quickly relieved the affected units.[99]

In general, senior officers tended to be pleased with the results of Special Brigade operations and recommended their continuance when the meteorological conditions were good. Edmonds noted that Haig was comfortable enough with gas to urge its frequent use upon his army commanders, and general headquarters believed that there was no better way to cause casualties and thus divert the enemy's reserves from the main battle. Cylinder operations, in particular, emitted a dense cloud of lethal vapor that penetrated deeply into the enemy's perimeter, not only killing front-line troops but also striking at headquarters, batteries, and other rear echelon units. Furthermore, cylinder discharges gave the British the means to strike at enemy soldiers in reserve positions, thus denying these troops the restorative rest they needed to rebuild their morale.[100]

Rawlinson's conclusions from the discharges during the preliminary bombardment offer a case in point. Despite the problems with the wind, he considered the results favorable. He credited gas for the sudden cessation of the enemy's trench mortars during III Corps's attack on 27 June, and his assessment of the discharges the following evening on X and XV Corps' fronts was equally positive.[101] Foulkes, while admittedly a prejudiced observer, was voluble in his praise for the success of gas at the Somme. In his history he wrote: "It is impossible to resist the conclusion that the German losses from gas were exceedingly heavy during the summer and autumn of 1916, especially in view of . . . the heavy concentrations of gas liberated, the deadly nature of the gas employed, the silence of its emission . . . and the frequency with which a complete surprise was effected."[102]

Of the various gas appliances tested during the Somme there was little doubt that the Livens projector offered the greatest promise. After their capture of Beaumont Hamel on 13 November, the British found over 300 Germans dead from gas poisoning, a discovery that might help explain the successful taking of the position. In investigating one of the shelters at Beaumont Hamel, the British came across a party of 15 dead Germans whose final poses the observers described as a "cinematographic series of photographs of German gas-mask drill."[103] Livens noted that it was possible to gauge how long it took for the gas to kill the Germans by the extent to which they had gotten their masks on. The three soldiers furthest from the entrance had fully positioned their masks, the fourth had his halfway on, the fifth had it on his face, the sixth had it out of his box, the seventh had the box open, and the eighth had his hand on the box lid, while the remaining seven—those closest to the entrance—had not found time to even think of their masks.[104] The power of the Livens projector suggests that Haig was correct in his demand of 17 July for lethal shell for use against the enemy's fortified positions. The projector also received a positive welcome by the army commanders, who demanded as large a supply as possible of the weapon.

While the Special Brigade did not dominate the battle as it had done at Loos, its performance during the Somme assured its position as an important auxiliary in the struggle against Germany. The British had succeeded in defining missions for the Special Brigade that corresponded with the methods they planned to employ to achieve decisive victory. The Somme proved that Foulkes's unit had the capability to contribute to the gaining of an advantage over the enemy. Gas, discharged from either cylinders, Livens projectors, or Stokes mortars, would continue to play a role in the wearing down process that eventually provided Britain with a superiority over Germany.

Shell gas, too, had established for itself missions within the fire capabilities of the Royal Artillery. Counter-battery was a vital objective of the gunners, since the suppression of the defender's firepower helped to ensure the survival of the infantry and the sustainment of an attack. The addition of chemical shell gave the gunners another dimension in their struggle with the enemy's artillery. Gas could blanket a target in a fog of dangerous vapors and its persistency would ensure the enemy's neutralization long after the effect of a conventional bombardment would have ceased. Furthermore, gas shell gave the gunners an effective area weapon so that they could bombard at night when precision was impossible. Having helped the infantry obtain their objectives, the use of counter-prep fire helped assure that the attackers could consolidate and hold onto their gains. Gas shell also performed an important role in the wearing down process and helped fulfill the British desire to never give the enemy a chance to recover their effectiveness.

The failure of the Somme to achieve decisive victory demonstrated that the wearing down process had not yet achieved its goal. The German army was still an effective fighting machine whose morale, though damaged, remained intact. The conflict would continue, and as more British factories and filling plants came into service the gas component of the war continued to expand. Haig, Foulkes, and others in the chemical war would look to 1917 for the opportunity to reestablish the vitality of the offense, to dominate the battlefield, and to crush the enemy.

CHAPTER 4

Institutionalization

Regard your masks as sacred, for gas causes as many casualties as artillery. – German Anti-Gas Lecture

The 1917 campaign began on a positive note for the western Allies. Britain's newly constructed munitions factories were turning out materials in abundance and, along with purchases from neutrals such as the United States, the Entente would soon have a resource superiority on the western front. The coming year would also confirm the growing British edge in many new war technologies, including the tank, predicted artillery fire, and gas. Regarding morale, Haig believed that the battles of the Somme and Verdun had exposed a sense of fatigue in the German soldiers' commitment to the war, which, with further pounding, would widen and lead to a collapse of the German army. The withdrawal of the enemy to the prepared positions of the Hindenburg Line in late February to mid-March seemed to confirm that the battles of 1916 had indeed left the enemy weakened. The year would not end on such an optimistic note; the collapse of Russia threatened to redress Germany's numerical inferiority on the western front, the French army mutinied after the botched offensive along the Aisne, Italy suffered heavily in its futile efforts on the Isonzo (culminating with their disastrous defeat at Caporetto), and the British campaign of Passchendaele became associated with drowning mud and a distant leadership and staff. Even with these failures, however, 1917 proved to be the turning point in the war. Germany's gamble on unrestricted submarine warfare failed to starve Britain into submission and predictably forced the world's greatest industrial power into the Entente's camp. The entry of the United States assured eventual victory for the Allies, though the vital question remained: how to achieve decisive victory.

The British in 1917 made great strides in institutionalizing the technologies and tactics that would bring victory the following year. By the campaign season of 1917 most infantry platoons had a Lewis gun, which, combined with bombers, rifle grenades, and rifles, gave the units formidable firepower and maneuverability.[1] Of equal importance was the spreading of attack principles outlined in training manuals such as *Instructions for the Training of Platoons for Offensive Action, Assault Training,* and *Instructions for the Training of Divisions for Offensive Action.*[2] In the air the Royal Flying Corps began the year outclassed by the enemy's machines, and at the Battle of Arras though the flyers paid a heavy price for technological inferiority they also displayed superb skill in aerial photography and artillery observation. The tank continued to undergo improvements and production numbers increased, but its effect remained relatively minor, except for its success at Cambrai in November. The artillery was where the most dramatic advances occurred. As Paddy Griffith notes in *Battle Tactics of the Western Front,* "by 1917 techniques had . . . been refined whereby the fire could be very precisely predicted merely from the map or an air photograph, without an observer at all."[3] Due to the combination of information gathered by map surveyors, aerial observers and photographers, sound rangers, flash spotters, and meteorologists, and armed with the knowledge derived from detailed analysis of gun and shell characteristics including calibration, British gunners gained the ability to fire indirectly with a high degree of precision. Predicted fire was a critical area of gunnery skill through which the British gained an advantage over the Germans, a lead they held to the end of the war.[4]

Contributing to this success was another important artillery innovation that came about from the recognition of the vital importance of counter-battery fire to the success of the infantry. By 1917 the British had created corps-level counter-battery offices under the command of a counter-battery staff officer charged with the location and destruction or neutralization of the enemy's guns. Attached to a typical office was a Royal Flying Corps squadron and a balloon company charged with making aerial reconnaissance and directing fire, an observation group of field survey engineers for flash spotting and mapping, and a sound-ranging group for the location of active enemy batteries. The counter-battery office also included intelligence officers to sift through the information collected from the above groups, along with data reported by forward observers and the infantry, and knowledge gained from the interrogation of prisoners and the study of captured documents. After Messines, Brig. Gen. G. Humphreys, Brigadier General Royal Artillery IX Corps, maintained that "the success of our counter-battery fire was largely due to the fact that control rested in the hands of one expert [the counter-battery staff officer] and his staff, who were free to devote their whole time, energy, brains to the one end of defeating enemy guns."[5] The combined efforts of these elements succeeded in giving the counter-battery commander a fairly accurate picture of the enemy's artillery and the effects of British counter-battery efforts. Gas featured heavily in the operations of this office and chemical shell became the preferred method for neutralizing the German artillery, especially at night when observed shoots were impossible.[6]

While gas had played a comparatively minor role in 1916, it would become ubiquitous on the battlefield by the end of 1917 and the importance and frequency of its use would correspondingly increase. Its dependence upon meteorological conditions still acted as a brake upon its employment, but improvements in weaponry and theory helped broaden its application and lessen the influence of weather. Increased supply, enhanced technology, and formalized ideas would lead to the institutionalization of gas within the British way of making war. As gas became more widespread the suffering it caused was intensified, particularly after the introduction of mustard gas by the Germans in July. There was no escaping from gas on the western front as it became an increasingly important component of all British operations.[7]

The Campaigns of 1917

The Chantilly Conference of 16 November 1916 laid the basis for operations in the following year. Allied commanders determined to seek a decision with a series of offenses in the western, Russian, and Italian theaters, timed so as to make it impossible for the Germans to shift reserves between fronts. France was to be the decisive sector but all other fronts would contribute to the weakening of the enemy. Haig and Joffre agreed to a combined offensive, straddling the old Somme battlefield with the French to the south and the British to the north. However, Joffre's replacement by Gen. Robert Nivelle in December led to a revision of the British role. Nivelle, one of the heroes of Verdun, intended to win the war with a massive blow from the entire resources of his army that would drive the Germans from the country. Whereas the Allies had intended to destroy their opponent's will through a series of hard blows leading to the rupture of the German line, Nivelle proposed to crush the enemy's main body in a single pitched battle. He envisioned the offensives as a two-stage process. First, the French army would break through the German line and then his reserve, the "mass of maneuver," would advance into the open and destroy the enemy's armies. The British contribution would be a preliminary attack to distract the enemy and use up German reserves. The Allies tentatively scheduled the battle for mid-March, but after various delays the British attacked on 9 April and the French seven days later. To maximize his resources Nivelle asked for and received British agreement to take over more of the French line so as to free up additional divisions for the attack. The role of the British was now a subsidiary one, with attacks alongside the River Scarpe, near Arras, aimed at the reduction of the Bapaume Salient and possibly an advance on the rail centers of Cambrai and Douai. Victory depended upon Nivelle's thrust, and if it failed the British efforts would be meaningless.[8]

Haig outlined the plan to his army commanders in a letter on 2 January 1917. He explained that the British would undertake operations with Gough's Fifth Army in the Ancre Valley, with Gen. E. H. H. Allenby's Third Army positioned opposite Arras, and with Gen. H. S. Horne's First Army against Vimy Ridge. While the British attacks held the promise of snipping off the Bapaume Salient, their principle function was to draw in German reserves so that the enemy would have fewer divisions to react to Nivelle's blow. While committed to supporting Nivelle, Haig remained unconvinced that French attacks would destroy the German army. Accordingly, at the London Convention of 16 January 1917, Haig extracted a promise that if the Anglo-French attacks did not lead to rapid victory then the British could shut down their operations and redirect their efforts further north to Flanders, the area where Haig preferred to seek the decisive battle. Throughout the winter the British worked on plans for a massive breakthrough offensive from the Ypres Salient, one that was coordinated with secondary operations around Nieuport along with a five-division landing by the Royal Navy on the Belgian coast.[9]

The German withdrawal to the Hindenburg Line caught the British by surprise and necessitated modifications in Haig's plans. The retirement obviated the need for Fifth Army's attack, but still left Allenby's attack at Arras as the principal thrust of the BEF's April battles. Originally scheduled for 8 April but postponed 24 hours to the ninth, the offensive had as its objective: "To strike the enemy on the Arras-Vimy front in the greatest possible strength with a view of penetrating his defences, outflanking the Hindenburg Line from the North, and operating in the direction of Cambrai."[10] The breaching of the enemy's defenses and the threat to a critical logistical center would force the Germans to divert reserves towards the British thrust, and thereby achieve the operation's principal mission: aiding Nivelle.

The Third Army's plan provided the infantry with powerful support for their assault, including over 1,100 field guns and nearly 600 heavy pieces. The bombardment to clear the wire and weaken the enemy lasted two weeks, although the gunners accomplished the bulk of their work during the last four days. But the 24-hour delay gave the gunners an extra day. The army also had the support of a brigade of tanks, 10 squadrons of the Royal Flying Corps, and the Special Brigade. The gas component of the battle was substantial. The artillery set as its objective the suppression of as many enemy batteries as possible at the battle's beginning. Accordingly, the 4.5-inch howitzers and 60-pounder guns would bombard enemy positions with gas from 7:30 P.M. on the evening preceding the attack to an hour after zero. The Special Brigade would contribute two discharges, one on the fourth and another on the sixth, to weaken the enemy's defenses.[11]

On the morning of 9 April soldiers of Third Army went over the top and advanced toward the Germans. The assault began brilliantly, with the British occupying most of the enemy's first line within 45 minutes and overrunning the second line two hours later. The British also captured 5,600 prisoners. However, the German third line remained, and the British attack slowed. By nightfall most of the area remained in enemy hands. Despite the failure to break through, the attack showed the effect of the changes the British had made in their tactics and the technological improvements, particularly in artillery, that were responsible for the increased firepower and accuracy of the guns. Gas, too, had served its purpose, and many German batteries were unable to respond to the British advance. However, once Third Army failed to reach the open the battle took on a familiar air. Increasing resistance and smaller gains followed the initial fast movement, until finally the advance ceased. Arriving German reinforcements spelled the doom of the offensive and Haig ordered it shut down on the fourteenth. While the first phase was over, Haig, determined to fulfill his commitment to support the French, required Third Army to make a series of further efforts throughout April and on until the end of May. The consequences of this support would be high. It cost Third Army nearly 90,000 casualties.

Coordinated with the start of Arras was the storming of Vimy Ridge by the Canadians of Horne's First Army. Unlike the battle at Arras, the British had conceived this attack strictly in terms of a limited action: once the ridge was in British hands the attack would stop. The four Canadian divisions also had considerable artillery and gas support. The gunners had over 1,000 pieces in the line and the Special Brigade planned to carry out a preliminary projector attack while its mortarmen would support the infantry with a smoke barrage. The artillery also planned to employ gas, and the gunners arranged a counter-battery bombardment for zero hour to neutralize the enemy's artillery. Tanks were also available but, as the Canadians had only eight and the ground was rough, planners did not attach much value to their presence.

At 5:30 A.M. the British artillery opened fire and engulfed Vimy in a storm of steel while tunnelers exploded two mines under the ridge. Simultaneously the Canadians began their advance and made it across no man's land with few casualties. The attackers quickly overwhelmed the enemy's front line and by 7:00 A.M. they had reached their intermediate objectives. The attack paused for consolidation but just before 10:00 A.M. the artillery redoubled its efforts and the Canadians resumed their advance. By the end of the day the entire ridge was in their possession except for the summit of Hill 145 (which they took the next day) and some other small objectives (which fell by the fourteenth). At the battle's end the Canadians gazed from the summit over enemy territory across the plain of Douai to the east, and the suburbs and slag heaps of Lens and the old battlefield of Loos to the north. The view dominated the enemy trenches below and left their approach routes exposed to British interdiction. So complete had been the Canadians' accomplishment that the Germans declined to launch a counterattack and instead accepted their defeat.

On 16 April, after the British battles had come to an end, Nivelle launched his war-ending offensive along the Aisne. The results were a catastrophe. Anticipating the blow, the Germans had positioned counterattack divisions behind their lines. As the French soldiers advanced into the German positions they came under increasing pressure and were forced back, many to their starting points. Having planned a gain of six miles, the French could barely manage 600 yards and that at a cost of nearly 100,000 men. Nivelle had promised not only victory but the end of the war. Instead, his attack led to the mutiny of the French army and the virtual collapse of France's offensive capability until the war's final campaigns. In the aftermath, the government later sacked Nivelle and place France's fortune in the hands of Gen. Ferdinand Foch.

With the near-collapse of the French army, future offensive operations on the western front devolved to the British almost exclusively. Foch did not resume significant operations until the war's final months, and America's first offensive was still a year away. Haig thus turned to his own ideas on how to win the war. Flanders had long held his interest as an area for a decisive victory. In January he had rejected a plan drawn up by Gen. Herbert Plumer as being too passive and demanded one "based upon rapid action and . . . the breaking through of the enemy's defences on a wide front without any delay."[12] He wanted a plan that aimed at the decisive defeat of the enemy and the freeing of the Belgian coast. Not only did a breakout from the Ypres Salient have the potential to clear the coast, thereby ending one of Germany's u-boat threats, but the capture of the Belgian rail net, upon which the enemy's logistics depended, would force his opponent from much of northern France.

Haig hoped that the offensive, which became known as the Battle of Passchendaele, would bring about the collapse of the enemy. Estimates of the enemy's manpower that had been drawn up in the summer and took into account the situation in Russia, suggested that Germany had reached the nadir of its personnel resources. The report announced that "Germany is now within four to six months of the total exhaustion of her available man-power, if fighting continues at the present intensity. At the end of this time, it can be definitely asserted, she will be unable to maintain the strength of her field units."[13] The report also concluded that worsening economic conditions in the enemy's homeland had brought about a decline in industrial production, with a corresponding effect upon the German army's resources.[14] Furthermore, both the morale of the enemy's civilian and military sectors had fallen, leaving no doubt about British ascendancy in that sphere. The report concluded that "given a continuance of circumstances as they stand at present and given a continuation of the effort of the Allies, then Germany may well be forced to conclude a peace on our terms before the end of the year."[15] Haig reiterated these points to the War Council on 17 June to justify his plan, to protest the diversion of resources to other fronts, and to reassure the reluctant government of David Lloyd George that the offensive was necessary and had a good chance of success. To not attack, Haig suggested, would allow the enemy to recover and result in the loss of any advantage gained from the wearing down process. Haig anticipated that if the British kept up the pressure, continued the exhaustion of the enemy, and inflicted a major defeat upon their opponent, the subsequent German collapse would end the war.[16]

However, before the breakout from the salient could commence, it was necessary to seize the Messines–Wytschaete Ridge to create a defensive flank and deny the enemy observation of the British preparations for Passchendaele. Undertaken by Plumer's Second Army, the Battle of Messines was one of Britain's most successful and cheapest victories. Preparations for the ridge's capture dated to September 1915 when the engineers put forth the idea of tunneling mines under the position. Although digging did not begin in earnest until 1916, eventually 24 tunnels, some more than 2,000 feet long, stretched from the British lines to under the enemy position. The British announced the battle's commencement on 7 June 1916 when they detonated 21 of the explosive-packed chambers, ripping the top off the ridge and annihilating the defenders, although only 19 of the chambers blew up.

Although the destructive and stunning effects of the explosives helped assure an easy victory, the mines were only one element of force that the British employed. Even without the mines the British had gathered an enormous amount of firepower. The artillery had 1,560 field guns and over 750 heavy calibers while the Royal Flying Corps provided more than 300 observation machines. The airmen photographed the enemy's battery areas every other day, which greatly assisted in locating German guns and providing an assessment of the British counter-battery effort. The gunners began their preliminary work on 21 May and intensified their effort at the end of month. The battle also featured important roles for the gas services. Throughout the buildup the artillery used chemical shells for harassment, attrition, and counter-battery, and at zero hour they unleashed a special gas bombardment on enemy gun positions so as to prevent a challenge of the advancing British infantry. The Special Brigade made contributions to the wearing out battle, including the projection of oil drums onto enemy positions, although poor weather conditions canceled many of their plans.[17]

At 3:10 A.M. on 7 June came the British detonation of the mines, which was immediately followed by the roar of the artillery. The explosion took the Germans completely by surprise as the British had maintained the secrecy of the scale of their digging. Twelve divisions of infantry rose and advanced on the ridge, obscured by dust and falling debris. The gunners firing gas and high explosives in their counter-battery missions succeeded in neutralizing the enemy's artillery, and the infantry crossed no man's land with little interference. The attackers found the defenders largely dead, wounded, or stunned, and the British, Australians, and New Zealanders quickly captured the enemy's first line. Resistance did increase and casualties mounted, but by 9:00 A.M. the ridge was in British hands and the infantry began the process of consolidation in anticipation of enemy counterattacks.

With Messines conquered the British began planning in earnest for a break out from Ypres and the decisive battle. On 30 June Haig explained to Gough his objectives: first, the occupation of Passchendaele

Ridge, and second, control of the coast. His ambitions were far too great, however, as the enemy defenses were extremely strong and their depth exceeded the effective range of the British artillery. Gough responded with a plan which, while it did not call for a breakthrough on the first day, still anticipated rapid success. The attackers aimed to penetrate about 3,500 yards into the enemy line in the initial surge, and then after a pause of a few days planned to bring forward their guns so that they could reach the enemy's final organized positions. Gough had preferred a less-controlled advance on the first day, but one where the infantry gained as much territory as possible to take advantage of the enemy's confusion in the attack's opening hours. However, on the eve of the battle Gough issued instructions that the infantry were to halt on predesignated stop lines, so that the organization for the second round could proceed in a more systematic fashion. When Fifth Army resumed the attack, they were to smash through the last of the enemy's defenses and push into the open beyond, first toward the rail hub of Roulers and then toward the coast. This grand sweep would trap enemy troops in Belgium and isolate much of the enemy's forces in northern France from their source of supply.[18]

The artillery preparation for the battle began on 16 July, and Fifth Army had at its disposal 1,422 field guns and 752 medium and heavy pieces. Second Army on its right would further augment the artillery resources. The gunners, packed into the salient, were under observation from enemy positions on the ridges and eventually suffered heavily, especially after the arrival of mustard gas. The counter-battery barrage reached its climax over the final three days and nights, with gas shells employed on as many targets as possible to neutralize the enemy gunners as the infantry moved into their jump-off positions. On the final night, from midnight to zero hour at 3:50 A.M., the artillery sent gas shells toward all known enemy batteries that they could reach. Additionally, over the final six nights of the preparation, the 4.5-inch howitzers sent gas shells into enemy strong points. German artillery power remained great but the British succeeded in suppressing their rival's guns during two critical maneuvers. The infantry reached their assembly positions without serious loss, and the enemy's defensive barrage was ineffective as the attackers crossed no man's land.[19]

The Special Brigade began their contribution to the preliminary bombardment on the fifteenth with a series of early morning wasting strikes against enemy positions all along Fifth Army's front. Foulkes's troops dispatched 2,696 projector drums and 3,622 gas-filled mortar bombs. They continued their bombardment the next night and at all subsequent opportunities when the weather was favorable. In total they would fire over 5,100 projector drums and 10,500 mortar bombs. At zero hour they switched from gas, and hit enemy strong points with thermite and incendiary bombs.[20]

At 3:50 A.M. on 31 July nine divisions of infantry rose, went over the top, and headed toward the enemy. Initially the British made good progress and the attackers quickly captured the German outpost and observation lines, but as they entered the enemy's strong points the assault slowed and casualties began to mount. The enemy's artillery also proved themselves not fully tamed as their barrages against the British center savaged the attackers. German resistance and counterattacks halted the offensive with the British less than halfway to their objectives. The losses were high, with Fifth Army sustaining 27,000 casualties during the first four days of the battle. The enemy had also suffered heavily, as the British had mauled nine German divisions and taken more than 6,000 prisoners.

Worse, however, was the rain that began as a drizzle but by evening had become a sustained downpour that lasted three days. The war had shattered the region's system of dikes and canals that normally drained the ground and, with nowhere to go, the water collected and converted the torn and shattered terrain into a wasteland of mud. The wounded, who had taken shelter in shell holes, slowly sank as pools of water collected and the mud drew them down to a slow, suffocating death. If the Somme is preeminent in the nation's collective memory for the tragedy of its first day, then Passchendaele should be a close second with the nightmare of its consuming earth.

The rain also altered the operational plan. In a sea of mud, Fifth Army could not quickly prepare their next blow, and instead of a pause of only a few days the next attack did not go off until 10 August, which allowed the enemy plenty of time to repair their defenses and move up reinforcements. Instead of a swift breakthrough, the campaign became a series of sharp, limited engagements with pauses in between, as the British fought their way up to the high ground. At each stage, gas attacks by both the Special Brigade and the Royal Artillery assisted in the preliminary bombardments and the assault. Haig, however, never gave up hope of eventually reaching the coast, and the British adopted a wearing down attitude toward the battle.

By October Haig sensed that the enemy was nearing the end of its resources and at a conference with Gough and Plumer on the second he

Table 7. Demand and Supply of Chemical Shell as of 31 December 1916

	4.5" lethal	4.5" lachrymatory	4.7" lethal	4.7" lachrymatory	60-pounder lethal	60-pounder lachrymatory
Weekly demand	18,450	3,000	2,300	—	9,250	2,000
Average receipt	3,890	1,985	1,695	285	276	1,594
Now needed	18,450	3,000	—	—	11,550	2,000

Source: "GHQ to WO," 31 December 1916, WO32/5174, PRO. The British had withdrawn the 4.7" gun and did not require any more ammunition.

questioned their preparations should the opportunity for exploitation arise. Haig wanted the reserve brigades of the attacking divisions for the Broodseinde assault of 4 October, along with corps cavalry units, tanks, and mobile batteries, all to be ready to advance on the initiative of local commanders. Gough and Plumer both agreed that signs indicated that the enemy was approaching the breaking point and that the British armies had to be ready for a rapid advance, but they also thought that the Germans required two more defeats.[21] On the sixth the Fifth Army ordered that "in case of a complete breakdown of the enemy's opposition, corps will be prepared to make a further advance,"[22] and Haig noted in his diary a discussion on the concentration of rolling stock and lorries for the rapid sending forward of reserves.[23] The collapse of the enemy never came about even though the battle cost the British nearly 240,000 men. Though pushed back, the Germans bent but did not break, and with the Canadian seizure of the Passchendaele Ridge, Haig brought the offensive to an end on 10 November. The only other British offensive of the year was Cambrai, but its objectives were strictly limited. Victory would wait until the following year.

The Supply of Gas

During 1917 an increased supply of chemical ordnance guaranteed a more visible and integral role for gas than had existed at the time of the Somme. While gas munitions were rarely available in the quantities desired by the army, ammunition for the Special Brigade and the Royal Artillery would become more regular and plentiful over the course of the year, allowing for a gradual intensification of gas operations. Objectives once thought impossible—such as the neutralization of every known enemy battery—became a reality. Table 7 outlines the status of supply as it stood at the end of 1916 and highlights the continuing discrepancies between request and receipt for shell gas. The widest gaps between what GHQ requested and what it received were for lethal shell, a reflection of the continuing shortage of production capacity of phosgene.

A report drawn up in late February further reinforces the image of the inability of the Ministry of Munitions to meet general headquarters requests. It showed that for the two-month period of January to February 1917, general headquarters desired 90,000 4.5-inch lethal shell, had been given a probable output estimate of 72,000, and had actually received just 27,608. The figures for the 60-pounder lethal shell were 52,000 requested, 34,000 promised, and 11,946 received. Production thus continued to fall well short of both requirements and guarantees. Despite the discrepancy, Haig raised his demands for the period of January to March to 165,000 and 100,000 lethal shell for the 4.5-inch howitzer and the 60-pounder gun, respectively. The number of lachrymatory shell produced was much closer to demand, and a mid-March report showed that the Ministry of Munitions exceeded GHQ's request for 3,000 rounds per week by 75 percent for the 4.5-inch howitzer, although they provided less than half of the requested 2,000 60-pounder shells per week.[24]

The arrival of mustard gas in June and the approval of a chemical round for the 6-inch howitzer complicated the British demand for gas shell. Table 8 outlines a revised general headquarters program for a weekly supply of chemical shells.

Table 8. Weekly Demand for Chemical Shell, September 1917

Caliber	Lachrymatory	Lethal	Mustard Gas	Total Weekly
a) 6" howitzer	10,000	4,000	36,000	50,000
b) 4.5" howitzer	7,500	7,500	15,000	30,000
c) 18-pounder	—	—	50,000	50,000

Source: Data taken from "Report of Conference on the General Gas Policy and the Chemical Shell Programme," 27 November 1917, MUN5/187/1360/10, PRO.

The demand for mustard gas, code named HS, underlines the scale of the impression the substance had made on general headquarters. Furthermore, its inclusion, and at such high rates of production, suggests that this agenda was a long-range goal, an observation reinforced by the fact that the Ministry of Munitions did not yet have a factory to make the chemical nor even a clear understanding of the necessary processes to do so. Table 8 also demonstrates the army's preference for the 6-inch howitzer since an approved pattern finally existed for the shell. The report did not include production targets for the 60-pounder gun since the British planned to replace it, especially for counter-battery, with the 6-inch howitzer. The addition of the 18-pounder also represents a desire to further diversify the capabilities of the British gas arsenal, even though a chemical shell was not yet available for this caliber. The field artillery would not fire an 18-pounder gas shell for more than a year.

The greatest logistical failure of Britain's chemical effort during the war was the great delay in the arrival of mustard gas shells. The British made mustard gas production a top priority and at a conference on gas policy Butler reflected that, "he [Haig] attached great importance to H. S. or any other gas which can be proved to be an equally good or better incapacitator; he [Haig] considered it to be the most effective gas used up to the present."[25]

At the same conference, the British agreed to expedite construction of one-third of the mustard gas factory's capacity with the rest built at a lower priority.[26] However, 14 months passed before the gunners had any shells to fire. The production of the substance required a complex chemical process, and although the British assigned a number of teams to work simultaneously on the task the secret of its mass manufacture proved difficult to solve. Scientific egos also entered into the picture, as competing researchers sought to advance their own solutions. One went so far as to appeal to Churchill to promote his process over that of his rivals. But the principal cause of the delay was the state of Britain's prewar chemical industry. Unlike the Germans, who had experience with producing these substances in industrial settings, the British simply lacked the capable personnel.[27] The British retaliated for this lack with some mustard gas attacks in 1917, such as the five projector drums they dropped near Armentières on 1 August, but they used materials in minuscule amounts that they had either captured from the Germans or extracted from dud enemy shells.[28]

The introduction of Blue Cross, the other German chemical innovation of 1917, had no effect on the British gas mixture since the substance proved to be one of the great gas fiascoes of the war. Blue Cross was an arsenic-based compound that acted as a powerful sternutator on the respiratory system. As an inert powder it could pass through the currently available British respirator, and if the Germans had designed a proper delivery system the gas would have had a devastating effect. Once inhaled, the irritation to the nose and throat, along with the possibility of nausea, forced the wearer to remove his mask, thereby exposing the victim to lethal agents which the Germans included in their gas bombardments. However, the substance was only effective if it was dispersed as a particulate cloud in the atmosphere. The Germans believed that the explosive force of the shell's detonation would be sufficient to pulverize the agent to the required fineness. Their error was to inadequately test the device, for on the battlefield the explosion failed to reduce the chemical to the size necessary to achieve airborne status and instead dispersed it in chunks that collected harmlessly on the ground. Never realizing their error, the Germans fired millions of Blue Cross rounds and wasted enormous chemical resources on a weapon that proved to have negligible effects. The British, who were also at work on an arsenic-based weapon, did not make the same mistake and did develop a dispersal system that properly suspended the chemical in a cloud. It was not ready until 1919, however.[29]

While General Headquarters did not get all they wanted, the army's stockpiles progressively increased over the year. At Vimy, First Army had an inventory of 40,000 gas shells and Third Army had 60,000 for Arras. Two months later, for the Battle of Messines, Second Army had on hand 120,000 gas rounds. By the end of the month Fifth Army had accumulated 154,000 rounds for use in the preliminary bombardment at Passchendaele and had expectations of receiving a further 34,000 a week. Though supply never caught up with demand, the Ministry of Munitions had certainly made progress in meeting the army's needs.[30]

Shortfalls also existed for the Special Brigade. Foulkes had wanted 22,000 rounds per week for the Stokes mortar, but for the three weeks ending 17 February he would get a total of 11,630 bombs, barely one-sixth of his request. Shipments for the Livens projector also failed to meet requisitions. Foulkes demanded 10,000 copies of the device but received only 5,800, and of the drums only 2,300 of the ordered 20,000. Another 6,000 devices came by mid-March and the Ministry of Munitions promised a regular supply of 5,000 Livens drums a week. However, on 20 March the Army Council saw fit to appeal to the Ministry of Munitions to provide as many Livens projectiles as possible, while Lieut. Gen. William Furse, the master general of the ordnance, wrote to complain that the Special Brigade was not getting the chemical munitions it needed.[31]

General headquarters reiterated the importance it placed upon chemical munitions in late February when it raised the percentage of gas shell to 12 percent of total supply of ammunition for the 4.5-inch howitzer and 60-pounder gun (from the previous year's establishment of 10 percent). In April the ratio was further increased to 12.5 percent, and Haig authorized the filling of chemical shell at the expense of both high explosives and shrapnel. By advancing gas shell ahead of high explosives and shrapnel, Haig signaled the value he placed upon these munitions.[32] However, despite the increased urgency, output by the Ministry of Munitions still lagged behind demand. By May it had only reached 7 percent of the total for the 60-pounder gun. In response, the director of ordnance services requested the acceleration of the supply so that this ammunition would reach its established level of 12.5 percent as quickly as possible.[33]

The shortages of materials had real operational implications, and on occasion the British had to curtail or cancel a discharge.[34] Yet to blame solely the Ministry of Munitions for its inability to meet general headquarters demands would be unfair, especially since this organization had to overcome Britain's tremendous prewar inferiority in chemical industries. Furthermore, general headquarters did not help matters by their frequent increases in demand and changes in the composition of the fillings. For example, on 17 March Haig eliminated the long-standing order for the lachrymatory agent SK as a shell material, and instead wanted half of the 4.5-inch and 60-pounder rounds to contain PS while the remainder could be any lethal substance such as phosgene. PS was the code for chloropicrin, a compound with lethal and lachrymatory properties that would become one of the mainstays of the British gas effort. It had gained in importance because the German mask was not entirely proof against it, and upon penetration PS had the effect of inducing vomiting. This forced the wearer to remove the mask and thereby become even more exposed to the lethal vapors. It became a standard tactic to combine PS with more-deadly compounds during bombardments of enemy positions.[35]

In July Haig modified the order for the howitzer to 25 percent lethal and 75 percent PS, while the 60-pounder would revert to 75 percent SK.[36] Later in the year general headquarters abandoned PS for the 4.5-inch howitzer and substituted either PG or NC, both of which contained chloropicrin but also contained other elements.[37] For the 60-pounder the army also replaced PS with PG and NC, but only to the proportion of 25 percent, while the remainder was to be 50 percent lethal and 25 percent KSK, a purer version of SK. In these shifts general headquarters was reacting to a tactical opportunity, seeking a mixture that would maximize the nausea effect of chloropicrin and increase an attack's casualty potential. The Ministry of Munitions did seek more predictability in the army's demands, but in March Furse acknowledged that a better forecast of requirements was impossible. This situation continued into the summer, and in July the Gas Service could still not definitely define the types of shell fillings it needed. [38]

The Special Brigade contributed its own confusion to the production situation by also reducing its requirement for SK, once in high demand, to zero. In April Haig changed the allocation for Stokes mortar bombs to 75 percent lethal and 25 percent lachrymatory, and he requested that if possible he wanted the lachrymatory agent to be PS not SK. By mid-May general headquarters determined that they no longer had a need for any SK mortar bombs and asked the Ministry of Munitions to cease its production. As of July the Special Brigade had 96,000 rounds of SK bombs in France, and Foulkes suggested the return of 80,000 to England for the reuse of the contents. [39]

The combination of its chemical properties and the capabilities of the delivery systems contributed to SK's fall from favor. It was among the most persistent agents used during the war, which complicated its use near friendly troops. The short range of the chemical mortar exacerbated the problem. However, its fall from grace was temporary, and as counter-battery increased in importance the British discovered that its persistency properties were ideal for the long-term incapacitation of the enemy's guns. Before the year was out there was a renewed call for the production of it and its successor, the more powerful KSK; it would continue to be an essential ingredient in Britain's gas arsenal until its replacement by mustard gas.

The Special Brigade in 1917

The lessons derived from the use of gas in 1916 helped to establish the methods by which the British waged chemical warfare for the rest of the war. Foulkes defined for the Special Brigade two broad principles to guide the Special Companies, and he disseminated his ideas through a lecture tour of British headquarters during 1917. He divided the combat environment into two sections: the assaulting front and the nonattacking front. On the assaulting front Foulkes believed that "the discharge from cylinders or projectiles is made so soon before zero that the enemy cannot, under the circumstances, replace his casualties. Resistance is thereby weakened and advantage is taken of resultant confusion."[40] General headquarters also accepted Foulkes's interpretation, and its planners concluded that "a discharge at . . . night preceding a general assault is likely to reduce very considerably the resistance to the assault." On the nonattacking front, Foulkes identified the objective of gas bombardments as the elimination of the enemy's potential reserves.[41]

Foulkes's distinction between these two situations helped fit Special Brigade operations within the overall principles outlined in the FSR and within Haig's concept of the phases of battle. Once the British army had agreed to a battle, it was necessary to weaken the enemy and gain fire superiority so that the infantry could successfully close with their opponent at the decisive moment. Foulkes sought ways for his engineers to contribute to this struggle by the discharge of poisonous vapors to kill, confuse, impair the efficiency of, or morally weaken the enemy. Furthermore, the Special Brigade could also strike at targets that were immune to destructive fire by the artillery, namely the defenders of strong points who were securely ensconced in their deep dugouts. British policy stressed that gas was more effective than high explosives in destroying these kinds of defenses. Finally, the Special Brigade would, through the use of ruses or attacks on defensive flanks, create diversions to assist the main attack. Through these actions gas would help to control the enemy's firepower and aid the infantry across no man's land and into the enemy's defenses.

On the nonattacking front, the Special Brigade would contribute to the overall wearing down of the enemy through a deliberate program of deadly discharges. The successful gassing of an enemy unit would lower its morale and also eat away at German reserves. When not supporting an attack by the infantry, gas became an attritional weapon, a pure auxiliary to the wearing down process. Interestingly, gas did not need to result in casualties in order to be effective. The British believed that simply forcing the enemy to wear masks resulted in a lowering of morale. Gas, along with other wasting activities on passive fronts (such as infantry raids or artillery harassment fire) would wear away the enemy's morale, and push the German army closer to the point when it would collapse under the pressure of a decisive battle. The largest discharge of 1917 occurred on a nonattacking front when the Special Brigade released 102 tons of gas between Givenchy and Hulluch on the night of 4–5 October.[42]

By the beginning of 1917 Foulkes had identified a number of missions that the Special Brigade was capable of performing and which contributed to the overall goal of gaining superiority over the enemy in order to be ready for the decisive battle. Attritional missions, both on attacking and nonattacking fronts, were the most common. Foulkes believed that the Special Brigade was the most efficient wearing down unit in the British establishment. After the war he calculated that the Special Brigade caused one enemy casualty for every cylinder, for every five drums, and for every ten mortar bombs discharged.[43] Harassment missions were similar to attritional missions, but instead of trying to kill or injure the enemy Foulkes designed them to increase the victim's misery and thereby lower their efficiency and morale. Counter-preparation missions on an attacking front were also vital in order to give the infantry time to consolidate before facing counterattack. Finally, the Special Brigade utilized ruses and discharges on defensive flanks to confuse the enemy and protect the infantry in the carrying out of its duties.

Foulkes also identified three ways to counteract the enemy's respirators, namely, surprise, exhaustion, and penetration. Surprise required the Special Brigade to envelop their target in a gas cloud before the enemy had a chance to put on respirators. Projectile weapons—the Livens drums, Stokes bombs, and artillery shells—which arrived with little warning, were highly effective means of obtaining this sort of success. Under the right conditions a cylinder discharge might also catch the enemy unaware. If the British secretly installed the appliances, covered the sound of the discharge with rifle or artillery fire, and attacked at night, the high concentration of gas obtained by a cylinder flotation could be devastating.[44] Even after the enemy had put on their masks it was possible for the British to exhaust the respirator's defensive capability. Foulkes pointed out that the German respirator's life expectancy was shorter than that of the British type, and that after an exposure of several hours the protective agents would become useless, thus rendering the soldier vulnerable. Foulkes also planned to take advantage of several design weaknesses in the enemy's issue which made exposure through the penetration of gas possible. General headquarters increased the demand for PS since that compound had some ability to pass through the German mask. Meanwhile, British chemists constantly sought other agents with similar properties, such as stannic chloride, known as KJ. Additionally, since the air intake valve on the German mask was fairly small it was possible to overload the protective agents. If the wearer took a breath in a cloud of extremely concentrated gas some of the toxic elements would escape reaction with the mask's active ingredients and pass into the victim's lungs. Finally, Foulkes had reliable intelligence that a significant percentage of the enemy's masks were defective.

In April 1916 the enemy had lost 1,600 men as a result of blowback from a lethal cloud they themselves had released. The British had captured a copy of a report in which the German investigators revealed that 35 percent of the masks in the area were unreliable. A wider search of the entire western front disclosed that 11.5 percent of unissued masks were not gas-proof. Foulkes hoped that the enemy would be slow to fix these deficiencies, and evidence suggests that he was correct. A projector attack at 2:00 A.M. on 21 July on Fifth Army's front in preparation for Passchendaele resulted in numerous enemy casualties. The doctor at the regimental dressing station revealed, in a captured document, that many of the injured complained that the gas went right through their masks. Upon investigation he found that the masks were too large for the men and that the loose fit had caused the casualties. In conclusion he recommended that the army give resting units facilities for testing masks, apparently something that the enemy's anti-gas organization had failed to do. Foulkes's intentions were dangerous for the enemy, in regard to both their survival and their morale. If gas could penetrate the German mask then the soldiers would lose faith in its protective value and feel that they were powerless against the deadly chemicals. Such a development had great appeal to the British because not only did it suggest moral superiority but, if German soldiers believed that their masks were worthless, gas discipline would break down and create a self-fulfilling cycle leading to more enemy casualties.[45]

Using Foulkes's methods, the Special Brigade frequently drew blood. A captured document dated 8 July 1917 from the 111th Division warned, "our losses have been serious up to now, as the enemy has succeeded in a majority of cases, in surprising us, and masks have often [been] put on too late."[46] Another document disclosed that "[we] cannot hope to prevent gas casualties owing to the surprise effected and the heavy concentrations of gas obtained."[47] Surprise was the most effective way to kill or injure the enemy, but if the chemical engineers could

establish a sufficient concentration then even protected soldiers would
fall victim.

Foulkes had three principal means at his disposal to strike at the enemy: cylinders, projectors, and mortars. During the year the chemical
engineers released 2,031 tons of gas. Table 9 illustrates how the Special
Brigade allocated the gas between the three delivery systems.

Table 9. Weight of Gas Discharged by the Special Brigade

System	Weight of Gas in Tons
Livens projectors	1,307
Stokes mortars	370
Cylinders	354
Total	*2,031*

Source: Data taken from "Report by DGS," 21 December 1917, wo142/98, PRO.

Throughout the year the British army debated the relative efficiency of
the three dispersal systems. The Livens projector gained the favor of
most leaders and it eventually eclipsed cylinders as the primary means
of discharging gas. Foulkes, however, preferred cylinders and they
therefore continued to play a role, if at a reduced rate.

Foulkes's support for the cylinder derived from its ability to deliver
the largest volume of gas on the broadest front, and therefore hold the
greatest potential for causing severe casualties. Projectors and mortars
were limited-area weapons which, while useful for causing casualties,
could not destroy the effectiveness of a whole unit. Cylinders had the
ability to force the enemy to withdraw entire organizations from the
line for prolonged periods of rebuilding. Cloud gas, however, continued to have a number of insurmountable drawbacks. Its dependency
upon the wind made it incapable of coordination with any of the other
arms, and the risk of blowback, i.e., the self-infliction of casualties, remained a prime concern. But the biggest problem for cylinders was the
extraordinary degree of preparation and labor required for their installation and discharge. The Special Brigade had to rely upon work parties, seconded from the infantry, to carry in the appliances, pipes,
valves, and other materials. It was then the infantry's responsibility to
share their positions with the gas and assume the risk of a leak or detection by the enemy while the chemical engineers waited for a suitable
wind. It was the infantry that also bore the brunt of the enemy's retalia-

tion as the Germans aimed their guns upon the point of discharge: the trenches. Infantry officers, therefore, tended to prefer projectors for which they did not carry the materials or prepare the site, nor share the risk, since the Special Brigade installed the devices in a retired, camouflaged position.

In his lectures Foulkes reiterated the value of cloud gas as a killing device and requested greater infantry support for his operations. To the Fifth Army staff he noted that "[the] present exclusive use of projectors is reducing the ability of the Special Brigade very much." He explained that the Special Brigade installed projectors without any infantry help and therefore his engineers could launch fewer attacks. He concluded that the main problem was the provision of labor, and he hoped commanders would make better utilization of the potential of gas by being more willing to provide work details.[48] To the Second Army he again spoke of the need for more support from the infantry for cylinder discharges. He explained that the cloud gas method was "by far the most effective for inflicting casualties, and by far the most profitable to employ." At the end of his lecture he suggested that "It is one of the ironies of fate, now that there is for the first time anything like a general demand for gas in the armies, that the demand should be for projectiles—which are less effective than cylinders."[49] Foulkes was fighting a losing battle, particularly since the demands upon the infantry's labor were already enormous. Even when moved out of the trenches for rest, British battalions engaged in all sorts of training and work details. His claims as to the superiority of cloud gas are also a little suspect. Cylinder discharges did cause casualties, and in large numbers, but it was the projector that apparently struck the greatest terror in the enemy's ranks. From the perspective of wearing down, Foulkes should have more firmly embraced Livens's invention.

To overcome opposition, Foulkes endeavored to make cylinder discharges more deadly and easier to launch. He arranged an issue of 500 small White Star cylinders, each weighing 50 pounds, to be carried by a single man in a sling. C Special Company carried them forward on the night of 17 April and discharged them the same evening without bothering to dig emplacements and without infantry assistance. However, even with reduced weight it still proved an exhausting operation as each engineer had to make two trips with a cylinder, and then assemble the pipes and discharge hoses. Foulkes would occasionally use this method but only for minor operations. On another instance the Special Brigade employed Yellow Star, a mixture of 70 percent chloropicrin and 30 percent chlorine. They opened 700 cylinders on the night of 6 November and the resulting cloud carried across to the enemy's trenches on a three mph wind. Captured enemy documents revealed that the chloropicrin penetrated the German soldiers' masks and caused heavy casualties in the 453rd and 10th Bavarian Regiments.[50] Foulkes also sought to utilize terrain to increase the efficacy of gas. In May, in support of the upcoming Messines battle, he suggested flooding the Lys valley with a massive flotation of gas. Foulkes believed that if pushed by the wind and held together by the shoulders of the valley, the gas would not disperse and a dense cloud of deadly gas would penetrate into the enemy's rear, bringing devastating damage to the enemy's artillery, headquarters, and support installations. Foulkes planned to release 3,700 White Star on about 21 May, 2,000 Green Star and 3,000 White Star on about 5 June, and a grand finale of 4,500 White Star on the eve of the attack. Poor winds forced the cancellation of the operation, however. Foulkes continued the debate into 1918 and would continue to experiment with other methods of cylinder attacks.[51]

Projectors became the mainstay of Special Brigade operations in 1917, and the chemical engineers fired nearly 100,000 drums during the year. Foulkes identified the most suitable targets as areas that the enemy held strongly and which contained underground shelters that were immune to artillery bombardment. The Special Brigade principally fired gas from their projectors, but on occasion they discharged drums filled with flammable oil or high explosives. When filled with gas each drum contained 30 pounds of phosgene.[52] Easily camouflaged, the projector was an ideal weapon of surprise, and if the enemy did not see the muzzle flash the drums arrived without any warning. Even if the German sentries were alert they still had only a few seconds to raise the alarm before the gas plunged onto their positions.[53] Captured enemy documents repeatedly stressed the devastating nature of the weapon and the difficulty in protecting the men from its threat. A memorandum of 4 June 1917 from German Fourth Army headquarters referred to it as a "dangerous weapon with a high degree of effectiveness," while another enemy report conceded that it was impossible to prevent gas casualties from the projector.[54]

The final branch of the Special Brigade's triad was the Stokes mortar. Unlike in 1916, the weapon now had an adequate supply of munitions along with a wide selection of chemical fillings. Initially the mortar companies could choose from PS, SK, and CG, as well as smoke and thermite bombs. However, improvements in agents led to the replacement of PS by PG and NC. Each gas bomb contained about seven pounds of chemicals.[55] So plentiful had ammunition become that Foulkes could write: "The most lavish expenditure of ammunition should be aimed at, and, if possible, every round allotted to the armies should be fired before the assault takes place as abundant fresh supplies are now being made available."[56]

In 1916 the Special Brigade used its mortars intermittently and only to fire smoke. In 1917 they launched over 90,000 gas bombs along with nearly 11,000 thermite rounds.[57] Foulkes welcomed the opportunity to be able to employ this weapon, finally, in the role that had been envisioned: both to help the infantry on the battlefield and to wear down the enemy.

The variety of bombs increased the mortarmen's ability to trick the enemy and inflict casualties. Foulkes, in *Gas!*, provides an example of an operation conducted by No. 1 Special Company on 1 December near Monchy-le-Preux. He wrote: "Forty-four mortars were engaged, and they opened with a half-minute bombardment with thermite, which brought the Germans hurrying out of their dugouts to man the parapet in anticipation of the infantry raid which they thought to be imminent. Then came one and a half minutes rapid fire with CG bombs, followed by 12 minutes with PS and NC for penetrative effect, with a final one and a half minutes with CG. The whole attack lasted for a quarter of an hour, during which 2300 rounds of ammunition were fired."[58] This method became a frequently used tactic from mid-July 1917 onward.[59]

The Special Brigade's projectiles had certain advantages over the cylinder. Both the mortar and the projector could quickly, if not instantly, establish a deadly concentration of gas on top of the target, and the rapidity of the arrival of the gas made the attainment of surprise highly likely. Though not unaffected by wind direction and velocity they worked best in a dead calm when the wind did not blow the gas away from its victims. The weapons also required less labor and were harder for the enemy to find, making retaliation more difficult and rendering them more acceptable to the infantry.[60]

The Battle of Messines can serve as a case study to illustrate how the Special Brigade applied Foulkes's principles on an attacking front. The preliminary bombardment began on 21 May and the chemical engineers made their first discharge during the night of the twenty-fourth/ twenty-fifth. At 10:35 P.M. No. 2 Special Company opened fire with a barrage of 1,000 PS and 992 SK Stokes mortar bombs on enemy trenches on the River Lys northeast of Houplines. The report on the operation outlined the objectives of the attack. The mortarmen used PS to inflict casualties and SK to force the enemy to wear their respirators for a prolonged period, interfering with their repair of the damage that the British artillery bombardment had caused. Masked soldiers found it difficult, if not impossible, to undertake any labor since the device impeded the flow of oxygen, a problem more pronounced in German models due to the small intake apertures they possessed. At 1:35 A.M. the next morning, the Special Brigade fired 100 rounds of thermite onto the enemy position in the expectation of causing confusion within the ranks of soldiers who had already suffered the fatigue of having to wear their masks for three hours, thereby producing displacement of respirators and adding to the enemy's casualties. The British were unable to ascertain the results of this attack but the conditions for a mortar discharge had been ideal.[61]

The Special Brigade had begun their contribution to the wearing down process and would continue these activities until the battle's commencement. On the evening of the twenty-fifth, L Special Company sent 179 drums of CG into the enemy's support lines in Bois Blancs. Their objective was not only to cause casualties within an area containing numerous dugouts, but also to disorganize the enemy's ranks so as to assist a fighting patrol of infantry who were out on a raid. After a pause of four days the Special Brigade resumed activity with a series of attacks on the II ANZAC (Australian–New Zealand Army Corp) Corps's front. Early in the morning, 45 rounds of thermite exploded over enemy positions around St. Yves. That evening the Special Brigade sent 644 drums of phosgene, along with 720 PS, 50 SK, and 50 thermite Stokes mortar rounds into enemy positions around Houplines.[62] On the thirtieth the Special Brigade sent 50 SK bombs into Le Touquet, 22 projector drums against Trois Tilleuls Farm, and 250 PS and 50 thermite bombs on enemy positions east of Armentières. Early in the morning on 1 June, No. 2 Special Company assisted a party of raiding Australians with a barrage of SK and smoke some distance on either flank of their target so as to mask their movements and interfere with interdicting fire by forcing the enemy to wear their masks. The next morning the same company fired over 500 PS and SK bombs into several enemy trenches with the intention of inflicting casualties.[63]

While most of the preceding operations were relatively minor affairs, the Special Brigade launched a large and quite novel gambit just after midnight on the morning of 4 June: operation "boiling oil." O and K Special Companies fired nearly 1,200 projector oil-drums into the woods of Grand Bois and Wytschaete with the intention of setting the trees and brush afire. In a scene that must have called to mind the burning pitch used during a medieval siege, the woods burst into flame and burnt for about 20 minutes. A prisoner of the 33rd Fusilier Regiment stated that the attack caused a mass panic throughout the position as soldiers stampeded to escape the fire. To increase the confusion and cause more casualties, the mortarmen added 173 rounds of ps to the conflagration. Simultaneously with the operation against the woods, No. 2 Special Company mortared 120 thermite bombs into enemy positions near Wytschaete with the intention of affecting the morale of the enemy and causing casualties. The results of the oil bombardment were sufficiently encouraging that the Special Brigade would repeat the method 23 more times in 1917 and continue the practice in 1918.[64]

On the day of the battle, the Special Brigade undertook a series of operations at zero hour to help the infantry get across no man's land. No. 3 Special Company sent 267 rounds of thermite into enemy positions near Wytschaete to cause casualties among the enemy as they manned their defenses. An inspection by the engineers that evening demonstrated that the bombs had found their target and that the enemy's trenches contained fragments of thermite bombs. Additionally, the bombs had set one dugout on fire, and inspectors found the remains of several Germans who had suffered burns. Another section of No. 3 Special Company fired 182 rounds of thermite into a different enemy trench in order to facilitate the advance of the 69th Infantry Brigade. Elsewhere, the same company used thermite to cause casualties and smoke to protect the advance of the 47th Division infantry from enemy machine gun fire. Finally, this company undertook a counter-preparation bombardment of Clonmel Copse with 295 sk, 188 cg, and 190 ps bombs to prevent the enemy from massing troops in the site for a counterattack. No. 2 Special Company also participated in the day's activity, attempting to establish a smoke barrage for the 3rd Australian Division located on the right flank of the attack, and disorganizing the enemy with sk gas so as to impede their interference with the ANZAC advance. They had to discontinue their smoke discharge, however, when the wind became unfavorable, and they were unable to fire any lachrymatory gas.[65]

The largest planned gas flotation of the battle also fell victim to the weather. Foulkes had intended to discharge 300 tons of gas up the Lys River valley at zero hour to protect the flank of the attack. Intelligence had correctly reported that the enemy had positioned two counterattack divisions in the valley. Foulkes had hoped to sweep the entire river bottom with gas, neutralizing the enemy's troops and any batteries that could have maneuvered or fired against the flank of the advancing troops. However, on the day of the attack the wind was such that it would have blown the cloud onto ground that the attackers had to traverse, so the discharge was aborted. Not only had the wind once again prevented the use of gas but it had also wasted the labor of four Special Companies who had installed, and would later remove, nearly 10,000 unused cylinders and projectors. [66]

Foulkes had allocated nearly one-half of his command to the Messines battle. The rest of his companies were by no means idle, contributing to the wearing down process by discharging gas on nonattacking fronts with the intention of inflicting casualties and fraying the enemy's morale. On First Army's front, the Special Brigade fired 687 projector drums of lethal gas along with 475 Stokes mortar bombs filled with PS into St. Laurent at 12:30 A.M. on 25 May. The combination of PS with phosgene might have accounted for the heavy losses the enemy suffered, as the affected regiment reported over 300 casualties. A smaller attack of 570 projectors launched at midnight on 31 May near Avion on the 4th Canadian Division front also netted a satisfying number of victims. From prisoner interrogations the British estimated they had caused 400 casualties, 130 of which were fatalities, including one platoon that lost 25 men. On the Third Army front on the night of 3 June the Special Brigade began its program with 189 PS mortar bombs into Havrincourt at 12:30 A.M. An hour later 180 phosgene-filled projector drums landed within the village, and at 2:10 A.M. nearly 200 more landed on enemy positions near Bullecourt (in addition to the nearly 1,000 projector drums and 750 PS mortar bombs the Special Brigade had sent into Havrincourt in the early hours of 29 May). During the Messines Campaign, in addition to their support of Second Army, the Special Brigade conducted 21 operations on other army fronts. [67]

During 1917 the Special Brigade conducted 540 operations; only a few more examples must suffice to illustrate the success of the brigade in fulfilling its mission. During the lead up to Passchendaele, Gough arranged for extensive discharges to wear down the enemy. On 15 July seven special companies released gas on enemy positions that lay in the path of the advance by the II, XIV, XVIII, and XIX Corps. Their targets were German strong points, trenches, concentrations of dugouts, and other positions that contained large numbers of enemy troops and that might impede the progress of the attack. They employed a total of

2,696 Livens drums and 3,619 mortar bombs, and virtually all of the gas they employed was lethal. On the evening of 20–21 July they repeated the attack, although with somewhat less weight, discharging 1,512 Livens drums and 2,723 mortar bombs.[68] The gas that exploded over the 90th Fusilier Regiment on the fifteenth struck at a particularly vulnerable time, as the unit was in the middle of a relief. A captured order from that unit dated 18 July noted that the gas attack caused considerable casualties and, it warned, "at the slightest indication of gas, masks are to be put on immediately."[69] Translated orders of the German 226th Reserve Regiment from the day after the attack also sternly reminded the unit of the need for strict gas discipline. This unit required a draft of 500 men to bring it back up to strength. A captured NCO in the 392nd Regiment from the strong point of Below Farm reported that his company had sustained at least 40 gas casualties, a figure that an enlisted man from the same outfit confirmed. After the subsequent discharge of the twenty-first, a report by the medical officer of this regiment revealed that he treated at least 62 casualties; others probably never made it to his aid post.[70]

The Special Brigade had even more success in causing casualties using discharges against the fortified village of Bullecourt just prior to the commencement of that battle on 10 April. The gas troops dropped 296 Livens drums and 340 PS-filled mortar bombs directly onto the enemy's position. The gas had a devastating effect upon the garrison, the men of the German 120th Regiment. A prisoner report estimated casualties to be at least 100 dead and nearly 200 wounded. One company had its establishment reduced to 25 soldiers, and the gas was so concentrated that some men died almost instantaneously. Shortly after the attack the British intercepted a German telephone conversation that described the gassing as a catastrophe and posed the question, "How could such an incident take place?"[71] Not surprisingly, Foulkes reported that the Germans withdrew the unit before its relief was due.[72]

The Special Brigade achieved a similar effect with a projector attack near Lens on a non-attacking front belonging to First Army. Nearly 1,200 Livens drums unleashed a cloud of phosgene in the early hours of 26 July. A captured letter described the effect: "Then all at one the gas projectors were discharged, and everyone swallowed gas. When we were relieved later our company was 24 men strong. . . . On account of our heavy losses our battalion went straight from the front line to rest."[73] Even on quiet sectors the Special Brigade could quickly inflict casualties on the enemy. The German 84th Regiment during the period

20 September to 16 October suffered 28 deaths. Of these, 21 were due to a 596-projector discharge onto Havrincourt on the night of 5 October.[74]

During 1917 Foulkes also continued a practice that he had begun during the Somme, one that aimed to irreparably reduce the morale of select units. He availed himself of intelligence reports at general headquarters on the disposition of enemy units and wanted his brigade to follow certain outfits, repeatedly gassing them as they operated in the British zone. The 1st Bavarian Reserve Regiment was hit 15 times, the 1st Guards Reserve Regiment 12 times, and the 156th Regiment 10 times.[75] Sometimes the Special Brigade gassed a German unit that was due to transfer to a battlefront so that the enemy arrived already weakened. This was the intention behind L Company's gassing of the 16th Bavarian Division which was about to move to the salient during the Passchendaele campaign.[76] Foulkes also tried to gas enemy units that had recently arrived from the east to take advantage of their lack of experience with the more intensive gas conditions in France. This practice resulted in a memorandum by the German general staff that called for units new to the English zone to receive instructions in the procedures necessary to survive the British gas attacks.[77]

The Royal Artillery in 1917

The Royal Artillery represented the second major means of conducting chemical warfare and, like the Special Brigade, the gunners developed principles by which to guide their gas operations. Although the gases were often the same ones used by the Royal Engineers, the different delivery systems necessitated a slightly different operational philosophy. The primary distinction between the two branches was that the Special Brigade placed their major emphasis upon causing the death of the victim (although they also defined success as causing casualties or lowering morale), while the artillery sought neutralization of the target (and causing casualties was a secondary concern). Haig identified the effect he wanted from his projectiles at a conference with the Ministry of Munitions in May 1917. He classified his weapons as:

1. Artillery Projectiles: Principally neutralizing effect, with a small proportion of killing effect.
2. 4-inch Stokes Mortar Projectiles: Principally killing effect, with a small proportion of neutralizing effect.
3. Livens Drum: Killing effect only.[78]

The conference did not consider cylinders, but since they only came with a lethal filling there is little doubt that the British perceived their role as principally to produce "killing effect."

The necessity for thus distinguishing between roles was due to the nature of the delivery systems, and the British conceded that a "killing effect" was difficult to obtain with shell gas alone. The manual describing the use of shell gas recognized two means to obtain a mortal effect. They were:

1. To take the enemy by surprise by bursting shells so close to him that he is overtaken by the vapour before he has time to put on his mask.
2. To keep up a bombardment for so long a period, either that the resistant capacity of the German respirator is exhausted, or that the physical exhaustion of the wearer consequent on wearing it so long forces him to discard it and so expose himself to the gas.[79]

The artillery had only a few seconds in which to cause casualties by the first method since, after the initial burst of shells, the enemy would naturally seek the protection of their masks. The second means of causing casualties was also difficult, since artillery shells held a small volume of gas when compared to Livens drums and Stokes bombs, and it was extremely difficult, and costly in shells, to establish a concentration of such density that the gas could overwhelm or penetrate the enemy's respirators. British gunners thus had only two practical choices by which to disable the enemy: they could employ sudden and short bursts of lethal shells to cause casualties or use slow prolonged bombardments with lachrymatory agents to neutralize the opposing forces. Both methods achieved success, but since the FSR defined artillery's primary responsibility as assistance to the infantry, neutralization, especially of enemy batteries, provided the greatest help to advancing troops.

The gunners also outlined the methodology necessary to meet these goals. While actual programs varied according to local conditions, the British did develop a typical neutralization program. The bombardment would open with a burst of 70 lethal shells followed by lachrymatory gas at a rate of 150 rounds an hour, interspersed with occasional bursts of lethal shell to catch those defenders whose masks might have failed. The shelling could last hours and force the enemy to remain masked, assuring their inability to properly man their pieces. If the objective was the killing of Germans then the attackers used a modified firing schedule. A number of batteries would fire concentrated salvoes of lethal shells for two minutes, after which they would switch to a different target. The gas consumed for either mission did not exceed several hundred rounds, far less than the up to 8,000 shells that policy had called for in 1916. The dramatic downward revision was derived from two key observations: first, once the enemy had their masks on additional lethal substances would be useless and hence wasted; second, it was virtually impossible for the artillery to build up concentrations of gas that could overwhelm the German respirator or penetrate their underground strongholds. Only the Special Brigade possessed weapons, that is, the Livens projector and Stokes mortar, that were capable of reaching the enemy within their refuges. In order to kill, the artillery had to surprise the enemy on the surface and strike before they had donned their masks. The persistency of lachrymatory agents such as SK or KSK also meant that the British needed only a few shells to contaminate an area enough to force the enemy into their respirators.

The manual *Instructions on the Use of Lethal and Lachrymatory Shell* outlined the operational specifications of gas munitions. Weather remained of paramount concern, and the best condition was dead calm. Shell gas was useless if the wind speed exceeded seven MPH for lethal gas and 12 MPH for lachrymatory agents. Both types were ineffective if used in freezing temperatures since the liquefied substances would not evaporate in extreme cold. The best targets were in valleys, woods, and other places that impeded the wind or positions that contained trenches, dugouts, cellars, or covered gun pits into which the gas could sink.[80]

The gunners defined three phases of battle during which they could contribute to victory: the preliminary bombardment, the infantry assault, and the consolidation after a successful attack. In the period leading up to the offensive the artillery used lachrymatory shell to neutralize enemy batteries, interdict roads, tracks, and junctions, and subject strong points to prolonged bombardments to tire the defenders. Second Army described the desired effect as, "his [the enemy's] front system must be cut off and starved. All means of supply and reinforcement must be reduced and his morale lowered by every possible means."[81] A post-battle lecture reiterated this point as the speaker explained: "Maintenance of harassment fire through the night on roads and approaches is of the greatest importance and guns should not be redeployed to other purposes. The danger is not the enemy's infantry in the front line but rather the weight of troops moving up from the rear."[82] During the same period British batteries fired brief barrages of lethal gas in order to cause casualties to small well-defined targets such as enemy battery emplacements, headquarters, and strong points.[83] Both methods had a similar objective. The British used lachrymatory gas to harass their opponent and lower enemy efficiency and will to resist, while the lethal agents thinned the enemy's ranks. If casualties were widespread enough it would render enemy units unfit for duty and force the German command to commit their reserves prior to the offensive.[84]

Once the infantry assault began, the guns not involved in the barrage concentrated on counter-battery. They employed bursts of lethal gas followed by lachrymatory substances to compel the enemy gunners to wear their masks and hamper their actions, and ultimately prevent the Germans from manning their pieces and hindering the British advance. After the British had secured their objectives, the artillery support reverted to the role they had played during the preliminary bombardment, with the additional objective of attempting to impede enemy counterattacks by firing upon likely approach routes and assembly points. Counter-preparation fire not only caused casualties within the ranks of the enemy massing for a counterattack but also bought time for the infantry to consolidate and prepare for the defense of their newly won positions. Gas was an ideal weapon with which to disorganize enemy troop concentrations and to prevent their advance. A report on Fifth Army operations during Passchendaele concluded that with good wind conditions a gas barrage beyond the final infantry objective "will have considerable effect hampering hostile counterattacks."[85]

While the gunners employed gas shell for a number of missions, including harassment, counter-preparation, and attrition, it was in counter-battery that chemical munitions achieved their most important function. British policy defined counter-battery as a fundamental operation of the artillery and its success was essential for the attainment of fire superiority and the survival of the attacking infantry. The training manual *Artillery Notes* explained the importance of counter-battery thus: "Unless the enemy's batteries are discovered and destroyed, not only may his barrage fire render the capture of an objective difficult and costly, but his subsequent bombardments may make its retention impossible."[86] It was therefore vital that at the moment the infantry left their trenches the artillery open fire "on every hostile battery, known or suspected, of a sufficient intensity to prevent the service of the guns."[87] By 1917, and largely due to their technical innovations, British gunners had achieved such a degree of competency in neutralization that they would attempt, and largely succeed, at silencing every German gun at the start of each battle.

Even though the Royal Artillery had obtained a high degree of accuracy, the elimination of an enemy gun by destructive shooting was still a slow and difficult task. Gas obviated the need for such precision since, as an area weapon, it only needed to land slightly upwind of the target so that the gas could drift over the enemy position. It therefore had a significantly greater allowance for aiming error than high explosive or shrapnel shells did. Additionally, it could be effective at night when the target was invisible and the Royal Flying Corps was unable to correct fire. If subjected to observed shooting during the day and gas attacks at night, the enemy would have no respite.

Furthermore, by 1917 the British had realized that the control of the enemy's firepower merely required the neutralization of hostile batteries—not their complete destruction—a crucial distinction. The support of the assaulting infantry required the removal of the enemy's weapons from the battle for a finite period of time only, that is, from the commencement of the attack through consolidation. A post-Passchendaele assessment concluded that it was possible to put a battery out of action for a varying length of time, generally up to a week. The Canadians agreed with this opinion in their own review of the battle and determined that the object of all counter-battery work is the reduction of enemy fire at critical points and for critical periods. Also, the Canadians identified gas shell as the most efficient munition to achieve this goal. [88] To remove the enemy's trench defenders from the battle the British employed the creeping barrage. To eliminate the German artillery the British refined the art of counter-battery and used prodigious quantities of gas.

The British defined neutralization as "the firing at batteries with the object of preventing the detachments from serving their guns, or, alternatively, causing the standard of their fire to be so lowered as to render their fire erratic and ineffective."[89] The report continued, "gas shell[s] . . . have probably the best neutralizing effect, especially on batteries sited in valleys and woods; the mere fact of the detachments having to wear gas masks renders the efficient service of the guns difficult."[90] The *Artillery Notes* series propagated the primacy of gas in achieving neutralization throughout the Royal Artillery: "Gas shell are particularly valuable in counter-battery work for neutralizing hostile batteries immediately prior to and during an attack, and should be employed in large quantities for this purpose. Recent experience has shown that this procedure has been attended with very excellent results, some hostile batteries so neutralized having subsequently remained silent for two or three days."[91] *Artillery Notes* also recommended an exhaustion method to render enemy gunners unfit to man their pieces. It suggested that employing gas shell night after night against certain targets would force the enemy gunners to wear their masks and "gradually produce physical exhaustion from want of sleep." Such methods would also keep the target isolated, making feeding, resupply, and relief difficult.[92]

The capabilities of the guns limited the scope of gas neutralization, however. The British admitted that the short range of the 4.5-inch howitzer restricted the number of targets that it could reach, and not enough of the longer-range 60-pounders were available to effectively strike at distant targets. For this reason the provision of gas shells for the more numerous and equally ranged 6-inch howitzers became increasingly important. The British eventually acquired even longer gas range when shells entered service for the 8-inch and 9.2-inch howitzers, but these did not become available until near the war's conclusion.[93]

As the summer approached, the need for effective counter-battery fire became even more paramount. Enemy plans, captured before Messines, indicated that the Germans intended to rely upon an artillery defense. Intelligence reported that the Germans hoped to catch the infantry in an annihilating barrage as they left the trenches. Furthermore, any troops that did get into German lines would be cut off from reinforcement by a curtain of fire and subsequently destroyed. To counter this threat, general headquarters intensified its emphasis on efficient counter-battery. Second Army arranged for each of its attacking corps to carry out two demonstration barrages to simulate an assault. Plumer also ordered an army-wide demonstration for 3 June. His objective was to trick the enemy into thinking that the attack had begun and thus reveal their counter-barrage program. Having obtained the location of their opponent's batteries, the British were able to refine their counter-battery agenda.[94] The enemy showed that the British fears were not groundless. During Messines an enemy gas barrage caught the 3rd Australian Division as it moved up to its assembly area. The Germans caused over 1,000 casualties and effectively eliminated two battalions from the offensive.[95]

As with the Special Brigade, the artillery campaign during the Battle of Messines can also serve as a case study for the gunners' use of gas. The battle's planners outlined the essential conditions necessary for the attack in a questionnaire regarding preparations. They wrote: "We must impose our will on the enemy. The upper hand must be gained by vigorous and controlled counter-battery work, by frequent raids of all descriptions, by accurate well placed harassment fire and by the destruction of OPs [observation posts], SPs [strong points], and L of Cs [lines of communication]." The authors listed a series of questions regarding the means to achieve these goals and concluded with the query, "What use are you making of your smoke and gas shell?"[96] The implication was that not only did headquarters believe gas had a role in assuring victory, it also expected subordinate commands to actively employ gas.

Second Army planners conceived of a number of applications for gas before, during, and after the assault. During the preliminary bombardment the gunners kept hostile batteries, sections of cleared wire, trench positions, roads, and tracks under the influence of lachrymatory gas in order to reduce the enemy's morale and efficiency and deter them from repairing defensive positions damaged or destroyed by British fire. They also employed bursts of lethal shell on limited objectives to cause casualties. During the assault the artillery focused upon counter-battery work with a concentrated salvo of lethal shell from a number of batteries followed by delivery of SK. Even if the gas found few or no victims, wearing a mask was tiring and greatly reduced a soldier's effectiveness. After the infantry had reached their objectives the artillery again changed its priorities and resumed firing upon the enemy's rear and communications to prevent a counterattack. The gunners also used lethal shells to cause casualties among the enemy's disorganized retreating troops, whose gas discipline was adversely affected by defeat and who were therefore more vulnerable to a chemical attack.[97] Whenever possible the artillery included shrapnel shells in the bombardment to force the defenders to take cover in shell holes or trench bottoms, the very areas into which the gas would sink and achieve its most deadly concentrations. At other times they fired shrapnel onto the perimeter of a gas attack to catch German soldiers who attempted to flee the poisonous environment. After the battle German prisoners admitted that they dreaded the combination of gas and shrapnel because it made it virtually impossible to find a safe refuge.[98]

All three corps that participated in the attack employed gas against a variety of targets on the three nights preceding the battle. X Corps conducted the broadest range of gas attacks by using chemical shells to undertake four mission objectives. They were:

1. To disturb and cause casualties—intense bursts of lethal shells at intervals throughout the night.
2. Firing at gaps in wire with SK to prevent repair.
3. Counter-battery work.
4. Lethal shells were used with smoke shells on Y day with the object of making the enemy put on masks when the smoke barrage was put up during the attack.[99]

The corps also selected 12 enemy batteries for neutralization at zero hour. The IX Corps target mix included as many support positions and headquarters as possible, and they conducted a special gas bombardment of the village of Wytschaete on 3 June. On the nights of w/x and x/y, IX Corps gunners employed lachrymatory shell for exhaustion purposes against the enemy batteries, then on y/z night they switched to lethal ordnance to eliminate the enemy whose masks no longer provided adequate protection. The II ANZAC Corps also directed its gas against enemy strong points and trench systems with the intention of causing casualties, preventing sleep, and reducing morale, while their counter-battery program commenced on the third and continued up to the battle's start. Each of these programs involved concentrated bursts of lethal shell generally lasting no more than three minutes, followed by at least an hour of lachrymatory shell.[100]

The attritional missions involved a combination of gas and shrapnel and a considerable numbers of shells. For their special bombardment of Wytschaete on 3 June, IX Corps employed 96 of their own heavy howitzers and 57 from II ANZAC Corps. The calibers ranged from 6-inch all the way up to 15-inch, and for 30 minutes they rained shells down onto the strongholds within the village. Additionally, three batteries of 60-pounder guns swept the exits of the village. Two hours later the 4.5-inch howitzer batteries of the 16th, 19th, and 36th Divisions opened fire with a concentrated bombardment of gas shells. Nine hundred lethal rounds landed in the first minutes, followed by 600 lachrymatory shells at a steady rate of fire. The British hoped the lethal gas would catch German work parties in the process of repairing the damage sustained during the high explosive bombardment. The British counted on the psychological effect of having survived the early round of shelling and the difficulty of having to engage in heavy labor to result in a lowering of gas discipline that might result in the harvesting of a rich crop of casualties. The purpose of the follow-up saturation with lachrymatory shell was to hinder the enemy's repairs by contaminating the environment and forcing the work crews to wear their masks.[101]

The Australians conducted an attritional bombardment of their own during Y/Z night on the eve of the battle. Against the strong point of Potterie Farm they allocated 750 4.5-inch gas shells and doused a concentration of enemy dugouts with 3,400 4.5-inch gas shells. The gunners also bombarded the approaches with shrapnel fired from 18- and 60-pounder guns.[102] Against the village of Warneton they planned to use over 2,700 60-pounder chemical rounds, along with shrapnel bursts on the perimeter. However, the artillery canceled the operations and the gunners instead used the gas shell for counter-battery.[103] II ANZAC Corps also conducted an exhaustion barrage against Messines. Divisional and corps guns interposed brief three-minute bombardments of lethal shell with lengthy steady barrages of SK or PS. The total program lasted from 11:00 P.M. on the third to 2:47 A.M. on the fourth and involved over 6,000 lethal and nearly 1,900 lachrymatory gas shells. The program orders provided options in case of meteorological problems. If the wind exceeded seven MPH the gunners were to replace the lethal component with high explosives. Winds greater than twelve MPH would have resulted in the cancellation of the action. Fortunately for the British, the wind proved compliant and the artillery fired the entire scheme. Similar programs were undertaken on the nights of w/x and Y/z.[104]

Gas also played an important role in wearing down the enemy through harassment fire. The traffic behind enemy lines was immense. The British realized that gas shells could profitably serve to dislocate these movements and make it harder for the enemy to repair the damage caused by destructive bombardments.[105] From U Day onward the harassing of roads, approaches, and communication became continuous. The artillery commander for II ANZAC Corps called for harassment fire 24 hours a day.[106] If the artillery succeeded in preventing the carrying forward of rations and ammunition or the removal of casualties and the advancement of replacements, the fighting efficiency of the enemy would suffer. Haig described the objective in simpler terms: "starve the enemy."[107] While the British fired harassment missions each evening it is difficult to ascertain which ones included gas because the gunners did not differentiate between types of ordnance in their reports. It is probable that they used gas more frequently than records indicate. The war diary of IX Corps showed gas harassment bombardments on the nights of 31 May, 2 June, and 4 June. The New Zealand Division used gas against enemy communications on 2 June. X Corps employed a lethal and lachrymatory program on 4 and 6 June, and the

Australians began a five-day program of shelling the enemy's rear areas on 31 May.[108]

The British made limited use of counter-preparatory fire, a mission that would see greater use later in the year. II ANZAC Corps did choose to target gas the night before the battle on enemy positions south of the River Douve on the battle's right flank. The Australians believed that the SK would prevent the enemy from counterattacking from that direction for 24 hours. (This was the same flank where Foulkes planned to pour gas on the Lys Valley to create a defensive chemical flank to protect the attackers).[109]

While the other missions were important, the success of counter-battery fire was absolutely crucial, the mission that Second Army headquarters identified as the one "on which so much depends."[110] Even with the explosion of the mines, had the German guns brought their fire to bear, the advance of the British infantry would have become, at minimum, a bloody affair. Originally Plumer did not want any gas counter-battery work before z Day, and he limited the use of chemical shell on days U to Z to missions that would cause casualties. Instead, he wanted gas counter-battery to commence at zero hour, when the British would attempt to neutralize all the German batteries.[111] Furthermore, the artillery plan reminded the gunners that even on the day of the battle they had to use care with gas since some of the enemy batteries lay within the zone which the infantry intended to occupy by zero plus 12 hours.[112] However, on 31 May Plumer changed his mind and authorized the use of gas for this mission from 2 June on. The demonstrations of 3 and 5 June had revealed the location of over 200 German battery positions, all of which received an intensive neutralization bombardment at zero hour.[113] Second Army subjected the enemy guns to a 24-hour trial, with high explosives during daylight and gas at night.

Plumer had several reasons for revising his instructions. Exposure to gas over many nights would deny the Germans a rest from the counter-battery efforts of the British.[114] More important, it would keep the Germans awake and force them to do their nighttime maintenance tasks with their masks on, thereby making this work even more laborious and increasing the exhaustion of the enemy gunners.[115] The British perceived these actions to be necessary if they were to foil the German plan of employing defensive artillery barrages to defeat the attack. The change in policy also provided the British with two additional benefits. First, it would be more difficult for the enemy to withdraw their pieces

in the face of advancing infantry. Second, the use of gas on all the preceding nights would not tip the enemy that the attack was soon to commence as it might have done if zero hour was the first occasion for
chemical counter-battery.

IX Corps was particularly active in its counter-battery work, allocat-
ing nearly 5,000 60-pounder chemical rounds and over 9,500 4.5-inch
howitzer gas shells to the task. They commenced their work on the
evening of U Day and fired missions each night. At zero hour Second
Army unleashed a special gas bombardment aimed at neutralizing the
enemy's batteries for those dangerous minutes while the infantry assaulted. It was the climactic moment of the battle, and, as the FSR outlined, the failure to suppress the German artillery could result in a repulse of the attack. The artillery instructions for II ANZAC Corps
explained that every howitzer that the gunners could spare from barrage duties was to assume counter-battery work. The counter-battery
staff officer had determined targets after two feigned barrages had revealed the enemy's defensive bombardment arrangements. The shelling took the form of neutralizing fire of sufficient intensity to inhibit or
stop the enemy from working their weapons. The Australians actually
committed only 1,000 gas rounds to this task, far less than IX Corps,
and this might suggest a reliance upon the Special Brigade to neutralize
German batteries in the Lys valley.[116] The British captured few gunners
during the battle, but the overall impression was that they had succeeded in neutralizing the enemy's guns, and Edmonds deemed the gas
shell as "very effective with a minimum of expenditure."[117] The German reaction to the infantry advance was slight, and the British gunners had to respond to only a few enemy artillery firing calls.[118]

The policies employed at Messines became the standard practice of
the Royal Artillery, and a few additional examples drawn from Passchendaele will help to highlight the value the gunners placed on gas in
achieving their missions. Counter-battery in Flanders was even more
critical due to the fact that the geography favored the enemy. On the six
nights preceding the battle, divisional howitzers and corps heavy artillery groups engaged enemy batteries with gas shells, except on the evening of 26–27 July when the wind was too great. On the final night the
gunners enjoyed excellent conditions, as the wind varied between dead
calm and three MPH.[119] In addition, during the last four hours before the
assault the gunners undertook a front-wide counter-battery neutralization program. The gunners received instructions requiring them to pay
particular attention to hostile batteries that the enemy planned to use in

its defensive barrage, as these posed the greatest threat to the advancing infantry.[120] The XVIII Corps engaged 30 hostile positions on their front while II Corps bombarded 33 locations.[121] In the XIV Corps sector each of its howitzer batteries engaged one of the enemy's, while the gunners of XIX Corps took on 37 enemy positions.[122]

Fifth Army also undertook a series of harassment and attrition gas attacks on the enemy. On the nights of 20–21 and 23–24, XIV Corps bombarded Arbi Wood with gas shell, along with a shrapnel barrage around its perimeter. On the evening of 22–23 the corps selected the four bridges over the Steenbeek River as the focus of a three-hour gas shelling. The bridges were choke points over which enemy traffic had to cross, thus providing good harassment possibilities. During the entire preliminary bombardment period, Fifth Army dispatched over 83,000 4.5-inch and 60-pounder gas rounds.[123]

The British continued to focus upon counter-battery at each stage of the Flanders campaign, and they preceded each phase with an attempt to neutralize the enemy's guns. In September a staff memorandum noted that "it is essential that sufficient gas shells are kept for neutralizing batteries for about four hours previous to zero hour."[124] Second Army's subsequent orders for the battle of Menin Road mandated the neutralization of hostile batteries using gas shells, for four hours immediately preceding zero hour. For example, in fulfillment of this order XVIII Corps fired a total of 9,345 4.5-inch and 7,542 60-pounder shells.[125] The order also required a second neutralizing bombardment three days prior to the attack, in conjunction with a practice barrage, in order to confuse the enemy as to the time of commencement of the battle.[126] Gas policy also suggested that hostile batteries near roads were particularly good targets since the bombardment gained the additional benefit of harassing enemy traffic.[127] XVIII Corps reported good results for these efforts with only a few of the enemy batteries active by the day after the battle.[128]

When the British attacked at Menin Road on 20 September, the artillery had subjected the enemy gunners to gas bombardments on the three preceding evenings, in addition to the zero hour neutralization. The artillery also fired counter-preparation missions against the most likely avenues of approach for the enemy's counterattack divisions. A postbattle report by Fifth Army concluded that with good wind conditions a gas barrage beyond the final infantry objective "will have considerable effect in hampering hostile counterattacks."[129] Prior to the battle Gough had requested that his corps commanders consider the "formation of a gas shell barrage for two hours after the objective had been taken."[130] The program they developed required the establishment of gas barrages at 8:15 A.M., 9:15 A.M., 1:30 P.M., and 4:00 P.M. In total, the gunners used 5,650 4.5-inch howitzer and 2,400 60-pounder chemical shells in counter-preparation. They carried out a similar program for the attack on Polygon Woods on the twenty-sixth.[131] In his history of the artillery, Rawlins stated his belief that the gunners had great success in breaking up enemy troop concentrations on these occasions. To further confuse the enemy the British had left certain avenues free of gas during the preliminary bombardment, assuming the enemy would use these routes to bring forward their divisions. These were then the subject of gas barrages once the battle was underway.[132] Captured documents also suggested that these gas barriers handicapped German counterattack preparations. For example, a German order noted that since Houthulst Forest was heavily gassed during an enemy attack, it was an obstacle to counterattack divisions and was to be avoided.[133]

In an assessment of 30 October, after the Canadian assault on Passchendaele Ridge on the twenty-sixth, the army concluded that the four-hour gas bombardment was effective and the corps commanders agreed that it had silenced much of the enemy's fire. One example cited was the fact that only three of 12 batteries neutralized with gas were able to fire by the next day.[134] As the battle ground down, the counter-battery staff officer of the Canadian Corps issued orders that "whenever weather permits, selected batteries will be subject of gas bombardment at night."[135] For their penultimate attack on 6 November the Canadians expanded the gas program from 4 hours to 10, a reflection of both the increasing availability of shell and an increased commitment to chemical munitions.[136]

The Infantry in 1917

While the infantry was a distant third as a user of chemical weapons, there were some advances in its weapons and tactics, especially for clearing dugouts. The British had found the high-explosive version of the Miles grenade ineffective in clearing out underground strongholds and instead found gas more successful.[137] Originally equipped with the white phosphorus P-grenade, the infantry now also had grenades filled with phosgene and KSK and, by the end of the year, KJ. The latter was particularly effective since the German mask offered little protection from its contents, stannic chloride. The phosgene bomb gave underground defenders only a few seconds to get their masks on or receive a fatal dose, while KSK left the position uninhabitable for at least 12 hours. In the confined space of the shelter the gas did not disperse as it did on the surface, and even the normally volatile phosgene remained deadly for hours. Furthermore, the gas remained highly concentrated and therefore was more readily able to exhaust the mask's protective ingredients or even overwhelm its ability to neutralize the poison. KJ was neither lethal nor persistent but since it went through the German mask the severe irritant effect upon its victim's nose and throat soon forced the defenders to the surface. In any case the nature of underground chemical warfare resulted in a rapid decline in the life expectancy of a respirator. The Australian journalist C. E. W. Bean observed the effect of a KSK grenade on a dugout. As soon as the bomb exploded the German inhabitants rushed out with their hands up even though they already had their masks on. Due to the potency of these gases general headquarters included in orders issued in preparation for an attack instructions that the troops were not to enter dugouts until they had been cleared of gas, because even if the surface had become free of chemical dangers underground installations were likely to remain highly toxic.[138]

By 1917 the British had assigned a portion of their assaulting troops to the duty of mopping up captured ground while the main part of the attacking wave continued on to the objective. Troops given this duty, as well as raiders, had only a few minutes in which to wreak as much havoc as possible, and they made great use of gas grenades. For example, the 11th Division issued 1,000 KJ grenades to its troops for their attack on 18 August at Passchendaele.[139] Their responsibility was to ferret out Germans who remained behind in their deep dugouts. These Germans posed a threat because they could emerge later, take British soldiers in the rear, and impede the progress of follow-up waves, thereby isolating and preventing consolidation by the initial assault force or assisting in an enemy counterattack.[140]

The Effect of Gas in 1917

At first glance 1917 appears to have been a disaster for the Allies. Russia had collapsed into revolution, the French Army had mutinied, and the British battles were costly and inconclusive. Decisive victory had eluded Haig at Passchendaele and instead both servicemen and civilians were left with the memory of a horrible, tragic campaign conducted by a remote and uncaring staff. While the British did not achieve their goal in 1917, the year did have important if not critical accomplishments. By the year's end the British army had successfully incorporated a host of new technologies into their principles of war, technologies that would help bring victory in 1918. Passchendaele had also been an unpleasant experience for the Germans, which, along with growing discontent among their civilian population, signaled the beginning of Britain's long-desired ascendancy in morale. Gas in particular was an area that, despite a lack of mustard gas, allowed the British to slowly gain the ability to dominate the Germans. The year did not bring victory, but with hindsight it is clear that it brought the basis for the establishing of a superiority over the enemy.

British gas tactics proved highly effective in helping the army achieve the necessary prerequisites for victory: the control of the enemy's firepower, superiority in morale, and the ability to maneuver on the battlefield. The reaction of the German officer corps to gas attacks suggest the degree to which the British were making progress in these areas. A captured German document from the Battle of Arras credited the British with considerable success in suppressing their batteries. It observed that gas greatly affected the fighting resistance of the men, and gas injuries to horses impeded the flow of ammunition to the guns. It suggested the substitution of horses with mechanical transport. The report concluded, "our artillery appears to have suffered heavily from hostile counter-battery work. . . . Material was badly damaged, and artillery activity seems to have been paralysed by the effect of the gas."[141]

The Livens projector caused the greatest concern to the enemy, who seemed powerless to prevent it from causing casualties and lowering morale. A German study of the device conceded that "The most thorough precautions must be taken against this mortar owing to . . . its high degree of effectiveness. . . . [T]he British possess a very effective means of throwing large quantities of highly poisonous gases, dangerously concentrated, onto our positions. . . . The most careful watch must be kept day and night in order to avoid casualties through surprise."[142] The projector was indeed a formidable weapon and the Germans estimated that it caused about 100 to 200 gas casualties per shoot and of those 10 percent were fatalities.[143]

The risk and prevalence of gas forced the German command to go to great and demoralizing lengths to protect its troops. In July the Germans recommended that soldiers carry around their neck a three-layer drum, without the mask. If a burst of fire occurred they were to immediately put the drum into their mouths while they retrieved the respirator from its canister. The idea was to save a precious few seconds in gaining protection.[144] A German intelligence summary from the same period contained the reminder that when hostile artillery was active in the vicinity the troops should put on their masks even if there was no evidence of gas present.[145]

After the war Foulkes would conclude that "it was evident that the German troops feared gas above all else, that it was a constant subject of discussion amongst them and that their losses from it had a profound effect both moral and material which seriously reduced their fitness for battle."[146]

1917 had passed without decision, and the British command, though disappointed, continued to believe in and pursue the decisive battle. Yet for gas the year proved a success. During the course of the year the British had battle-tested their delivery systems while the nation's chemical factories had finally begun to deliver agents in significant quantities. Even more important, gunners of the artillery and engineers of the Special Brigade had discovered the principles by which to use the weapon, and they had disseminated their techniques throughout their respective regiments. In 1917 gas had become a mature weapon. The next year would bring victory.

CHAPTER 5

March to Victory

Gas! Gas! Quick, boys!—An ecstasy of fumbling,
Fitting the clumsy helmets just in time;
But someone still was yelling out and stumbling
And flound'ring like a man in fire or lime . . .
Dim, through the misty panes and thick green light,
As under a green sea, I saw him drowning.
– Wilfred Owen

For more than three years the combatants on the western front struggled to find the means to overcome the superiority of the defense and the stalemate of trench warfare. Then quite suddenly in spring 1918 positional warfare came to an end and mobility returned to the conflict. The characterizing trait of the Ludendorff offensives beginning in March and the Allied attacks commencing in July was rapid movement and the partial return of the open warfare that had not been possible since the war's opening months. Mobility did not mean the cessation of casualties, as the cost of war remained as high, if not higher than during the period of trench warfare. Yet the ability to advance and drive the opponent from the field of battle did create a greater sense of purpose and hope.

With Russia prostrated and having dealt Italy a devastating blow at Caporetto in October 1917, the Germans turned their attention to the critical theater of the western front. Ludendorff knew that the consequence of the German resumption of unrestricted submarine warfare was the entry of the United States into the war. If Germany was to emerge victorious from the conflict it had to defeat France and Britain before the United States mobilized. The Germans struck on 21 March with specially trained storm troopers, who, advancing behind a hurricane barrage of shells, tore a huge hole in the thinly defended line of the British Fifth Army astride the Somme in Picardy. Gough's army nearly dissolved under the onslaught and subsequent retreat. In desperation the western Allies established a unified command under Foch to share reserves and coordinate their movements, which brought the threat to an end. Ludendorff had engineered an impressive advance, the largest since the onset of trench warfare, and Germany occupied a further swathe of French territory. Yet for all its brilliance the offensive was bereft of strategic purpose. Unlike the British who had focused on fire superiority, supremacy of morale, and maneuver, Ludendorff had not conceived of an objective, either tangible or intangible, that was capable of bringing ultimate victory.

The Germans maintained the initiative with a series of attacks lasting into mid-July, but the results did not change. The stroke against the French on 27 May along the Aisne—the Chemin des Dames Offensive—also netted a considerable amount of territory, but the *poilus*, though bent did not break. Further offensives in Champagne and Flanders were less successful and became outright defeats as the British and French adjusted to the new tactics. When the furor of the German army was finally spent, Ludendorff had not only failed to end the war on favorable terms but had lost an enormous number of irreplaceable men and broken the spirit of his troops. The casualties left the German army weakened, and the territorial reward created a longer line to defend. Finally, through it all American troops were pouring into channel ports by the hundreds of thousands.

Though the United States provided a seemingly endless amount of manpower, the Allies did have to survive until the Americans had readied themselves for battle. The situation in anticipation of and during the German attacks did appear quite grave to many Allied leaders, both military and political. As the prospect of the enemy's spring attack loomed, Lloyd George asked Robertson to report on whether the general staff saw any hope of winning the war either in 1918 or 1919.[1] After Haig had begun his march to the Rhine, Churchill, too, continued to expect the war to last until at least 1920.[2] Even after Ludendorff's efforts had peaked, Robertson's replacement as chief of the imperial general staff, Gen. Henry Wilson, predicted the collapse of Italy and the prolonging of the struggle into 1920.[3]

While an alarmist tone was understandable, it did not represent the reality of the situation. The Ludendorff offensives would actually do more harm to the German army than to Germany's opponents. By June, astute Allied leaders, notably Lieut. Gen. John Monash, Australia's senior commander, noted the dire state of the enemy's troops. He confirmed this observation at the brilliantly planned Battle of Hamel on 4 July. The German army was shaken and the British had firmly established a superiority over their opponent. Hamel demonstrated that Britain had achieved the prerequisites needed for decisive victory: an ascendancy in morale, the ability to maneuver, and a superiority in the technical application of firepower. The situation had so improved that Haig could comment to Wilson on 11 July that the "present position is much more satisfactory than it was in March before the first great German attack."[4] From the time of Hamel on the synergy of a variety of weapon systems, especially artillery, tanks, and gas would enable the British to open up the battlefield and push the enemy back in a relentless series of attacks that culminated in the enemy's acknowledgment of defeat.[5]

The State of Gas in 1918

In the final year of the war the supply of gas, with one exception, reached proportions that firmly established it as a weapon for the artillery and the Special Brigade to use whenever conditions permitted. While the army would receive only about half of what it requested, it was the weather and the tactical situation—not the availability of gas— that became the primary determinant of its use. The only agent for which a lack of supply hindered operations was mustard gas, which would not be available to the British Expeditionary Force until the war's final months.

In November 1917 general headquarters hosted a major conference to determine the army's gas needs for the following year. Participants made it clear that they would use as much gas as the government could produce. The conference resulted in a renewal of emphasis on lachrymatory agents over lethal substances, due to a better understanding of both the needs of counter-battery operations and the broader meteorological conditions under which gases such as KSK were effective. The renaissance of these substances would be short-lived, however, as mustard gas would prove more effective than any lachrymatory agent. On 12 November Haig set the weekly request for the 6-inch howitzer at 40,000 lethal and lachrymatory shells, an increase of 26,000 from just two months earlier. For the 4.5-inch howitzer he asked for 35,000 lethal and lachrymatory shells, an increase of 20,000. These demands were still beyond the capacity of the Ministry of Munitions to deliver. It advised that it would take until May 1918 before it could reach the requested level of production. The following week, taking little account of the Ministry of Munition's difficulties in meeting the army's demands, general headquarters again revised estimates upward. On 17 November general headquarters recommended the establishment of the 6-inch howitzer at 51,000 rounds, the 4.5-inch howitzer at 34,000, and the 60-pounder gun at 1,000 rounds. It also requested that the Ministry of Munitions allocate production at 75 percent lachrymatory and 25 percent lethal. The ministry continued to express interest in a chemical round for the 18-pounder gun but general headquarters did not put forth any specific figures at this time. By midsummer the Ministry of Munitions production rate provided approximately half of the requested amount for the 6-inch howitzer shell and two-thirds of the 4.5-inch howitzer request, and would exceed the demand for 60-pounder chemical rounds.[6]

Mustard gas, however, greatly affected the desired distribution of substances employed by the Royal Artillery. Table 10 outlines the estimated weekly delivery of all chemical shells from midsummer into the autumn and illustrates the influence of mustard gas upon chemical shell requisitions.

Table 10. Estimated Weekly Deliveries of Chemical Shell, 1918

Caliber and Gas	Week Ending 27 July	Week Ending 31 August	Week Ending 28 September
18-pounder HS	8,000	24,000	32,000
4.5" howitzer HS	5,000	22,500	22,500
4.5" howitzer NC	26,500	5,000	4,000
4.5" howitzer CG	7,500	7,500	7,500
4.5" howitzer total	*39,000*	*35,000*	*34,000*
60-pounder HS	—	—	2,000
60-pounder NC	1,000	1,000	1,000
6" howitzer HS	6,500	10,500	34,000
6" howitzer NC	27,000	27,000	3,500
6" howitzer SK	6,000	—	—
6" howitzer CG	9,000	12,500	12,500
6" howitzer total	*48,500*	*50,000*	*50,000*
8" howitzer HS	—	—	1,500
9.2" howitzer HS	—	—	1,500
Grand total	*96,500*	*110,000*	*122,000*

Source: "Estimated Weekly Deliveries of Chemical Shell," n.d., MUN5/198/1650/30, PRO.

A second report of estimates drawn up later in the year, which projected needs for 1919 as well, also illustrates the growing dominance of mustard gas. Table 11 outlines these figures.

Table 11. Weekly Requirements in Chemical Shells, 1918–19

Nature	Presistent (Mustard Gas)	Non-Persistent (Lethal Agents)	Total
18-pounder	50,000	—	50,000
4.5″ howitzer	22,500	7,500	30,000
60-pounder	20,000	7,000	27,000
6″ howitzer	37,500	12,500	50,000
6″ gun	4,000	—	4,000
8″ howitzer	7,000	—	7,000
9.2″ howitzer	6,000	—	6,000
Grand total	147,000	27,000	174,000

Source: "Weekly Requirements in Chemical Shells, 1918–1919," n.d., MUN5/198/1650/30, PRO.

Both tables reveal a definite trend in the type of chemicals that the British planned to employ. Not only did mustard gas continue to increase in actual amounts but it also represented a greater proportion of all chemical agents. Additionally, they intended to provide mustard gas for all major ordnance types, except for the super-heavy calibers, giving virtually every battery a chemical potential. The allocation of mustard gas to the long-range weapons helped widen the scope of the chemical war as these guns could reach more deeply into the enemy's lines thereby extending their harassment and counter-battery capabilities. Despite the potency of mustard gas, however, the British had decided that it could not be the only agent used. When released HS had a delayed action, as it took time for it to evaporate and have its corrosive action take hold. If it was necessary to quickly neutralize an enemy position, such as a hostile battery that was firing on a British position, then it was essential to use phosgene with its almost immediate effect.[7] If the Ministry of Munitions had met the production figures of table 11, mustard gas would have accounted for nearly 85 percent of British chemical munitions, with the remainder mainly phosgene. British production never reached these levels, but their requests did represent the direction the British intended to take with chemical agents.

Despite this enthusiasm there would be little HS available until late September. Both Thuillier and Foulkes undertook missions to England to get an explanation for the delay and to spur the Ministry of Munitions on to greater efforts. Foulkes reported in February that production for the 6-inch howitzer shell would commence in June and that demand would be met within three months.[8] The startup was subsequently delayed to July, but a breakthrough in the manufacturing process did result in a modest savings of time.[9] W. J. Pope, one of the key scientists working on the project, outlined the problems as the combination of a multistage manufacturing process and the range of chemicals required, both of which placed a strain upon the nation's resources. Further complicating the issue, the British process produced a compound with a high percentage of impurity.[10] Additional reports in March and August provided greater insight into the problems but also implied that full production would not begin until the following year.[11]

Throughout 1918 the British continued work on another chemical that promised to be a great success, although it was not available until just after the war. As discussed in the previous chapter, the German introduction of Blue Cross was a complete failure, due to dispersal problems, although the agent—diphenylchloroarsine—was a highly effective sternutator. The blast effect of an artillery shell was unable to pulverize the substance finely enough to create the required particulate cloud. The British, who gave the compound the designation DA along with DM, a related material composed of diphenylaminechloroarsine, focused their research on the use of candles, which, when heated up would release the agents into the atmosphere. By March the Ministry of Munitions had placed an order for DA for experimental purposes.[12] By mid-September DA had entered production in limited quantities and the chemical warfare committee anticipated the large-scale manufacture of DM within a few weeks.[13] The British were on the right track, and candles proved an effective way to create a particulate cloud. The weapon's initial victim, however, would be not the Germans but the Soviets, when the British used it against the Red Army in 1919.

The potential of DA and DM lay in their ability to penetrate respirators. As inert solids they were not neutralized by the protective agents contained in the wearer's mask; the only way to prevent their inhalation was with a filter. The German mask of 1918 afforded no such protection, and indeed neither did the British mask. Therefore, DA and DM offered a potential means to injure enemy soldiers even after they had donned their masks. To protect their own troops, British chemical researchers also sought the means to improve the protective value of the small box respirator just in case the enemy won the race to develop these weapons. Such an enhancement was relatively easy to effect. However, an additional filter would increase the resistance to breathing and lower the flow of oxygen to the wearer. Researchers had a solution in place by March, but as feared it did decrease the breathability of the small box respirator by 25 percent. They hoped to have an improved pattern that allowed the unobstructed flow of air. While developing increased resistance was of concern to the British, it was even more critical for the Germans due to the design of their mask. The German equipment already had a considerably lower airflow rate than the small box respirator; a further decrease would impair the efficiency of the soldier. The British were therefore on a promising path in chemical warfare research. The successful introduction of DA or DM would have made the continued wearing of a mask impossible, forcing the defender to remove the device and thereby expose himself to other toxic agents. The decision to employ an aerial delivery system also meant that German installations located well beyond the range of British artillery were vulnerable to chemical attack.[14]

As with gas shell, the army also reassessed the needs of the Special Brigade. Foulkes wanted to radically change the direction of his unit's operations for the following year to an emphasis on cylinder discharges instead of projector attacks. He eventually lost this argument since the projector's greater ease of use, lower demands on labor, and proven effectiveness won out. Nevertheless, the reasons he advanced for the use of cylinders do illustrate the evolving nature of chemical warfare ideas. Foulkes outlined his plans in a document issued on 1 April 1918 in which he compared the capabilities of both cylinder discharges and projector attacks against the changes in the enemy's defensive tactics.[15] The German decision not to hold the front line strongly but to keep the bulk of their forces further back meant that the center of the enemy's strength lay beyond the range of the Special Brigade's projectile weapons. If the Special Brigade was to maximize its ability to inflict casualties upon the enemy and retain a role in the wearing down process, Foulkes believed he had to have the means to strike in depth at a more distant foe. At a conference in November 1917 Foulkes pointed out that, "it is necessary that cloud gas should be toxic after travelling long distances."[16] Cylinders offered this potential because the cloud, borne by the wind, could penetrate deeply into the enemy's lines and, with sufficient quantities of gas would retain its potency. Foulkes had also tried to alter the gas mixture to achieve a cloud that would not disperse as readily as pure phosgene. He requested experiments to determine if the addition of KJ to PS and Red Star would achieve this goal. However, the effort failed as there was no chemical solution to the problem of cloud spread.[17]

The difficulty was to create a cloud that was concentrated enough to pose a threat to the enemy's rearward troops. Another possibility was to massively increase the amount of cylinders in the attack so that the cloud kept its strength deep into the enemy's lines. At a conference regarding gas policy, with Churchill in the chair, participants discussed the possibility of gas attacks employing up to a half million cylinders. The objective was to cleanse an entire front of the enemy's troops. Several problems immediately arose which suggested the hopelessness of the suggestion. Due to the steel shortage and the need to share the cylinder supply with the navy, the Special Brigade could never accumulate such a stockpile. Furthermore, even if 500,000 cylinders were to become available, Foulkes lacked the personnel to install and manage such a number in a single attack. Although Churchill discussed the expansion of the Special Brigade, the shortage of manpower prohibited such an increase. Finally, the French would have objected to an indiscriminate release of gas as the wind could blow it into territory behind the enemy line that was inhabited by civilians. While the British could flippantly suggest that French civilians had to take their chances just as Londoners did in the face of German bombs, the government in Paris would no doubt have taken a different view.[18]

With a grand attack impossible, Foulkes proposed to achieve the concentration of gas needed for a deep penetration not by increasing the number of cylinders but by narrowing the discharge front. Instead of discharging from a trench as standard tactics required, Foulkes suggested tightly packing as many cylinders as possible into light rail trucks and discharging them from a position directly behind the front line, after the withdrawal of the local British troops. He termed this kind of flotation a "gas beam" attack. The simultaneous opening, by an electrically fired charge, of more than 1,000 cylinders would create a cloud of incredible density that would remain lethal, despite dispersion, for several miles behind the enemy front. The concentration would be so great that it would overwhelm the protective agents in the defender's mask. Furthermore, the potential for surprising the enemy's rearward installation was great since they would not hear the noise of the discharge.

On the night of 23–24 May the chemical engineers undertook a typical gas beam attack on XVIII Corps's sector of Third Army's front. The objective was to produce a cloud that would "penetrate in lethal strength to a great depth behind the enemy lines up the Scarpe Valley."[19] The plan required 20 10-ton rail trucks, each loaded with 120 cylinders for a total of 2,400 cylinders. With a discharge front of only 140 yards, the ensuing cloud would be incredibly dense and would be lethal to a depth of at least 10,000 yards.[20] Technical details modified the plan so that the Special Brigade had to employ a broader front, but they were also able to increase the number of cylinders as well. The cloud, while not as dense as proposed in the initial plan, was still of impressive concentration. The planners had to split the attack among three rail spurs, and the corps's engineers had to extend some of the lines and ballasts sufficiently to bear the great weight of the trucks. Tractors pulled the trains most of the distance but the infantry had to provide 900 soldiers to pull the heavy rail cars the rest of the way and into position. Instead of the original 20 cars the operation now consisted of 75 cars containing 4,725 cylinders evenly divided among the three railheads. Nearly 2,000 yards separated the left and right discharge points but general headquarters estimated that the beams would merge into a single great cloud within one mile of discharge. The Special Brigade succeeded in firing only 3,789 cylinders, as a rail collision and the overturning of a number of cars damaged the delicate firing apparatus on the others. At 1:30 A.M., covered by the sound of Lewis guns firing, the chemical engineers detonated the charges that held the cylinder heads closed. They released over 120 tons of phosgene into the atmosphere which the southwest wind of 10–12 MPH swiftly carried toward the enemy.[21]

Despite there being no need to install cylinders, beam attacks still required an investment of considerable labor and the effects of the operation were difficult to evaluate since the victims lay well behind the enemy's front. For the discharge on the night of 23–24 May, Foulkes had to allocate six of his companies, the infantry had to provide 900 troops to haul the cars into position, and the engineers had to undertake considerable construction of track and strengthening of line. Additionally, there was the work at the depot, the loading of the gas tanks into the railcars, and the task of attaching the fuses and the delicate electrical wiring to the cylinder heads. The Special Brigade conducted a number of other beam attacks, such as the release of 2,011 cylinders on the 49th Division's front on the morning of 24 July, but the procedure did not supplant the projector as the unit's most important method of attack.[22]

The beam attack was the most complete of Britain's chemical innovations in 1918 but it was not the only one. The British conducted experiments in a number of other areas to discover and exploit an advantage over the enemy. Throughout the spring and summer scientists attempted to jam enemy machine guns by exploding an 18-pounder corrosive shell over them. The substances used in these tests were titanium chloride, aloxite, and carborundum. They all failed.[23] The chemical warfare committee considered an antiaircraft shell filled with liquid chlorine peroxide, a substance that theoretically would explode on contact with an airplane. Tests found that this substance was impractical and that explosives were more effective at downing planes. The committee also attempted to render the enemy's respirator ineffective by clogging its air intake with silicon tetrachloride, but these experiments also failed.[24]

Between October 1917 and June 1919 researchers in Britain investigated a wide range of materials, seeking any that were more effective than the agents already in use. Substances tested included the oil from poison ivy (rejected as being too seasonal), the pepper-derivative compound capsicine (which received another look but was turned down due to difficulty of supply), and powdered glass (found harmless when dispersed as a cloud). They passed on nicotine, too, not because it was not deadly but because it was less so than the established war gases.[25]

The desire to get DA into service led to the suggestion of floating pans filled with the compound in the Moselle River and pouring flammable liquid onto the water. Once the mixture reached the logistical center of Metz, the proposal was to ignite it with incendiary shells. The burning oil would heat the pans and generate a toxic particulate cloud.[26] Less fantastic, and more feasible, was a plan for an aerial incendiary weapon. Since 1916 the Special Brigade had employed Livens drums filled with oil to set fire to woods and cause casualties just before an attack. This new idea, however, had the potential of being a much more devastating weapon, as its aerial detonation would also consume the oxygen in the target perimeter. The chemical warfare committee investigated the use of coal dust as the fuel. The goal was to create an inferno by bursting a pattern of drums filled with the powdered coal over a target and, while the dust was still airborne, igniting it with an incendiary charge. During testing in late September the researchers succeeded in setting fire to a wooden hut 30 yards from the point of propagation. The committee was sufficiently satisfied with progress to order further tests using dummies and live animals to measure its destructive effect, but the end of the war interceded before they completed the next stage of tests.[27]

The British continued to employ chemical weapons within the mission objectives that they had defined after the Somme. Gas participated in the wearing down process by inflicting casualties and misery upon the enemy, both to lower German morale and efficiency and to use up reserves prior to the commencement of a battle. Gas also assisted in all phases of battle. First it helped reduce the enemy's fitness and firepower during the preparatory bombardment, then it aided in neutralizing the enemy's artillery during the infantry assault, and last it established interdiction zones to prevent enemy counterattacks during consolidation. In 1918 gas maintained these roles both on attacking and nonattacking fronts. The only difference was that gas was now much more available and therefore more readily used. Unlike at the beginning of 1917, when the gunners had to stockpile gas munitions in order to have sufficient quantities available for the battles of Arras, Vimy, and Bullecourt, the artillery in 1918 could freely use gas whenever the situation permitted. Accumulation remained necessary for big offensives, just as it did for other shell types, but Britain was producing gas rounds in numbers that still permitted the artillery to fire chemical ordnance in wearing down missions during nonattacking situations. Gas was now pervasive.

As a percentage of total shell expenditures by all types during the entire war, the share of chemical munitions is quite modest. Gas first had to overcome its late start, and the British did not really begin to use it in shells until the Battle of the Somme. Chemical shells were not available in large numbers until spring 1917. Additionally, chemical supplies were so constrained and the demand for high explosives so great that, until the war's final year, gas shells were not available for most gun types, including the 18-pounder, which was easily the most voracious consumer of munitions. While the overall share of gas munitions remained small, a definite trend existed and gas represented an increasing percentage of shell composition as the war progressed.

By 1918 the artillery routinely exceeded the 1916 standard of 10 percent chemical shell for the calibers for which chemical munitions were available, and in some instances the share of gas actually reached 50 percent. The 6-inch howitzers of the 36th Australian Heavy Artillery, Royal Garrison Artillery, conducted such a bombardment when they fired a mix of 50 percent gas and 50 percent high explosive shells in October in support of a feint infantry attack.[28] Another instance occurred on 7 July when the 11th Australian Field Artillery, as part of a larger gas program, fired 72 high explosive and 300 NC 4.5-inch howitzer shells for a chemical composition of 80.6 percent.[29] On 10 July the guns of the 2nd Australian Division fired 240 high explosive and 472 gas shells, resulting in a chemical presence of 66.3 percent.[30] More typical was the performance of the Fourth Australian Division, whose expenditures over a six-month period were representative of the trend toward a greater use of gas. During the month of June the division's 4.5-inch howitzers fired 5,573 shells, of which only 698 were gas (a percentage of 14.3 percent), but the ratio for the year through 1 July revealed a higher chemical share of 21.3 percent (39,604 high explosive versus 8,428 gas shells).[31] For the Battle of Hamel the division increased the ratio further, and at the end of June it set the number of rounds for the batteries at 250 high explosive and 300 gas (a chemical allocation of 54.5 percent). The artillery commander shortly ordered his batteries to fire gas at every favorable opportunity.[32] For one exceptional mission the gunners received orders that on the night of 23–24 June the 4.5-inch howitzer contribution to the harassment program was to be 95 percent chemical and 5 percent smoke, while other calibers were to provide the high explosives.[33]

On occasion gas shell appeared to be available in such quantities that its abundance brought comment. The chemical adviser of XI Corps complained to his superior at Fifth Army headquarters that the 6-inch howitzers were receiving only chemical munitions and the absence of high explosives forced them to waste "stinks" by firing them on unsuitable targets in poor weather conditions.[34] While this was perhaps a temporary situation, W. A. Rigden, a sergeant in the 196th Siege Battery, believed that his unit had an enormous supply of chemical munitions, and he was glad to finally be able to give the Germans more gas than he received.[35] The general officer commanding Royal artillery of Canadian Corps summed up the situation with his recommendation that artillery headquarters should use gas freely in support of an aggressive policy to inflict casualties upon the enemy at every opportunity.[36]

On other occasions gas shells dominated a bombardment. On 7 and 8 June, Fourth Army blasted enemy positions with a heavy barrage of gas and other shells. Table 12 lists the number of rounds and percentage of chemical shells expended by those caliber guns that had gas. Nearly half the shells deployed on the seventh were gas, with the figure for the 4.5-inch howitzer an extraordinary 72 percent, while on the eighth chemical munitions represented a reduced but still considerable 25 percent. The Fourth Army carried out a similar shoot on 30 July with an even heavier use of gas.

The March to Victory

The first signs that the German army was nearing collapse came on the Australian front. Starting in May, while guarding the approaches to the

Table 12. Shell Expenditure and Percentage of Gas Shell Fired by the Fourth Army, 7–8 June 1918

Caliber	Expended on 7 June	Percentage Gas Shell	Expended on 8 June	Percentage Gas Shell
4.5″ howitzer HE	2,000		2,844	
4.5″ howitzer gas	5,043	71.6	1,669	37.0
60-pounder HE	522		1,132	
60-pounder shrapnel	1,410		1,439	
60-pounder gas	212	13.1	—	0.0
6″ howitzer HE	4,036		3,882	
6″ howitzer gas	2,412	37.4	1,421	26.8
Total	15,635	49.0	12,387	24.9

Source: Data taken from "Summary of Operations," 7 June 1918 and 8 June 1918, Montgomery–Massingberd Collection, 69, LHCMA.

critical rail junction of Amiens, the Australians resumed a policy of "peaceful penetration" that the Germans had interrupted with their spring offensives. Peaceful penetration was anything but what its name suggested. It involved the nightly dispatch of small groups of men, frequently as few as three or even a single individual, into no man's land to inflict casualties on or take prisoners from German observation posts, machine gun posts, and patrols. The Australian method brought in a steady stream of prisoners, identity badges cut from bodies, and captured documents that kept intelligence officers sated and provided detailed information of the enemy's dispositions and condition. Peaceful penetration also had another objective: the domination of no man's land, a feat the Australians quickly accomplished. The enemy's inability to oppose the Australians in this deadly game signaled to local commanders that they had gained a superiority over the Germans.

The British recognized the need to test the degree of their superiority in order to evaluate the true strength of the enemy and gauge the potential for large-scale offensive action. Monash had begun work on a plan for the capture of part of the enemy line in late May, and on 23 June Rawlinson sought approval from general headquarters for an attack by Australian Corps to seize the village of Hamel and the Vaire Woods.

In the official history Edmonds describes the attack on Hamel as a minor affair—an accurate assessment if derived solely from the size of the forces involved.[37] Hamel was, at its heart, a limited-scope, division-scale operation and at no point in the planning or implementation did the British consider it a breakthrough or decisive battle. The presence of four companies of Americans fighting alongside the British for the first time since the Boxer Rebellion was a harbinger of things to come, but it did not in itself represent anything of striking importance. Yet the battle was far more significant than its size, style, or the employment of American troops would suggest. Hamel represented the successful convergence of a number of technological and tactical innovations that the British had begun after the Somme and had refined during the campaigns of 1917. The integration of tanks into the infantry assault, the mastery of precision indirect artillery fire, the perfection of the role of the counter-battery staff officer, and the incorporation of gas into all aspects of the attack, along with increases in the infantry's integral fire power and its training in fire and movement tactics, led to a system that maximized the offensive potential of the attack and enabled the British to overcome the inherent advantages modern firepower vested with the defense. The British had combined man and machine into a methodology that restored maneuver to battle.

Rawlinson described the essence of the plan as a reliance on surprise, and accordingly the Australians eliminated the preliminary bombardment. The British had previously used this bombardment as a means to clear the defender's wire obstacles and to reduce the enemy's numbers and morale. These necessities did not exist at Hamel since the Australians already enjoyed a considerable advantage in morale and the enemy had not bothered to strongly fortify or wire their defenses after their spring offensives had advanced them to their current positions. The German failure to undertake the construction of defensive works, whose strength in the past had enjoyed a justifiable reputation, was taken by the British as a further sign that a rot had set in within the German army. Monash, who was to have 60 tanks for the attack, believed that these vehicles were sufficient to clear paths through the wire, although if necessary the infantry were prepared to cut it themselves. The ability of tanks to clear obstacles for the infantry and the decision to forgo the preliminary bombardment meant surprise was feasible and that the British could gain all its advantages over an unprepared and unalerted opponent.[38]

Although there would be no preliminary bombardment, the Australian gunners undertook a considerable harassment program on enemy trenches, dumps, headquarters, and other targets for about two weeks preceding the attack. The artillery kept their fire within normal ranges while reinforcement batteries maintained their silence until the battle's commencement so as not to alert the enemy to the attack's imminence. The operation's initial plans also recommended the extensive use of gas in order to continue to attack the enemy's morale and thereby maintain a British advantage. Once the preparations were underway the Fourth Australian Division required that "full use will be made of chemical shell and every opportunity taken when conditions are favourable to include 4.5-inch howitzers with chemical shell in all harassment concentrations."[39] An additional component of the harassment program was "morning hate," a special early-hour bombardment consisting largely of gas shell, with some smoke and high explosives. Its objective was to condition the enemy into putting on their masks and to lull them into complacency, thereby helping the attackers achieve surprise. On the day of the attack the artillery fired its morning hate routine but the gunners substituted smoke for gas. The British hoped that the enemy would put on their masks and thereby be at a disadvantage to face the attackers.[40]

The wind did not always allow the artillery to include gas in their harassment and morning hate bombardments, but the evidence suggest that they did so at every opportunity. The 14th Australian Field Artillery Brigade employed it in their program on the nights of 15–16 and 18–19 June, although poor weather conditions forced its deletion from the bombardment on the night of the third–fourth.[41] The 10th and 11th Australian Field Artillery Brigades used gas on 24–25, 25–26, and 26–27 June, as well as on the night of 30 June–1 July.[42] The five batteries of the right group mixed gas into their harassment fire on the evenings of 24–25 and 26–27 June.[43] The Fourth Australian Division's intelligence report noted the inclusion of gas in bombardments on the nights of 16–17 June against Hamel and Vaire Woods, while on 23–24 June the targets were various trenches and dugouts.[44] The Second Australian Division's guns, to the right of the battle zone, assisted with the harassment agenda and contributed its own chemical munitions on 1 through 4 July.[45] Additional gas bombardments no doubt occurred, but the records frequently did not distinguish between chemical and ordinary shells. However, battle instructions insisted that, weather permitting, the batteries were to include gas in their plans. The conditioning of the enemy also appeared to have had an effect as Australian units, once in the enemy's positions, reported finding opponents wearing masks.[46]

Monash scheduled zero hour for 3:10 A.M. on 4 July and he forbade the artillery from firing gas during the final night so as not to interfere with the forward movement of the infantry.[47] The gunners staged their normal morning hate on battle day except that this time it did not include any gas. Starting at zero minus eight minutes, a limited portion of the artillery fired a program of 90 percent high explosives and 10 percent smoke. The objective was to mimic a gas discharge and cause the enemy to put on their masks, while the firing also served to cover the noise of the tanks. Only at zero hour did the full weight of the Australians' artillery preparation reveal itself. The gunners intensified their fire and the silent batteries commenced to shoot. The Australian Corps had considerable gunnery resources, especially for such a limited operation. General headquarters had reinforced the Fourth Army with seven brigades of guns, allowing Rawlinson to allocate to the attack 326 field guns and howitzers and 302 heavy weapons. The near equality between field and heavy guns represented an exceptional concentration of fire power and helps to explain the fury of the attack's counter-battery fire.[48]

The field artillery, with the assistance of some heavier calibers, formed a creeping barrage of high explosives, shrapnel, and smoke, behind which the infantry advanced.[49] Simultaneously, the heavy artillery commenced its counter-battery program. Intelligence had accurately noted that the enemy had concentrated their artillery in groups located in the Lamotte-Cerisy Valley two miles to the east of Hamel. The neutralization of these weapons was essential for ensuring the survival of the exposed infantry as they crossed no man's land and for preventing the enemy from using their guns in any counterattacks. Furthermore, dealing successfully with the enemy's artillery was more critical than usual since, for the sake of obtaining surprise, there had been no preliminary bombardment by which to physically destroy the German guns and battery positions and exhaust their personnel.[50] Accuracy, both in the location of the enemy's batteries and in the firing, was therefore essential. To preserve surprise Monash had even forbidden the use of registration rounds. To ensure targeting precision, at the end of June the Fourth Australian Division issued detailed instructions for accurately fixing the location of the division's guns, and required the artillerymen to undertake a detailed inspection and repair of each weapon's platform, aiming gears, range dials, and clinometers.[51]

Monash had allocated two-thirds of his heavy guns to counter-battery and the gunners had planned for the extensive use of gas. The Australian Corps Heavy Artillery headquarters ordered the 6-inch howitzers to commence fire with lethal shell followed by lachrymatory rounds. The program was to last from zero to zero plus 150 minutes. While it is not possible to ascertain the exact number of gas shells dedicated to the neutralization of the enemy's guns (since the British also employed gas in counter-preparation missions the same day), on the fourth the 6-inch howitzer did fire 8,573 stinks along with 12,360 high explosive shells for a chemical composition of 41 percent. If one extends the comparison to include all heavy caliber weapons, 60-pounder guns through 12-inch howitzers, the figures become 25,543 high explosive and shrapnel and 8,573 gas, for a chemical percentage of a still-considerable 25.1 percent. The counter-battery program proved a complete success as the enemy gunners in the Cerisy Valley failed to fire their defensive barrages and were unable to affect the conduct of the battle. The British had indeed achieved neutralization, and for some time after zero they could report that the hostile artillery was practically silent. The divisional 4.5-inch howitzers did fire some gas on the fourth but the plan limited its role principally to the direct support of the infantry.[52]

Coinciding with the commencement of the battle, the Special Brigade made its own contribution to the attack. The mortarmen of No. 1 Special Company dropped over 720 WP and 154 NC bombs onto the high ground just north of the Somme and a further 612 smoke rounds on the southern flank of the attack. The northern attack was the more important because from the heights the enemy could observe the assault. These bombardments were meant to isolate the battle zone from adjacent enemy positions, a mission in which the Special Brigade was entirely successful. The III Corps to the left and the French army on the right provided additional assistance by firing artillery missions to neutralize the enemy guns on their fronts that could enfilade the Australian advance, while the III Corps also simulated an attack as a diversion.[53]

The infantry left their trenches promptly at 3:10 A.M. and, protected by the creeping barrage and the counter-battery fire, had one of the easiest advances of the war. By 5:00 A.M. the attackers had reached all their final objectives and had begun to dig in. While the British plan had called for a limited advance—at its greatest depth it was no more than 2,000 yards—its complete success was still an impressive accomplishment. The casualties were also relatively minor. The total, for the Australians and Americans combined, was slightly more than 900 officers and men. Exact German losses are not known but prisoners alone exceeded 1,450 men.[54]

Having reached their goal, the infantry began to dig in and prepare their defenses while the artillery began counter-preparation fire in order to provide the troops with the time they needed to consolidate their gains. When the creeping barrage reached the final firing line, the participating 6-inch howitzers switched to chemical shell.[55] The gas enveloped the Australians' new front in a protective toxic cloud and deterred enemy counterattacks. The artillery staff officers had also prepared two plans in anticipation of the need to repel enemy counterattacks and thereby prevent a repetition of the embarrassment that occurred after Cambrai when the enemy retook the ground they had lost to the British attack. Counter-preparation phase IA provided for a heavy concentration of fire upon known hostile batteries and was under the control of the counter-battery staff officer. Counter-preparation phase IB included plans to fire upon likely enemy assembly points and communications and was under the direction of the commander corps heavy artillery.[56] Plan B contained a list of 48 targets, including railway cuttings, roads and road junctions, bridges, other concealed positions, and transportation chokepoints, and noted that the batteries were to use gas, weather permitting.[57]

The British implemented both IA and IB on the evening of the battle. Commencing at 10:00 P.M. the heavy artillery opened fire with gas on German artillery positions in the La Motte–Cerisy Valley. Seventy 6-inch howitzers shelled 24 targets containing one or more enemy batteries. The program, fired at intervals, consisted of each gun shooting five rounds; the attack lasted until 3:20 A.M. Each target received three bursts of fire, and in total the British expended over 1,000 rounds. Additionally, the heavy artillery silenced enemy batteries four times during the night when they began to fire. The Fourth Australian Division's 4.5-inch howitzers also contributed to these bombardments. The British undertook neutralization missions on subsequent nights and the 6-inch howitzers continued to fire large quantities of gas shell through 10 July.[58]

The divisional 4.5-inch howitzers also commenced harassment fire according to counter-preparation plan IB on the evening of the fourth. On the morning of the battle the division's artillery commander ordered each battery to have 300 gas rounds on hand in anticipation of the bombardment. During a preplanned 27-minute program, 12 batteries expended 3,600 chemical rounds onto potential enemy assembly points in anticipation of the Germans concentrating their local reserves for a counterattack. The 18-pounders contributed shrapnel and high explosives to the bombardment. The artillery completed another gas harassment mission on the sixth. The division's howitzers remained active with larger-than-normal expenditures of gas shells up to 10 July, when they doused enemy positions with a further 2,216 rounds.[59]

The British continued to invoke counter-preparation plans 1A and 1B on each evening after the battle until 10 July when firing patterns resumed a more normal pattern. Over the course of the battle, Fourth Army consumed nearly 10,000 4.5-inch howitzer and 15,210 6-inch howitzer gas shells, an extraordinary amount for a battle of this size. On some days the consumption of chemical shells challenged high explosive munitions for dominance. For example, on 6 July 48.5 percent of the 6-inch howitzer shells fired were gas, and on 10 July the ratio for the 4.5-inch howitzer reached 49.2 percent chemical. In addition, the Special Brigade made a modest contribution to the counter-preparation programs with two small projector shoots on the mornings of 6 and 7 July. The Australian planners had drawn up their counter-preparation programs both to protect their own infantry and to upset the enemy's offensive plans. In this mission they were absolutely successful; the Germans did not retake the ground.[60]

The success of Hamel suggests two conclusions. The first, and more obvious, is that the British had indeed gained a superiority over the Germans and that the wearing down process had worked. Since the Somme, the British had inflicted such damage, both through casualties and harassment, that in summer 1918 the enemy's morale precipitously declined to the extent that it adversely affected the efficiency of their army. By the Battle of Hamel, the British had achieved one of their essential preconditions for decisive victory: a superiority in morale over the enemy. The enemy's soldiers no longer had the stomach to resist the British with the same determination that they had had in the past, and frequent doses of gas in the morning hate and other forms of harassment fire ensured that low enemy morale continued. The second conclusion regarding Hamel is more far reaching. The ability of the Australian infantry to leave the protection of their trenches, survive passage into no man's land, and speedily penetrate into all their final objectives (and at a minimal cost) indicate that the British had also succeeded in neutralizing German defensive firepower and thus restored mobility to battle. At the Somme the British artillery had attempted to obliterate the enemy with brute force so that the infantry could simply move forward and occupy their objectives. The bombardment's failure resulted in 60,000 casualties. At Hamel, the artillery had a far easier task. Instead of aiming for complete destruction, Monash aimed merely to neutralize the defenders during the brief, critical period when the infantry assaulted. In their prewar principles the British assigned to firepower a number of tasks, including the gaining of a fire ascendancy over the enemy and the preventing of the defender's weapons from interfering with the attack. By Hamel the British had developed the means to suppress the enemy's fire so that the infantry could advance and close with their opponent.

Hamel demonstrated that the British had indeed solved the essential problem of the western front: the ability of the defender's firepower to control the battlefield. The British method of assault redressed this imbalance, and shifted it in favor of the attacker. Hamel represented the culmination of a painful learning process as well as the successful incorporation of new technologies, weapons, and tactics into the British method of waging war. The first new element was the tank, although, after the battle, Rawlinson did exaggerate the improvements incorporated into the Mark V model when he wrote that "it arrives in time, keeps well up with the infantry sometimes in front of them and is handier than a polo pony twisting and turning whenever it likes."[61] While the tank's cannons, machine guns, vast bulk, and daunting appearance certainly played a role in overwhelming the enemy positions, its more mundane ability to clear lanes through the wire was its most important contribution. The presence of the tank meant that the British no longer needed to destroy the enemy's defenses with a prolonged bombardment, a move that would have alerted the enemy to the immediacy of an attack. Furthermore, dispensing with a preliminary bombardment also meant that the British did not have to accumulate massive amounts of ordnance. The enemy might have noticed the enormous stockpiles of shells, or, at the very least, deduced the possibility of an attack by the proportionally increased levels of logistical activity behind the British line. Either occurrence would have resulted in the loss of surprise. The importance of preserving surprise cannot be minimized, as its achievement typically helped the attacker gain a position of superiority over the defender. Furthermore, if caught by surprise the enemy's high command would not have foreseen the need to bring reinforcements to the sector or prepare counterattack divisions. Thus, surprise at Hamel had both tactical and operational implications, and Rawlinson was right to value it so highly.

Improvements in British gunnery accuracy, intelligence gathering, and target allocation were other areas of important advances. The ability to fire with precision obviated the need to shoot registration rounds,

rounds that might have warned the enemy of a potential attack. Accuracy also freed the artillery from dependence on aerial observation, which was not only slow but could suggest to the enemy that something was in the wind. Furthermore, these advances in gunnery technique permitted the reinforcement batteries to remain silent until zero hour. Finally, the British mastery of state-of-the-art artillery technology gave them a decided edge over the opposition and assured that at the required moment they could eliminate the enemy's guns from the battle.

British coordination of artillery intelligence collection and analysis in the office of the counter-battery staff officer was another major breakthrough in the application of gunnery firepower. Its staff, relying upon information collected from its many observers, successfully located virtually all of the enemy's battery positions. The British knew not only that the German artillery was somewhere in the Cerisy Valley but also precisely where in the valley it was. The combination of improved accuracy with the ability to locate the enemy proved devastating to the German guns. At zero hour the enemy artillery remained silent.

What, then, did gas, the final critical technology, add to the mix that tanks and improved gunnery did not already provide, and what was its contribution to victory? At zero hour the tanks rolled forward to clear paths through the wire, while the divisional artillery established a creeping barrage to suppress the enemy's small-weapon defensive fire from the trenches and machine gun strong points. Meanwhile, the Special Brigade and the artillery created smoke clouds and obscured the enemy's line of sight. Simultaneously, the Australians rose up and attacked across no man's land fully exposed to the wrath of the enemy's defensive fire. Tanks could clear the way but they could not protect the exposed soldiers. The barrage upon the enemy's defensive works did minimize the normally lethal rifle and machine gun fire, and the smoke did hide the Australians from the view of enemy observers posted on the heights above the Somme River. However, the enemy's strongest defensive weapon—their artillery, whose preprogrammed defensive barrages could obliterate anything that attempted to traverse no man's land—still posed a threat. The Australians made it across, into the enemy's defensive works and on to their final objectives, because the German gunners were choking in clouds of gas from British counter-battery fire and could not fire their weapons. The Australians succeeded so easily because they had countered every capability of the German defensive fire.

Was gas an essential ingredient of the counterattack? Certainly, because it was the most effective method of neutralizing the enemy's guns. If the wind had been too strong, that is, stronger than 12 MPH, the British would have had to substitute high explosives, since gas was still weather dependent and therefore a difficult weapon to employ. However, it is possible that the use of explosive munitions in place of chemical shell would have resulted in greater activity by the enemy's artillery, resulting in a higher level of Australian casualties. Consequently, publications, reports, orders, and training materials of the time make it abundantly clear that gas was the preferred shell for counter-battery, counter-preparation, and harassment fire and, if more munitions had been provided more would have been used.

Gas afforded a number of advantages that traditional ordnance did not possess. It had a wider tolerance for aiming error than high explosive shells, since gas was an area weapon and its cloud spread to engulf all in its path. In effect, gas was inherently more accurate that any other type of ordnance, with the possible exception of smoke. Gas also had a prolonged length of effectiveness and was capable of causing casualties until dissipated by the elements, unlike high explosives that ceased to be dangerous once they exhausted their kinetic energy. Another advantage was that a concentrated burst of gas shells silenced the firing of a weapon more quickly than explosive munitions, since the targeted personnel had to stop, put on their masks, and attempt to continue to fire in an encumbered state. Once a gun crew had put on their masks their efficiency, both in rate of fire and accuracy, declined dramatically. If the concentration of gas was high the manning of the weapon became impossible, and the artillerymen either had to flee the position or seek the shelter of their dugout. Finally, the likelihood of the continued working of an artillery piece was greater during a high explosive or shrapnel barrage than during a gas bombardment since gun pits afforded a degree of protection from virtually anything but a direct hit. Gas, however, sought the lowest point of land and tumbled into emplacements, converting them to death traps filled with extremely concentrated toxic vapors.

Gas had one additional major benefit: like the tanks, it made surprise possible. It had the power to stop a firing battery, or prevent a battery from beginning to fire almost instantly, as opposed to explosive-based munitions that relied on the incremental addition of casualties and creation of damage to reduce the efficiency of a gun crew. This final advantage was critical for the sake of the advancing infantry. At Hamel, since surprise was such an important factor in the plan, the British artillery had to ensure the silence of their opponent's guns at zero hour. Without gas the British artillery would have had to commence their counter-battery bombardment before the instant of the attack, perhaps even days earlier. The gunners would have needed time to master the enemy's artillery through the methodical destruction of the enemy's pieces using aerially observed locators. Destructive shooting was a time-consuming procedure that would have cost the British the advantage of surprise and given the Germans sufficient warning to have taken counter-measures in anticipation of an attack. The consequences were high, as the lack of surprise would have changed the nature of the operation and raised the specter that its outcome would resemble the blood-baths of 1916 and 1917.

Gas also served another role. As soon as an advance came to a halt the guns established a protective barrier of gas. Monash chose to rely upon artillery fire, including large quantities of gas shell, to deter enemy attempts to regain their lost positions. His attention to this phase of the battle was probably due to his fear of a repetition of the aftermath of the hollow victory at Cambrai, when a subsequent German counterattack regained the lost ground. Accepting the possibility of a counterattack, the Australian gunners undertook harassment and counter-preparation missions on the seven nights following the battle. In reality, the opposition's efforts to regain their original positions never became terribly vigorous. Although the Germans did not test the Australian defenses, counter-preparation fire acted as a form of insurance and its presence would have impeded any serious enemy effort. Only on the eleventh did the artillery cease its exertions.

After the battle wound down, it became increasingly obvious that the German army's morale was in a serious state of collapse. On the eleventh a patrol of four men from the 1st Australian Division entered the German line near Merris at midday and captured 15 prisoners. By the end of the day succeeding excursions by Australians in pursuit of peaceful penetration brought the total number of captured to three officers and 69 other ranks. Disconcerting for Ludendorff, the evidence of the next few days suggested that the German malaise had spread far beyond the Australian zone. The 31st Division, on the Second Army front in Flanders, netted a number of prisoners on the eleventh, followed by 58 on the thirteenth. The following day brought further success when a minor operation undertaken by the Second Army's 6th Division near Dickebusch, also in Flanders, resulted in 268 captives.[62]

However it was on the French front that the Germans provided the most visible evidence of their decline. Ludendorff's final offensive began on 15 July against the French Fourth, Fifth, and Sixth Armies in Champagne as 43 German Divisions attacked on both sides of Reims. Expecting the attack, the French to the east of Reims held the Germans to virtually no gain, while to the west of the city the defenders contained the enemy's advance. By the following day the Germans had lost their momentum, and French counterattacks, accomplished with American assistance, began to drive them back. On the evening of the seventeenth the German high command admitted the attack's failure and brought it to a halt. However, the French had not only prepared a defense they had also planned a massive counterstroke. On the eighteenth, the French 10th and later the 6th Armies struck back on the western side of the Château-Thierry salient. Overwhelmed, the Germans quickly gave way before the attackers. A few days later the French extended their attacks to the eastern and southern faces of the salient. The battle lasted until 3 August as the French, with British and American support, pressed the enemy back. At its conclusion the German army had retreated nearly 20 miles and its troops had received another drubbing.[63]

Encouraged by the battles at Hamel and Château-Thierry, Haig sought a further success on the Fourth Army zone in front of the important rail hub of Amiens. The Australians had already demonstrated the enemy's weaknesses, and Rawlinson reported to general headquarters that the Germans had done little to rectify their defensive deficiencies. He noted that the enemy's lines were disorganized and were not properly protected by wire. Furthermore, Rawlinson continued, the opposition's units were severely under-strength and had few reserves with which to counter an attack. Finally, he pointed out the great superiority in morale that the Australians had established and the advantage this would confer on their soldiers. Haig required little convincing of the desirability of another attack. Two of his most strongly-held beliefs were that only through the attack could a combatant achieve decisive victory, and that an injured foe should never be given the opportunity to rest and recover. The British needed to maintain the initiative, press the Germans, and increase their superiority. They would attack.

On 17 July, at the request of general headquarters, Rawlinson submitted a plan for a major offensive. On the same day Haig approached

Foch for assistance from the French army to widen the attack to the south. Foch ordered General Debeney, the commander of the First French Army, to cooperate with Rawlinson.[64] Rawlinson's plan was simple and basically a repetition of Hamel except on a grander scale. Instead of 10 battalions and 60 tanks Rawlinson wanted to employ nine divisions and 400 armored fighting vehicles. Additionally, Haig promised Rawlinson the powerful Canadian Corps. With their arrival and addition to the already present Australians, Fourth Army contained most of the best fighting troops available to the British Expeditionary Force. Although he possessed a strong offensive force, Rawlinson kept the objectives limited and essentially defensive in nature. In his letter to general headquarters Rawlinson outlined the attack's advantages as:

1. Assuring the safety of Amiens, and driving the enemy out of shell range of the town.
2. The improvement of our position as regards its junction with the French.
3. The gain of further valuable observation [posts] and the improvement of our positions defensively.
4. The shortening of the Allied front.
5. The possibility of inflicting a serious blow on the enemy at a time when his morale will be low owing to the failure of the Champagne Offensive.[65]

Only one of the stated goals—inflicting a serious blow on the enemy—suggests the offensive potential of the attack, while the rest focus upon the advance as a means to improve the defensiveness of the British line and strengthen the hinge with the French. The absence of ambition to set bolder objectives suggests that the British leadership had not fully grasped the seriousness of the enemy's ravaged condition. The outcome of the battle would make Ludendorff's dire situation patently clear.

On 5 August Haig held a conference with Rawlinson, Debeney, and Lieut. Gen. Sir C. T. McM. Kavanagh at Fourth Army's headquarters in Flixecourt. Haig explained that he and Foch had decided upon a more extended operation in light of the success the French were having in driving the enemy from the Château-Thierry salient. While the first day's objective was to continue to focus on the old British Amiens defensive line, about five to seven miles in length, Fourth Army and the First French Army were to attempt to press the advance further the following day. Kavanagh's Cavalry Corps was to ready itself for open warfare, and general headquarters placed some mounted units, whippet tanks, and horse artillery at the disposal of the Canadian and Australian Corps, whose commanders would be in a better position to exploit any local successes. Haig still did not describe the battle in terms of breakthrough or decisive victory but he had certainly revised his expectations.[66]

Like Monash at Hamel, Rawlinson believed that the key to the operation's success was the attainment of surprise. Once again the gunners would not conduct a preliminary bombardment and the army would rely upon the tanks to clear paths through the enemy's thin wire screen. To move the enemy out of shelling range of the Amiens rail lines, however, Rawlinson did require a deeper penetration than the two miles the Australians accomplished on 4 July. Consequently, he drew the final stop position to include the German gun line. While he hoped for a rapid advance that would capture most of the enemy's batteries before they could escape, the inclusion of the German artillery positions within the advance zone did raise some complications for the British counter-battery program. Gas was the most effective means for neutralizing hostile artillery. However, if the infantry were to advance beyond the German gun line the British artillery could not use gas shells to silence the enemy's pieces. Contaminated ground within the advance zone would pose a risk to the attacking troops and channel the British advance away from the enemy's guns, thus allowing them to escape. The desire for rapid movement limited the opportunities for the employment of gas, and the artillery fired just under 3,000 chemical shells on the first day of the attack. On the days following, when the attackers hoped for a further advance, the artillery continued to employ gas but in modest quantities.[67]

Rawlinson had at his command three corps consisting of, from right to left, Canadian Corps, Australian Corps, and III Corps. The attack by III Corps was the least significant of the three, as its role was to establish a defensive flank on the north side of the battle to protect the advance of the Dominion troops. This section's terrain was rough and not suitable for tanks, and Rawlinson did not plan for as large an advance as he expected from the Australians and Canadians, who would benefit from flatter ground. Since the troops on the left would not move as rapidly as those on the center or right, Rawlinson decided that gas could support the northern flank. Therefore, only on III Corps's sector did Fourth Army authorize the use of gas by the artillery in order to neutralize the enemy's guns. However, while the Australian and Canadian gunners were not to fire chemical munitions in the zone-of-advance, the use of gas by III Corps's artillery was more significant than the minor role its infantry played in the advance. A disproportionate amount of the enemy's batteries remained positioned in the Cerisy Valley, which lay within III Corps's counter-battery zone. Although limited to only one-third of the front, gas would still play an important role in neutralizing hostile firepower that could interdict the exposed Canadians and Australians as they advanced through the enemy's lines. Once the attacking infantry had reached their final stop positions, the artillery would fire a protective bombardment of high explosives and gas, beyond the furthest advancement point, to disrupt enemy counterattacks while the army consolidated along their new line. Finally, the artillery had prepared a counter-preparation scheme for use after the battle against concentrations of enemy troops or likely points of assembly. Periodically the gunners would fire bursts of shells. On suspected targets these shells could be up to 50 percent gas.[68]

To secure surprise Rawlinson ordered his artillery to maintain normal firing patterns during the leadup period the week before the battle. Artillery commanders carefully monitored the expenditure of ammunition and checked that the character of harassment and counter-battery fire remained unchanged. The gunners fired measured doses of gas shell on each of the seven nights preceding the assault.[69] The Special Brigade's contribution, both before and during the battle, was also quite modest. On 6 August they fired 570 Stokes mortar bombs against the village of Sailly Laurette on the extreme left of the attack perimeter, and dispatched 240 projector drums against the Bois d'Arquaire in front of the Australians. On the next day they sent a further 175 drums of phosgene into enemy positions near Morlancourt, on the III Corps front. Fourth Army's plan did call for additional minor discharges of gas and smoke on the day of the battle although the special companies did not fulfill these operations.[70]

At 4:20 A.M. on 8 August, Fourth Army's artillery suddenly unleashed a furious bombardment of shells on the enemy's front line and battery positions. Once again the British filled the Cerisy Valley with lethal gas, choking the German gunners, which the enemy had kept in this locale despite the lesson of Hamel. Simultaneously, the tanks rolled forward, followed by the infantry who advanced behind a creeping barrage. The outcome of the battle was remarkably similar to that of Hamel. The infantry rounded up large numbers of prisoners and the advancing battalions reported no interference from the German guns.

In one instance the infantry captured an intact 8-inch howitzer battery whose masked crew lay dead around their weapons. Apparently the gas had penetrated their respirators and suffocated them before they could escape. The force of the British counter-battery program had nearly silenced the enemy and only a few hostile batteries eluded capture.[71] Intelligence proved critical in this success as the British had successfully plotted the location of most of the enemy's artillery. Again the infantry succeeded in crossing no man's land and pressed into the enemy's defenses. The advance of the Canadians and Australians went swiftly and deeply into the German lines, and by day's end had reached its objectives. Only on the left, in III Corps's zone, did the attackers fail to reach their goals. The next day the British and French renewed their attack. They continued to make gains but by the eleventh it was clear that the enemy had succeeded in bringing up reserves and that the opportunity for an even greater success had passed. Fearing the steep rise in casualties that typically occurred after an attack had lost its impetus, Rawlinson closed down the offensive.[72]

The attack on the eighth succeeded brilliantly, and Ludendorff was completely justified in calling it Germany's blackest day. At a low cost, not more than 9,000 casualties, Fourth Army had secured the safety of Amiens and its rail lines. More important, it had inflicted a massive defeat upon the enemy. During that first day nearly 17,000 Germans entered the prisoner cages. A further 10,000 were killed or wounded, and the German army also lost over 400 guns and a huge number of machine guns and mortars. More important, the attackers had inflicted upon the enemy's morale a blow from which it would not recover, and the ease of the Australian-Canadian success removed any remaining doubts about the efficiency of the German army at this stage of the war. Amiens convinced Haig that the war could be won in 1918 if the enemy were given no opportunity to recover. The British had achieved superiority in morale and they would use the initiative they possessed to hammer the enemy relentlessly during the war's remaining months, as they exploited their opponent's weaknesses and drove the Germans backward.[73]

In addition to revealing the extent of the enemy's weaknesses, Hamel and Amiens also suggested that mobile warfare would hinder the use of gas. If the infantry were to advance, then the artillery could not contaminate the ground over which they were to attack. After Amiens the Australian Corps instituted a scheme for mobile warfare that prohibited the use of gas shell unless specifically ordered.[74] Casualties caused by "friendly gas" had been a great concern for British planners since Loos, and they did not want to risk the potential loss of morale and their superiority advantage through the indiscriminate use of chemical munitions. The British would continue to practice chemical warfare but its employment had peaked. Fourth Army's expenditure of chemical munitions, except for a few instances such as the crossing of the Hindenburg Line, would remain modest and on many days they would not fire any gas at all.[75] The operations of the Special Brigade also suffered a decline, and Foulkes complained of lost opportunities and wasted effort as his men prepared their attacks only to have the enemy retreat before his engineers could discharge the gas. From Amiens to the armistice the Special Brigade installed but failed to discharge 9,000 cylinders and 8,000 projector drums when the enemy repeatedly fell back from the target.[76] In September there was a small rise in the number of projector operations but this proved temporary and the overall trend was one of decreasing activity. Table 13 summarizes the scale of Special Brigade attacks as the war came to an end.

Table 13. Number and Size of Special Brigade Operations, July–November 1918

Type of discharge and amount	*July*	*Aug.*	*Sept.*	*Oct.*	*Nov.*
Cylinder Attacks	6	2	0	0	0
No. of cylinders	8,263	3,197	0	0	0
Projector Attacks	42	33	41	13	4
No. of drums	13,464	12,365	13,069	3,443	630
Mortar attacks	11	8	5	2	2
No. of bombs	6,399	5,833	2,914	345	1,645
Total Operations	59	43	46	15	6

Source: Data collected from "SB Ops," wo142/266, PRO. Table includes only those attacks that involved gas, thermite, or oil. The Special Brigade also undertook in this period a number of Stokes mortar bombardments that exclusively involved smoke.

Further contributing to British hesitation to use gas as freely as they had in the past was the increasing likelihood of civilians being present in the target zone. As the Germans retreated they did not evacuate the civilian populations, who remained behind awaiting liberation by the western armies.

While these prohibitions impeded the employment of gas, there was nonetheless a place for its employment in the British method of waging war. Whenever the campaign returned to trench warfare, however temporarily (such as when the Germans retreated into the Hindenburg Line), the opportunity for the full employment of gas returned, particularly as part of a preparatory bombardment. Gas still retained its potency as a harassing weapon to attack the enemy's morale and to cause casualties on nonattacking fronts, or when the British did not anticipate an advance by the infantry. In addition, low-persistency lethal gases such as phosgene could dissipate in as little as an hour or less, depending upon the terrain and weather. Foulkes, in particular, sought ways to keep his unit relevant. He was able to motorize a few extemporized parties that could keep up with the advance, and in September he received several supply tanks to carry projectors and drums across the devastated roads of northern France.[77]

The final months of the war, known collectively as the Campaign of the 100 Days, featured relentless pressure upon the enemy by the combined armies of the western Allies. A series of major battles, with smaller engagements taking place in between, forced the enemy back upon their defensive bastion, the Hindenburg Line. Second Army resumed offensive operations in Flanders on 18 August when it seized Outtersteene Ridge. On 21 August Third Army opened the Battle of Albert. Third Army was joined a few days later by the Fourth and First Armies, leading to the occupation of Bapaume and Péronne. On 2 September the Canadians stormed the Drocourt-Quéant Line, throwing the enemy's defenses into disarray and causing a rapid retreat along the entire German line. As the enemy fell back, the British pursued, attacking whenever the Germans attempted a stand. The Third Army dislodged the enemy from Havrincourt on 18 September, and Fourth Army, with French assistance, gained Epéhy. By the end of the month, the British had reached the approaches of the Hindenburg Line and prepared to breach its defenses. First and Third Armies began the assault on the twenty-seventh towards Cambrai and Fourth Army pierced the fortifications on the twenty-ninth. Elsewhere, the Americans, with French assistance, finally attacked in force and cleared the enemy from the St. Mihiel salient on 12 September. At the end of the month they commenced the Battle of the Argonne.

The Hindenburg Line, the fortified positions the enemy had retreated to in spring 1917, represented the last refuge of the German army. If the Germans could stem the Allied advance in front of its defenses they would have the upcoming winter in which to rebuild their army. If the British breached the line, however, only the Rhine could serve as a barrier behind which to reorganize. From the Allied perspective, there could be no pause. If the Germans were given a lengthy interval of quiet they would succeed in improving their army's efficiency, which would fulfill London's prediction of the war lasting at least into 1919. Despite its imposing strength, Haig was determined to push through the Hindenburg Line and win the war before winter shut down the offensive season. While the British would attack the line at several points, it fell to Rawlinson's Fourth Army to make the most important breach.

Rawlinson did not intend to pursue surprise, which his army had used to such effect at Hamel and Amiens. Attaining surprise would have been an impossibility, for the enemy understood that the blow would fall and fall soon. Although not occupied since earlier in the year, prior to Ludendorff's spring offenses the Hindenburg Line was an extremely strong defensive system. Augmenting the interlocking fire of machine gun posts and strong points, the several belts of wire, and multiple lines of trenches was the St. Quentin Canal, which lay as a moat directly in front of the German works. Where the canal ran underground through a tunnel from Bellicourt to Vendhuille was one exception to the German stronghold; realizing it was the weak point in its natural defense, the Germans guarded the gap with particularly tenacious fortifications including several layers of wire and six systems of trenches. Despite its strength, the gap was precisely the point that Rawlinson selected to make his principal effort. It fell to Monash's Australians, along with two American divisions, to batter their way through the heart of the enemy's defenses. Leading the way would be the American 27th and 30th Divisions followed by the Australian 3rd and 5th Divisions. The "diggers" would then leap-frog past the Americans, enlarge the hole, and push through the enemy's defenses, allowing the waiting cavalry and armored cars to break into the open. In support, IX Corps would force a passage across the canal to the south of the tunnel while III Corps would establish a defensive front on the left and maintain contact with Third Army to the north.[78]

In lieu of using the element of surprise Rawlinson planned a powerful preliminary bombardment. He gave its objectives as: "(a) To complete the demoralization of the enemy, [and] (b) The destruction of the enemy's defenses, including wire and dug-outs."[79] Fourth Army had at its disposal over 1,000 field guns and nearly 600 medium and heavy pieces, and the artillery would begin its work on the evening of 26 September. Rawlinson divided the artillery's role into five concentrations: a special gas (BB) bombardment, counter-battery fire, harassing fire, wire destruction, and the shelling of select strong points and localities.[80]

The most unusual aspect of the preliminary work was the use of BB (the British designation for shell mustard gas). The Battle of the St. Quentin Canal was the first use of mustard gas by the British, more than 15 months after the German introduction of the compound.[81] The army had in its stores over 26,000 18-pounder and more than 6,200 6-inch howitzer rounds. Additionally, the gunners fired an unknown amount of German yellow cross shell using captured enemy guns.[82] Rawlinson scheduled the BB bombardment from 10:00 P.M. on 26 September to 6:00 A.M. the following morning. The targets were the enemy's artillery and centers of communication, such as headquarters and phone exchanges. After the conclusion of the BB bombardment the British fired only a handful of additional mustard gas shells because the planners estimated that it would take two days for the gas to fully evaporate and for the ground to be safe to cross. Infantry units did issue an additional warning to the assaulting troops not to enter cellars and dugouts as the gas would remain dangerous underground for two to three weeks. The infantry advanced 50 hours after the end of the bombardment and did so without any inconvenience.[83]

The British were greatly pleased by the results of the BB bombardment. They silenced many enemy batteries and inflicted a great number of casualties over a wide area. Some enemy companies lost over one-quarter of their complement, although a more-dispersed pattern of injury was typical. Besides causing casualties, the British had another objective. They wanted to increase the misery, and thereby lower the already weak morale, of the German soldiers. Mustard gas was an insidious weapon, and although a mask afforded protection from fatal poisoning, its ability to blister made its effect on the skin and eyes a torment for its victims. The British had two additional reasons to employ mustard gas at the time. The first was simply that it was finally available and they had the opportunity to pay back the enemy for all the suffering they had undergone at German hands. The second reason was less vindictive and more strategic. Haig believed it was absolutely essential to provide the enemy with no respite. If the Germans succeeded in holding the Hindenburg Line, the line would act as a bastion behind which they could recover their morale and rebuild their forces. Blasting through this position was critical in order to deny the enemy a refuge short of the Rhine. Mustard gas could provide additional power to the attack and, by its ability to cause casualties and misery, make the task of Fourth Army easier. Such was the determination to use mustard gas on this occasion that the gunners received orders instructing them to ignore the meteorological conditions, even if the wind was too strong for the effective use of gas, and to instead commence the program despite the weather.[84]

The rest of the preliminary bombardment represented the application of firepower in areas that had become routine. After the end of the special BB bombardment, Fourth Army's guns commenced intensive harassment fire, counter-battery fire, and the bombardment of selected strong points, all of which incorporated large quantities of gas shells. Only the shelling of the enemy's wire, a purely destructive mission, was free of gas.[85] The gunners maintained harassing fire along the whole front, day and night, right up to zero hour, firing burst of shells at irregular intervals. Its effect was to disorganize the enemy and to lower morale through the cutting off of units, the interruption of reliefs and resupply, the prevention of ration parties from reaching their units, and the causing of casualties. The counter-battery schedule also ran around the clock, hitting targets identified by the counter-battery staff office. Once again the program was highly successful and the enemy's guns inflicted few casualties on the attackers on the twenty-ninth. The final task was the bombardment of the enemy's strong points in order to inflict casualties upon their garrisons and physically destroy their defenses. Some targets, such as the entrances to the canal tunnel, were impervious to high-explosive shells, so that gas was the only means by which the British could reach the defenders. The British were aided in the planning of the destruction of the enemy's positions by the fortuitous capture of a complete set of drawings that detailed the layout of the defenses and the location of German dugouts and strong points. The demoralization of the enemy was so complete that on the day of the attack many enemy soldiers failed to man their defenses and emerged from their deep dugouts only to surrender. For all of these operations the artillery fired a mixture of high-explosive shells, gas—either CG or NC—and smoke. However, the British did not fire any gas onto the path of advance after zero minus six hours in order to protect the infantry.[86] The Special Brigade's role in the battle's preparations was virtually nonexistent, and they undertook only one small projector discharge on the twenty-sixth on III Corps's front. The only other contribution occurred at zero hour when mortarmen of No. 4 Special

Company established a heavy smoke screen to protect the attack from enemy flanking fire.[87]

The assault did not succeed as well as Rawlinson had hoped, as he was unable to employ the cavalry or armored cars for exploitation into the enemy's rear. The 27th and 30th Divisions did mostly reach their objectives but the Australians, who were to pass through the Yank forces, were delayed by German holdouts that the American "mopper-uppers" had failed to eliminate. However, the Australians pressed sufficiently far into the Hindenburg Line position to render its continued defense by the enemy an impossibility. IX Corps also succeeded in leaping the moat and had even captured a bridge over the canal, winning a close race with an enemy demolition team. Over the next few days Fourth Army pressed the enemy back further and widened their footholds in the German defensive system until the breach became irreparable. Combined with the breakthroughs further north in the zones of the First and Third Armies, during the Battle of the Canal du Nord, the British had broken the Hindenburg Line. The Germans no longer had a refuge from which to defend and reorganize their army and they would face defeat in 1918.

The final six weeks of the war witnessed a further collapse of the enemy's army as it recoiled from the incessant attacks of the British, French, Belgian, and American armies. During the war's final days the enemy's retreat accelerated and the cohesion of its army continued to unravel. The German position on other fronts was even more grave as its allies deserted and sought terms with the western democracies. Bulgaria capitulated on 30 September, the Ottoman Empire on 31 October, and Austria-Hungary on 4 November. As the Allied advance reached ground that they had not seen since August 1914, such as Mons and Le Cateau, Germany finally conceded the inevitable. At last, on 11 November, the western front fell quiet.

During the previous spring, Ludendorffs's offenses had forced the Allies back, bringing forth dire predictions in London and Paris on the war's indefinite continuation and ultimate outcome. However, less than six months later, at Amiens on 8 August, the immediacy of the Allied victory became apparent. While this radical change of fortune came suddenly it was not due to a novel turn of events, but rather was a result of the British army's incremental mastery of the problems of the western front. Victory came from the officer corps' incorporation of new ideas into their ethos, their integration of weapons and other components into operations, and their mastery of combined arms coordination. The British had begun the processes of adaptation in 1915 and it had taken nearly four years for the ingredients to reach maturity.

By the beginning of 1917 the British had in place the weapon systems and intellectual controls that would lead to victory the following year. The Special Brigade continued to discharge gas both to kill the enemy and to make their opponent's troops lives' miserable. Although it was hard for Foulkes's engineers to keep up with the advance, once the German army began its collapse the chemical troops did fight the enemy to the Armistice. Furthermore, during the Campaign of 100 Days, whenever the Germans attempted to stem the Allied advance and reestablish a stable position the Special Brigade entered the line and released their poisons. If Foulkes found it difficult to maintain his unit's operations in the war's closing months, the position of the artillery in the chemical war reached new heights. The Ministry of Munitions had successfully guided the enormous expansion of Britain's chemical plants, and the army now benefited from a consistent supply of gas shell. While mustard gas would arrive nearly too late, the stocks of other agents were at least approaching desired levels.

However, it was when gas was employed in conjunction with other arms that the British realized its full effectiveness. Without its incorporation into the combined arms matrix, gas would have remained a mere accessory, useful for wearing down the enemy but unable to contribute directly to victory. However, when employed upon the integrated battlefield, gas became an important player in the phases of battle, in the struggle for fire supremacy, and in the destruction of the enemy's determination to resist. Utilizing the intelligence-gathering and coordination functions of the counter-battery staff office, the artillery gained the ability to silence the enemy's artillery quickly at zero hour, thereby making the achievement of surprise a reality. Without this contribution the task of the infantry would certainly have been more bloody, if not impossible. The victories of 1918 showed that gas had aided the British officer corps in achieving the preconditions they believed essential for the decisive battle. When used to lower morale, gas proved to be a formidable weapon and a crucial component of the wearing down process. Furthermore, during the assault gas denied the Germans the use of their defensive fire and helped to restore the power of the attack, which permitted the infantry to assault across no man's land relatively unscathed.

Once the Allies had withstood the German attacks at the beginning of 1918, the way became clear to finish the destruction of the German army's morale and secure the restoration of the mobility which would lead to the enemy's collapse. After the experiment of Hamel, Haig authorized a full test of the enemy's capabilities. The great achievement of Amiens and the French success at Soissons indicated that the conditions were right and that their opponent's troops were in a dire state. The British had achieved their critical superiority and the defeat of the German army soon followed.

Conclusion

Ample and generous provision must be made for the continuous study of chemical warfare both as regards offence and defence during peace, in order to ensure the future safety of the fighting forces of the Empire. – Holland Report, July 1919

After four years of carnage, peace once again returned to the fields of northern France and Belgium. While peasants would soon resume their traditional cycle of planting and harvesting, the course of the war had forever changed the nature of battle. The combatants had entered the struggle with an understanding of the dangers of modern weapons, but they had not clearly or fully thought through nor prepared for the implications of these weapons. Warfare in 1914, however, had been on the brink of a major change that previous conflicts, such as the Boer War and the American Civil War, had suggested but which would not become truly apparent until viewed from the perspective of a colossal struggle such as the Great War. If operations during the opening stages of the war had a flavor of the Napoleonic era, by 1918 they much more closely resembled the experiences of World War II. This transformation was revolutionary in effect, and it continues to underpin to this day the operational art of contemporary armies. But its achievement was incremental, a product of a lengthy process of problem identification and solution implementation. World War I is often identified as a great technological or industrial war, and while these descriptions are true it was also, and more important, an intellectual war. In preparing for the conflict, the German strategist Gen. Alfred von Schlieffen had dismissed the British army with contempt as being irrelevant and unworthy of consideration in his plans. It was ironic, therefore, that it was the British army which emerged at the forefront of this revolution and which came most fully to grips with the nature of modern war.[1]

Victory in the Great War was neither easily nor cheaply obtained. The prolonged nature of the conflict was a result of the numerous difficult problems that defined warfare on the western front. As outlined earlier, the most significant of these problems was the enormous firepower capability of modern weapons which for most of the war gave the defender the ability to prevent the attacker from gaining a decisive victory. Defensive firepower was at the heart of the difficulties of waging war on the western front. Any attempt at victory, therefore, had to address this issue. For most of the war the Germans had used firepower to maintain an equilibrium on the western front that denied the British the superiority they needed to secure victory. As has been shown, the British gradually modified their operations in order to counteract German defensive advantages and consequently achieved the favorable relationship they required. Their success at countering the enemy's firepower at every level opened the way for the battlefield victories the British enjoyed during the war's final months.

In the course of explaining the British success on the western front and the mechanisms they employed in their quest for victory, a number of subthemes have also been examined here. While the full study of these themes is beyond the scope of this work, it is hoped that their inclusion will spur greater attention from the historical community. Part of the explanation for their success was the skill of the British officers as tacticians, especially in the area of artillery firepower. Despite their accomplishments it has been fashionable in some historical circles to make claims for superior German tactical skill while deprecating British efforts.[2] A good example of this tendency to overrate German achievements occurs in connection with the territorial gains they achieved in March 1918. Bruce Gudmundsson has interpreted the German employment of storm trooper tactics as an indication of the degree to which the German leadership responded to the nature of warfare on the western front.[3] Putting aside the fact that these operations did not bring victory, that the Ludendorff offenses left the German army in a worse position strategically than it had been in at the beginning of the year, and that the Germans were only able to retrain a small part of their formations in the new doctrine, these tactics were also unable to significantly negate the defender's firepower advantage and were therefore doomed to fail. Holger Herwig's comment that the attack on 21 March was more of a gambler's desperate last throw of the dice than a well-conceived and integrated operation that had any chance at victory, is the more balanced assessment.[4]

The storm troopers relied on mass, maneuver, and portable firepower to negotiate the enemy's defenses. However, the German army of 1918 did not have the technical sophistication, equipment, or training to neutralize British defensive strength completely through these means. Furthermore, German gunners were particularly deficient at counter-battery fire and were not nearly as adept as the British at locating and neutralizing the enemy's artillery. The gains against Gough's Fifth Army in March were indeed large, and did cause tremendous concern among allied leaders, but once the situation stabilized they also became meaningless as the Germans had struck against an overextended defender protecting a strategically unimportant zone. The real test of the new German tactics came in Flanders in April when they made a similar effort against the much stronger British defenses that guarded the channel ports. Then the inability of the Germans to master British firepower soon resulted in the collapse of the attack; its failure revealed the feebleness of their bid for victory. Historians are therefore wrong to give too much credit to German tactical genius and overlook British accomplishments, especially if, by comparison, one considers how easily Rawlinson's Fourth Army penetrated the Hindenburg Line—the strongest defensive position on the western front—and within a few hours made the position untenable for the Germans.

The British incorporation of technology into their operations is another area of debate in need of reassessment. All too often scholars have judged the British way of war-making in terms that are based purely on morale; some writers have suggested that in their attacks the British emphasized the role of man over the role of machine. Even concerning the war's last months when the British had fully integrated highly technical weapons such as the tank and gas into their tactics, the allegation is still made that the British defined their priorities in terms of morale.[5] Indeed, superior morale was an important concept to the British. As has been made clear, however, it was never an end in and of itself. Instead, morale was a tool that fit within the army's principles of war and which played a role in the struggle to gain fire superiority. The British desire to develop a superiority in morale was part of a broader scheme to overcome the advantages modern weapons conferred on the defender. Only within this larger framework is it possible to discern and evaluate the true nature of British intentions.

The British accomplishments in chemical warfare also suggest the extent of their capabilities at technical endeavors and their willingness to advance technology in their method of waging war. The British entered the war's gas race at a great disadvantage. Germany possessed the largest chemical industry in Europe, while by comparison the British infrastructure was terribly inadequate. Like most European countries, Britain had depended upon German imports for most of the chemicals (except for chlorine, in their case) that would emerge as war agents.

The British not only developed a chemical industry of their own but developed the tactics and dispersal systems by which they would wage the gas war as well. By the war's end they had bested the enemy both on the battlefield and in the struggle to dominate the chemical war. By the time of the Armistice the German soldiers, not the British, had the most to fear from gas.

Additionally, too little scholarly effort has been devoted to studying how the combatants actually used gas and its place within an army's conception of how to wage war. Instead, scholars have tended to overlook the pervasiveness of the weapon and have focused their attention on more-riveting although more-marginal weapons such as the tank. Evidence presented here should help to redress this imbalance and demonstrate that by 1918 there could be no escape from gas. Furthermore, in a period when chemical warfare might again be under consideration in places such as the Persian Gulf, a reminder of how widespread chemical warfare can become is warranted.

Moreover, the role of gas in 1918 only begins to suggest the scale of British reliance upon the weapon. Had the war continued into 1919, as many decision makers believed it would, the role of gas would have increased even further. Churchill planned to treble the 1918 capacity of Britain's chemical weapons infrastructure, and in the following year the Allies would have completed the expansion of their chemical manufacturing plants. By the time of the Armistice, Allied production of chemical agents had already drawn abreast that of Germany, and, at maturity the production programs of Britain, France, and especially the United States would have vastly exceeded Germany capacity. The consequences for the Germans were indeed grave, particularly in the competition over mustard gas. By 1 May 1919 the production of mustard gas by the United States would have reached 200 tons a day, Britain's would have reached 100 tons a day, and France's increased to 80 tons a day (whereas German production had averaged only 14 tons per day since they had introduced the substance). A ratio of 380 to 14 would have rendered the war a merciless disaster for German soldiers.[6]

The British chemical intentions for 1919, however, went far beyond the issue of supply. The weapon system that dominated the war was the artillery, and its role as a gas delivery system would have become even more significant. The British planned to increase the availability of gas shell by providing chemical munitions for every caliber up to and including the 9.2-inch.[7] Additionally, the British would have had the DM device, an airborne candle which, when ignited, released the substance as a particulate cloud. German masks offered no protection from this agent's sternutator effect. DM would have permitted the Royal Flying Corps to enter the gas war for the first time in an offensive role, as the newly arrived Handley-Page bomber with its long range and relatively high lift capacity could have served as a formidable delivery platform. The intensification of chemical warfare and the attack from the air with poison gases that Giulio Douhet and other interwar air power theorists predicted, would have become a reality.[8]

In an effort to further intensify the chemical war and increase the mobility of his unit, Foulkes planned to deploy a sled-mounted projector carrier for 1919. Easily positioned and fired, it carried a battery of 16 projectors. The crew could then reload, drawing materials from their supply tank. The sled also saved labor because it absorbed the recoil, obviating the need to bury the device in the ground and thereby freeing the Special Brigade from its reliance upon the infantry for work details. Since the weapon never saw action its effect can only be guessed at, but it would most likely have resembled the German Nebelwerfer of World War II.[9] The widespread availability of mustard gas, the increased range of the larger-caliber guns, the penetrative power of the bomber, and the enhanced mobility of the Special Brigade would all have contributed to making 1919 the year in which gas became unavoidable.

While these subthemes are interesting, the British ability to correctly deduce and react to the problems of the western front is of much greater significance, not only as an explanation of their success in the Great War but also as an example of how any army should react to the stress of change in war. The issues of adaptation and innovation are among the most critical for all professional military leaders, because it is impossible to fully anticipate the requirements that a conflict will impose upon one's forces until war actually occurs. Therefore, unless a combatant possesses a superiority of such great magnitude that victory is immediately guaranteed, an army's leaders must allow for the need to modify their method of waging war in the face of unanticipated problems that might impede the attainment of their objectives.

How the British army interpreted the nature of modern warfare and how it then evolved and implemented the methods that brought it victory is a cautionary tale of the complexity of adaptation, especially in conflicts where the problems are so great and the costs of failure so high, such as the fate of Germany, Austria-Hungary, and others suggest. British reaction to the introduction of chemical warfare can be used as a mechanism to detail both the parameters of Britain's intellectualization of war and the interpretive processes that its leaders employed to address and solve the conflict's problems. It is a story that takes place on two levels. First, how the British used gas during World War I in order to establish the prevalence of the weapon, identify the tactics, agents, and dispersal systems needed for its use, and how the they incorporated it into their method of waging war; the second part of the story, which builds upon the first but is more far-reaching, is how the British army interpreted the problems of waging war on the western front and then how they underwent the process of innovation and adaptation as they sought the means that would bring them victory. The two themes are interrelated, as gas played an important part in the integrated style of warfare that the British began to envision after the Somme and which reached maturity in 1918, as the victories in the war's final months demonstrated. Throughout, the key issue is the question of how the British army changed its operations as it pursued victory, and how it did so with such success that by the war's final months it was capable of routinely defeating the German army on the field of battle.

As has been shown, the British proved to be talented adaptors to the demands of modern war and throughout the conflict their trenches seethed with practical experimentation and intellectual fervor. However, these activities did not occur in a vacuum. Instead, the British modified their methods of waging war within an objective-driven structure which their principles of war defined and which their ethos disseminated throughout the institution. The objective they sought was, of course, decisive victory, a goal they shared with their rivals. However, the British experience was unique in the unwavering tenacity with which they held true to their principles and the prerequisites they identified as necessary to create the superiority required for decisive battle.

The British expected a decisive battle to unfold in a series of phases, each building upon its predecessor, until the moment arrived for the launch of the blow that would dislodge the enemy from their position and cause the defender to rout. However, the key requirement before the infantry could assault with any chance of success was the attainment of an advantage in firepower capability that favored the attacker over the defender. The enormous firepower of the weapons which the defense possessed on the western front made attempts at attaining this fire superiority more difficult, more prolonged, and even more essential. To create the required relationship the British embarked upon a lengthy program of offensive action in order to wear down the defender's fire power. Haig and his generals focused on three elements: the attainment of an advantage in morale, the pursuit of the means to maneuver, and the development of superior techniques in the application of firepower. Their success in these areas contributed to the collapse of the German army's military effectiveness and resulted in the British victories that ended the war.

When evaluating the operational performance of the British army in World War I, or of any force in any conflict, it is essential to define the parameters that shaped its leadership's decision making. Scholars have all too commonly dismissed the British performance derisively as having been an unvarying saga of mindless attrition. As demonstrated clearly in the previous chapters, this is simply not the case. The British conduct of the war centered around the need to establish the conditions necessary to fulfill their objective of decisive victory. Haig's emphasis upon morale, his repeated entreaties regarding maneuver, and the tremendous advances his army achieved in gunnery control can only be correctly judged if viewed from their function within the framework of how the British army perceived the nature of modern war. From this perspective, British operations no longer appear as exercises in attrition, stolidity, or unimaginativeness but rather become institutionally accepted mechanisms that formed part of an extensive plan that slowly but surely brought about the enemy's defeat.

Despite their dedication to their objective, the British never did succeed in achieving the decisive battle, at least not within the terms of their prewar expectations. The opportunity never came about for Haig to direct the cavalry onto the German line of communications, which would have converted the enemy's defeat into a rout that would have won the war in an afternoon. At times he did come close, such as during the rapid advances undertaken by the light tanks during the Battle of Amiens, but the mobile forces of the time simply did not have the ability to maneuver against the firepower of a comparable opponent in the midst of a withdrawal. However, the British were able to modify their expectations of decisive battle as they had modified other aspects of their principles, as when they redefined the struggle for fire superiority in temporal terms more suited to the realities of World War I rather than those of the Napoleonic era. In the war's closing months, assisted by her allies, Britain repeatedly attacked the enemy and drove the Germans back toward the Rhine. Each round led to a progressive weakening of the enemy so that by November the German army was impotent and had no choice but to request peace and accept the opponent's terms, despite the onerous conditions. Neither the failure of Versailles to result in lasting peace, nor the German army's success in establishing its "stab in the back" legend, should detract from the reality that Britain had defeated Germany on the field of battle. Haig may never have had the opportunity to fulfill the prewar image of a decisive battle but he had certainly orchestrated a decisive victory.

Although the British were highly skilled adaptors their record as innovators is a considerably different one. Innovation involves the modification of the intellectual fabric of how a military institution perceives the nature of war and, hence, how it plans to achieve victory. Throughout the war Haig and his officers remained loyal to their principles, with modifications occurring only in scale not in their conception of the problem. If any aspect of World War I should have caused the British to reconsider their interpretation of the nature of war it should have been the introduction of chemical warfare, an entirely novel and unexpected weapon system which the British had not even conceived of when they wrote the *FSR* and other training manuals. In fact, despite the outward manifestations of relentless change and the constant struggle for new gases, delivery systems, and defensive appliances, the British did not utilize chemical warfare to make a radical departure from their principles nor to make any central alterations in how they approached the problems of the western front and the pursuit of decisive battle. Successful innovation needs both a modification in how an army perceives the nature of war and in how it changes in the method of inculcating these values throughout the institution. For most combatants this would have required a reassessment of doctrine, but for the doctrineless British it would have meant the creation of a new ethos. Instead, the British remained true to their principles of war and to their ultimately astute perception that superiority was an essential precondition for victory.

Rather than seeing gas as a driving force for innovation, the British interpreted it as an auxiliary to use in obtaining superiority in the areas of competition upon which they had already chosen to focus. Instead of forcing innovation, gas underwent a process of incorporation. Its function at Loos might suggest a partial exception since Haig entirely relied on the effectiveness of gas for the success of the battle. However, gas still operated completely within the existing framework for waging battle, its principle function at Loos being to induce panic in order to prevent the enemy's soldiers from firing their weapons and thereby instantly establishing the superiority in firepower that the British desired.

Nor was this failure to innovate, to reassess their method of waging war, an indication of British inability to master technology-driven weapons and tactics. The British had a superb record of inventiveness and a proven ability to incorporate new devices and tactics into their operations. Due to new appliances, such as the tank, or improvements in existing weapons, such as in the artillery, the British came to dominate the correlating German arms. Even within coordinating agencies, such as the counter-battery staff office, and within intelligence collection units, such as the technology-dependent sound-ranging engineers, the British were pioneers and kept well ahead of equivalent efforts by the enemy. The failure to embrace fundamental innovation was not due to an aversion to seeking and trying new technologies but instead lay at the heart of how the British army thought.

As discussed in chapter one, the army's leaders accepted that a few timeless, inviolate principles guided the practice of war. Throughout the carnage of the western front neither Haig nor his staff and other senior officers questioned the correctness of these principles. For innovation to have occurred the army would have had to undertake a review of these principles, an intellectual exercise that did not take place. Without this process of introspection innovation was impossible. The prewar mental attitude of the British set the parameters within which adaptation was allowed to happen. Furthermore, the army had firmly rooted their principles in the cultural context of late Victorian and Edwardian Britain. The ideas that guided the army during the war were in place well before the war began and could not be separated from the nation's cultural milieu.

This should not suggest that the British army suffered from an ossification of ideas or that during the war its leaders pursued a rigid interpretation of the strategic and tactical environments. The army's loyalty to its principles would not prove to be a liability; instead, this loyalty provided the necessary focus for the process of adaptation through which its leaders successfully modified their operations. The durability of the British principles also provided the army's decision makers with other benefits. Armies are social institutions that operate within the cultural environment of their parent society. To speculate, what are the consequences for a military institution that during the course of a war attempts to disregard or violate the controlling boundaries set by the overarching culture? In a time of war, overturning the existing mental order would be equivalent to a collapse of the social fabric of the nation. Within the perspective of the parent culture, a military institution would no longer have a frame of reference by which to analyze new problems or to pose new solutions. For the British to have jettisoned their prewar principles would have required the abandonment of the ethos by which the officer corps defined itself. Had the British undertaken this task, had they thrown away their existing principles, they would also have lost their cultural connection with British society. The result of such an innovation would have been serious. Lacking an ethos and bereft of principles, they would no longer have had the mechanisms for adaptation. The army would no longer have been able to rise to the challenges of the war or find the modifications in implementation that would bring victory.[10]

What historians must do when assessing the military effectiveness of an army in wartime is to identify the combatant's objective and the methods, resources, and force structures employed to reach this objective, then evaluate the degree of correlation between these inputs and goals. It is readily apparent that the British army had the perceptiveness to employ their resources consistently in such a manner as to bring them continually closer to their goal. An assessment of the German army's performance in World War I is less flattering. After the failure of the Schlieffen Plan, Germany was strategically bereft of any understanding of how to bring about the conditions that would make victory possible. Fatally, on the western front the Germans spent more effort preventing their opponent's victory than in obtaining victory themselves. Furthermore, when they did attack they demonstrated an inability to think ahead to the objectives of their assault. For example, when they attacked at 2nd Ypres they failed to allocate any reserves in order to take advantage of the potential opportunities of the employment of gas for the first time. This tendency had not disappeared by 1918 when Ludendorff described the objectives of his war-winning offensive as, "we shall punch a hole into [their line]. For the rest, we shall see."[11]

Unlike the British, who placed every aspect of all their offensives within the context of their struggle for superiority, the phases of battle, and the decisive battle, the Germans were consistently unable to integrate warfare at all its levels—strategic, operational, and tactical—with their war objectives. Lupfer has argued that the German ability to reinvent their doctrine three times during the course of the war was an advantage and an example of their skill. However, he fails to correlate his findings with effectiveness, and thus his claims appear hollow. By contrast, the strength of the British system was the army's ability to adapt its operations within the preexisting context of its ethos, so that new methods conformed to institutionally accepted and understood standards. This was the methodology that the army's leaders had insisted on during the general staff debate over doctrine before the war, and it would prove its worth during the Great War. The difference between the British and the German armies is that the British got it right from the beginning, whereas with every restatement of their method of waging war the Germans remained unable to coordinate operations, objectives, and methods into a system that would create the conditions by which they could achieve victory.[12]

Not even the advent of something as radical and unforeseen as chemical warfare could change the direction of British policy. Instead, despite its dynamic potential to establish an entirely new form of war, gas became, like all the other accessories of war, an adjunct to the existing British interpretation of the nature of war. They made the right decision. The choice allowed the British to react more rapidly to the German chemical challenge and to develop the agents, dispersal systems, and tactics of employment more quickly than would have been possible if they first had had to conceive an entirely new policy definition. Gas would also prove readily adaptable within the British method of waging war, and they skillfully exploited its attributes to advance their objectives. Although gas would never again achieve the degree of operational dominance that it had at Loos, it would continue to be an important instrument that the British increasingly relied upon in their efforts to defeat the Germans.

Throughout the war the British army moved relentlessly toward the institutionalized objective of decisive victory using means understood by all. It was a bloody route, but not nearly as bloody as for some of the other combatants, and it was a sure road that led to victory. The potential result of systemic, intellectual innovation is the loss of the vision necessary for victory without the guarantee of finding a suitable substitute. War is a dynamic forum, and an army without an ethos is a force adrift and lacking in the means to identify, analyze, and solve problems. Armies cannot afford to be static and must possess the means to adapt to the changing nature of war. Innovation can be a dangerous process. Its results are unpredictable and are best left to a period of peace when there is opportunity for reflection and thorough inculcation. The ultimate potential consequence for the British, if they had thrown away their principles, was not only the loss of the ability to adapt but, even more gravely, the prospect of defeat.

Notes

ABBREVIATIONS

ANZAC	Australian–New Zealand Army Corps
AWM	Australian War Memorial (Canberra)
CAC	Churchill Archives Centre (Cambridge)
FSR	*Field Service Regulations*
GOC	General Officer Commanding
GOCRA	General Office Commanding Royal Artillery
HA	Heavy Artillery
HQ	Headquarters
IWM	Imperial War Museum (London)
LHCMA	Liddell Hart Centre for Military Archives (London)
MUN	Munitions
NAC	National Archives of Canada (Ottawa)
NAM	National Army Museum (London)
NLS	National Library of Scotland (Edinburgh)
OC	Officer Commanding
PRO	Public Records Office (Kew)
RAI	Royal Artillery Institute (Woolwich)
WO	War Office

INTRODUCTION

1. For examples see L. F. Haber, *The Poisonous Cloud: Chemical Warfare in the First World War* (Oxford: Clarendon, 1986); Victor Lefebure, *The Riddle of the Rhine: Chemical Strategy in Peace and War* (New York: Chemical Foundation, 1923); B. S. Haldane, *Callinicus: A Defense of Chemical Warfare* (New York: E. P. Dutton, 1925); Henry F. Thuillier, *Gas in the Next War* (London: Geoffrey Bles, 1939); and Edward M. Spiers, *Chemical Warfare* (Urbana: University of Illinois, 1986).

2. See Martin Samuels, *Command or Control?: Command, Training and Tactics in the British and German Armies, 1888–1918* (London: Frank Cass, 1995); Denis Winter, *Haig's Command: A Reassessment* (London: Viking, 1991); and Alan Clark, *The Donkeys* (London: Hutchinson, 1963).

3. An example of this literature would be Timothy Travers, *How the War Was Won: Command and Technology in the British Army on the Western Front, 1917–1918* (London: Routledge, 1992).

1. CONFRONTING THE WESTERN FRONT

1. Shelford Bidwell and Dominick Graham, *Firepower: British Army Weapons and*

Theories of War, 1904–1945 (London: George Allen & Unwin, 1982), 1–2; and C. E. Callwell, *The Tactics of To-day* (Edinburgh: William Blackwell and Sons, 1909), 3–5.

2. For the effect of the Russo-Japanese War on British thought see T. H. E. Travers, "The Offensive and the Problem of Innovation in British Military Thought, 1870–1815," *Journal of Contemporary History* 13, no. 3 (July 1978): 531–53; and Keith Neilson, "'That Dangerous and Difficult Enterprise': British Military Thinking and the Russo-Japanese War," *War & Society* 9, no. 2 (October 1991): 17–37.

3. Michael Howard, "Men against Fire: The Doctrine of the Offensive in 1914," in *Makers of Modern Strategy, from Machiavelli to the Nuclear Age*, ed. Peter Paret (Princeton NJ: Princeton University Press, 1986), 510–27.

4. Bidwell and Graham, *Firepower*, 2–3; Tim Travers, *The Killing Ground: The British Army, the Western Front and the Emergence of Modern Warfare, 1900–1918* (London: Unwin & Hyman, 1990), 54; and Brian Holden Reid, *War Studies at the Staff College, 1890–1930* (Camberley, England: Strategic & Combat Studies Institute, 1992), vii.

5. "Report of a Conference of General Staff Officers at the Staff College," 9–12 January 1911, 5–9, 28, Haig Collection, 3155/87, NLS; and "The British Army and Modern Conceptions of War," *Journal of the Royal United Service Institution* 55 (September 1911): 1182–84.

6. Bidwell and Graham, *Firepower*, 2–3.

7. Reid, *War Studies*, vii.

8. Jack Snyder, *The Ideology of the Offensive: Military Decision Making and the Disasters of 1914* (Ithaca: Cornell University, 1984), 27.

9. John Gooch, "Military Doctrine and Military History," in *The Origins of Contemporary Doctrine*, ed. John Gooch (Camberley, England: Strategic and Combat Studies Institute, 1997), 5.

10. Timothy T. Lupfer, *The Dynamics of Doctrine: The Changes in German Tactical Doctrines during the First World War* (Fort Leavenworth KS: Combat Studies Institute, 1981), vii.

11. The *Oxford English Dictionary* defines ethos as "the characteristic spirit, prevalent tone of sentiment of a people or community; the 'genius' of an institution or system." See *The Compact Edition of the Oxford English Dictionary* vol. 1 (Oxford: Oxford University Press, 1986), 314.

12. Samuel Hynes, *The Edwardian Turn of Mind* (Princeton NJ: Princeton University, 1968), 7–8.

13. J. O. Coop, *The Story of the 55th (West Lancashire Division)* (Liverpool: Daily Post, 1919), 8–9.

14. Henry Rawlinson, "Forward" to *The Story of the Fourth Army: In the Battles of the Hundred Days, August 8th to November 11th, 1918* by Archibald Montgomery (London: Hodder and Stoughton, 1919), x.

15. W. H. F. Weber, *A Field Artillery Group in Battle: A Tactical Study Based on the Action of 2nd Brigade, R. F. A. during the German Offensive, 1918, the 100 Day's Battle, and the Battle of Cambrai, 1917* (London: Royal Artillery Institute, 1923), 131.

16. While the antitraditionalist Fuller identified these as the army's characteristics he did not think too highly of them. He continued: "As soldiers they lacked one thing only—a knowledge of their profession." J. F. C. Fuller, *The Army in My Time* (London: Rich & Cowan, 1935), 39.

17. General staff, *Field Service Regulations, Part 1: Operations* (London: HMSO, 1909), 42. (Hereafter cited as FSR.)

18. "Conference of General Staff Officers," 9–12 January 1911, 5–9, 28, Haig Collection, NLS.

19. "Infantry Training," *Army Review* 1 (July 1911): 86.

20. W. D. Bird, "Infantry Fire Tactics," *Journal of the Royal United Service Institution* 49, no. 332 (October 1905): 1175.

21. J. F. C. Fuller, "The Tactics of Penetration: A Counterblast to German Numerical Superiority," *Journal of the Royal United Service Institution* 59 (November 1914): 389.

22. Tim Travers, "The Hidden Army: Structural Problems in the British Officer Corp, 1900–1918," *Journal of Contemporary History* 17 (1982): 524. For the benefits of amateurism see John Baynes, *Morale: A Study of Men and Courage* (London: Leo Cooper, 1987).

23. John Keegan, "Regimental History," in *War Economy and the Military Mind*, ed. Geoffrey Best and Andrew Wheatcroft (London: Croom Helm, 1976), 10–11.

24. Keith Simpson, "The Officers," in *A Nation in Arms: A Social Study of the British Army in the First World War*, ed. Ian F. W. Beckett and Keith Simpson (Manchester: Manchester University, 1985), 63–90.

25. Simpson, "The Officers," 69–71; and Edward M. Spiers, "The Regular Army in 1914," in *Nation in Arms*, ed. Ian F. W. Beckett and Keith Simpson (Manchester: Manchester University, 1985), 39.

26. Michael Glover, ed., *The Fateful Battle Line: The Great War Journals and Sketches of Captain Henry Ogle, MC* (London: Leo Cooper, 1993), 152.

27. Peter Parker, *The Old Lie: The Great War and the Public School Ethos* (London: Constable and Co., 1987).

28. Geoffrey Best, "Militarism and the Victorian Public Schools," in *The Victorian Public School: Studies in the Development of an Educational Institution*, ed. Brian Simon and Ian Bradley (Dublin: Gill and Macmillan, 1975), 140–41; and Simpson, "The Officers," 78.

29. Parker, *The Old Lie*, 17.

30. Simpson, "The Officers," 65; Best, "Militarism and Public Schools," 140–41; Parker, *The Old Lie*, 17, 56, 99; and Spiers, "Regular Army," 42.

31. Basil Williams, *Raising and Training the New Armies* (London: Constable and Co., 1918), 63.

32. Williams, *Raising New Armies*, 64.

33. Parker, *The Old Lie*, 34, 157–62.

34. Simpson, "The Officers," 65–66; and Spiers, "Regular Army," 43.

35. A. Hilliard Atteridge, *The History of the 17th (Northern) Division* (Glasgow: Robert Maclehose, 1929), 10–11; Peter Simkins, *Kitchener's Army: The Raising of the*

New Armies, 1914–1916 (Manchester: Manchester University, 1988), 88–89; and Glover, *Fateful Battle Line*, 154, 166.

36. FSR, 107.

37. J. H. Boraston, ed., *Sir Douglas Haig's Dispatches (December 1915–April 1919)* (London: J. M. Dent & Sons, 1979), 325.

38. Boraston, *Haig's Dispatches*, 319–20.

39. "Strategy II," Haig Collection, NLS.

40. "Tactics, Staff College Books 1896–97," Haig Collection, 3155/17, NLS.

41. "The Present Situation and Future Plans," 1 May 1917, OAD 428, Haig Collection, 3155/113, NLS.

42. Boraston, *Haig's Dispatches*, 319–20.

43. FSR, 113.

44. General Staff, War Office, *Infantry Training* (London: HMSO, 1914), 133.

45. "Strategy II," Haig Collection, NLS.

46. FSR, 111, 119.

47. General Staff, *Infantry Training*, 134.

48. "Report by OC 11th Infantry Brigade to HQ 4th Division," 3 November 1916, Montgomery–Massingberd Collection, 48, LHCMA.

49. "Strategy II," Haig Collection, NLS.

50. "First Army Conference," 6 September 1915, Haig Collection, 3155/174, NLS.

51. General Staff, *Infantry Training*, 147–48.

52. FSR, 132.

53. FSR, 133.

54. The manuals clearly envisioned the infantry starting their advance at some distance from the enemy's position, a situation trench warfare obviated.

55. General Staff, War Office, *Field Artillery Training* (London: HMSO, 1914), 246–52.

56. General Staff, *Field Artillery Training*, 230.

57. General Staff, *Field Artillery Training*, 230. The FSR summed up the artillery's objective simply as "to assist the infantry advance." See FSR, 115.

58. General Staff, *Artillery Notes, No. 4—Artillery in Offensive Operations* (General Headquarters, February 1917), 5, 15, 21; and General Staff, *Instructions for the Training of Divisions for Offensive Action* (London: HMSO, 1916), 9–15.

59. For a discussion of a role of the cavalry see Philip Chetwolde, "The Employment of Cavalry," *Army Review* 3 (July 1912): 41–50; and Sir John French, Preface to *Cavalry in War and Peace*, ed. Freiherr von Bernardi, (Fort Leavenworth KS: U.S. Cavalry Association, 1910). For a discussion of the lessening of the role of the cavalry see, Callwell, *Tactics of To-day*, 18–19.

60. For an example see "Haig's Great War Diary," 9 September 1916, 3155/97, NLS.

61. Haber, *The Poisonous Cloud*, 17.

62. FSR, 119.

63. FSR, 111–12.

64. Quoted in F. W. Bewsher, *The History of the 51st (Highland) Division, 1914–1918* (Edinburgh: William Blackwood & Sons, 1921), 142–43.

65. J. Campbell, "The Training of Infantry in the Attack," *Army Review* 6 (April 1914): 423.

66. C. W. Battine, "The Proposed Changes in Cavalry Tactics," *Journal of the Royal United Service Institution* 54, no. 393 (November 1910): 1426.

67. Lupfer, *Dynamics of Doctrine*, viii–ix.

68. General Staff, *The Training and Employment of Divisions, 1918* (France: Army Printing and Stationery Services, 1918), 5.

69. "Haig's Great War Diary," 8 January 1916, Haig Collection, 3155/97, NLA.

70. "Robertson to Haig," 28 January 1916, in *The Military Correspondence of Field-Marshal Sir William Robertson*, ed. David Woodward (London: Army Records Society, 1989), 33.

71. Gerard J. De Groot, "Educated Soldier or Cavalry Officer? Contradictions in the pre-1914 Career of Douglas Haig," *War & Society* 4, no. 2 (September 1986): 60–61.

72. For a discussion of the general constraints to innovation see Stephen Rosen, *Winning the Next War: Innovation and the Modern Military* (Ithaca: Cornell University Press, 1991).

73. Quoted in David French, "The Military Background to the Shell Crisis of May 1915," *Journal of Strategic Studies* 2, no. 2 (September 1979): 197.

74. C. R. M. F. Crutwell, *The Role of Strategy in the Great War* (Cambridge: Cambridge University Press, 1936), 13–14.

75. One historian dates the animosity to the appointment of the first Secretary-at-War in 1782. See W. S. Hamer, *The British Army, Civil Military Relations 1885–1905* (Oxford: Clarendon Press, 1970), 41.

76. Sir John French, "Memorandum," *Army Review* (April 1912): vii–ix.

77. Travers provides estimates of German losses in *How the War Was Won*, 108.

78. The FSR state that "Decisive success in battle can be gained only by a vigorous offensive." See FSR, 107. Major C. Ross at a lecture at Aldershot concluded that if overpowering force at a vital point is a true principle, then offense is the only safe defense. See C. Ross, *The Principles of Success in War—The Application of Overpowering Force at the Vital Point* (n.p.: Aldershot Military Society, 1906), 8.

79. B. C. Dening, *The Future of the British Army: The Problem of Duties, Cost and Composition* (London: H. F. & G. Witherby, 1928), 24–25.

80. John Keegan, *A History of Warfare* (New York: Alfred A. Knopf, 1993), 258.

81. Howard, "Men against Fire," 520.

82. See the description of the assault in FSR, 134–40.

83. Quoted in John Terraine, *Douglas Haig: The Educated Soldier* (London: Hutchinson & Co., 1963), 432–33.

84. "Haig's Great War Diary," 18 January 1916, Haig Collection, 3155/97, NLS.

85. Russell Weigley, *The Age of Battle, The Quest for Decisive Warfare from Breitenfeld to Waterloo* (Indianapolis: University of Indiana Press, 1991), xiv–xv.

86. For examples see H. de B. De Lisle, "The Strategical Action of Cavalry," *Journal of the Royal United Service Institution* 56 (June 1912): 787–806; C. V. F. Townshend, "The Strategical Employment of Cavalry," *Journal of the Royal United Service Institution* 56 (1912): 1172–78; E. C. Bethune, "The Uses of Cavalry and Mounted Infantry in Modern Warfare," *Journal of the Royal United Service Institution* 50 (1906): 620–36; and C. B. Mayne, "The Lance as a Cavalry Weapon," *Journal of the Royal United Service Institution* 49 (1905): 119–40.

87. General Staff, *Field Artillery Training*, 257.

88. David T. Zabecki, *Steel Wind: Colonel Georg Bruchmüller and the Birth of Modern Artillery* (Westport CT: Praeger, 1994).

89. "Report on Attack at Messines, 26 June 1917," Monash Collection, folder 962, item 493, National Library of Australia.

90. "Robertson to Haig," 10 April 1917, in Woodward, *Correspondence of Robertson*, 168.

91. "Robertson to Haig," 14 April 1917, in Woodward, *Correspondence of Robertson*, 170–71.

92. *FSR*, 107.

93. "War Diary, Volume X, Haig to Chief of the Imperial General Staff," 1 August 1916, Haig Collection, 3155/107, NLS.

94. "Haig to Joffre," September 1916, Haig Collection, 3155/108, NLS.

95. Quoted in J. R. Byrne, *New Zealand Artillery in the Field, 1914–18* (Auckland: Whitcombe and Tombs, Ltd., 1922), 130.

96. Byrne, *New Zealand Artillery*, 146.

97. "Haig to GOC Armies," 22 August 1918, Haig Collection, 3155/130, NLS.

98. "Haig to GOC Armies," 23 August 1918, Haig Collection, 3155/130, NLS.

99. Montgomery, *Story of Fourth Army*, 240.

100. General Staff, Great Britain, *Notes for Infantry Officers on Trench Warfare*, 7.

2. INTRODUCTION AND REACTION

1. Technically speaking, 2nd Ypres was not the first use of gas during World War I, as the Germans had employed various substances in artillery shells on at least three previous occasions. Those attacks, however, were so ineffectual that the targeted troops were not even aware that the Germans had subjected them to a chemical bombardment.

2. A. Fortescue Duguid, *Official History of the Canadian Forces in the Great War, 1914–1919*, vol. 1, *From the Outbreak of the War to the Formation of the Canadian Corps, August 1914–September 1915* (Ottawa: J. O. Patenaude, 1938), 228–29.

3. For a chronicle of the Battle of 2nd Ypres see James L. McWilliams and R. James Steel, *Gas! The Battle for Ypres, 1915* (St. Catharines, Ontario: Vanwell, 1985), and Daniel G. Dancocks, *Welcome to Flanders Field: The First Canadian Battle of the Great War, Ypres, 1915* (Toronto: McClelland & Stewart, 1988).

4. Duguid, *Official History*, 408.

5. V. F. S. Hawkins, ref. 55, Liddle Collection, University of Leeds.

6. Cotton Collection, IWM

7. Cotton Collection, IWM

8. "Transcripts of Notes Dictated by Lt. Col. S. L. Cummins," 12 June 1917, 1, WO142/266, H.7. GI, 1–5, PRO. Cummins was the assistant director gas service, defensive. For more information on the Black Veil respirator see "Transcripts of Notes by Cummins," 12 June 1917, 6. For McPherson's work see "Transcripts of Notes by Cummins," 12 June 1917, 3. For more on Barley's work see "Field Respirator—May 1915," WO95/158, PRO; "Barley to Hartley," 4 July 1963, Hartley Collection, box 31, CAC; James E. Edmonds, *Military Operations, France and Belgium, 1915,* vol. 1, *Winter 1914–15: Battle of Neuve Chapelle—Battle of Ypres* (London: Macmillan, 1927), 217; and Haber, *The Poisonous Cloud,* 41–82.

9. James Brown Scott, *Texts of the Peace Conferences at the Hague, 1899 and 1907* (Boston: Ginn & Company, 1908), 81–83.

10. Edmonds, *Military Operations 1915,* 1:326, 357.

11. "Kitchener to French," 24 April 1915, Hartley Collection, box 42, CAC.

12. "Rawlinson to O. A. G. Fitzgerald," 29 April 1915, Rawlinson Collection, 5201–33–17, NAM.

13. Quoted in Simon Jones, "Under a Green Sea: Moral and Military Aspects of the Introduction of Poison Gas during the First World War," dissertation presented at Sunderland Polytechnic, May 1987.

14. "French to War Office," 23 April 1915, and "Kitchener to French," 24 April 1915, Hartley Collection, box 42, CAC.

15. Haber, *The Poisonous Cloud,* 81.

16. "Circular Letter from War Office," 11 May 1915, WO32/5173, PRO.

17. "Robertson to von Donop," 26 May 1915, Foulkes Collection, 6–1, LHCMA.

18. The War Office identified them as 186, 187, 188, and 189 Special Companies, R.E. In fact they tended to be rather large organizations for a company designation. On 12 January 1916 their complement consisted of: 186 Special Company—7 officers and 373 men; 187 Special Company—8 officers and 369 men; 188 Special Company—9 officers and 442 men; and 189 Special Company—9 officers and 335 men; for a total of 34 officers and 1,519 men. For a discussion of the formation of these units see Donald Richter, *Chemical Soldiers: British Gas Warfare in World War I* (Lawrence KS: University Press of Kansas, 1992), 24, 107; and C. H. Foulkes, *"Gas!" The Story of the Special Brigade* (Edinburgh: Blackwood & Sons, 1936), 46. See also "Gas in Trench Warfare: Summary of What We Have Done to Date," 27 June 1915, WO32/5171, PRO.

19. See "Memorandum on the Use of Gas, etc., in Trench Warfare," 27 June 1915, WO32/5171; Maurice Hankey Diary, 14 May 1915, 1/1, CAC; Haber, *Poisonous Cloud,* 51; and Richter, *Chemical Soldiers,* 18. Some of the bombs were designed to be thrown by catapults or spring guns. See "Memorandum on the Letter of F. M. C.-in-C.," 20 June 1916, MUN5/198/1650/16, PRO. The memorandum also makes reference to the use of gas in artillery shell, mortar ammunition, and airplane bombs.

20. Atteridge, *History of the 17th Division,* 38–39; and James E. Edmonds, *Military Operations, France and Belgium, 1915,* vol. 2, *Battles of Aubers Ridge, Festubert and Loos*

(London: Macmillan, 1928), 104–5. For Haig's impressions see Douglas Haig, *The Haig Papers from the National Library of Scotland*, part 1, *Haig's Autograph Great War Diary* (Brighton, Essex: Harvester Press Microfilm, 1987), 2 and 15 August 1915.

21. "Australian and New Zealand Army Corps Memorandum on Gas Attacks," 11 July 1915, AWM25/371/8.

22. "Instructions for Defence against Asphyxiating Gas," 9 June 1915, 38, 3DRL8042, item 101, AWM.

23. *Defensive Measures against Gas* (1915), 1.

24. "Tradition," 16, Montgomery–Massingberd Collection, 159, LHCMA; and Edmonds, *Military Operations 1915*, 2:340–53.

25. Bidwell and Graham, *Firepower*, 73; and Robin Prior and Trevor Wilson, *Command on the Western Front: The Military Career of Sir Henry Rawlinson, 1914–18* (Oxford: Blackwell Publishers, 1992), 31.

26. "Notes at Conference on 5 March 1915," Haig Collection, 3155/171, NLS.

27. Quoted in Prior and Wilson, *Command on the Western Front*, 25.

28. Edmonds, *Military Operations 1915*, 1:149.

29. Edmonds, *Military Operations 1915*, 1:149–50.

30. "Rawlinson to Clive Wigram," 25 March 1915, Rawlinson Collection, 5201–33–17, NAM.

31. "Report by I Corps," 22 March 1915, and "2nd Divison Report on Operations at Givenchy on March 10th & 11th, 1915," Haig Collection, 3155/171, NLS.

32. "Rawlinson to Wigram," 25 March and 24 April 1915, Rawlinson Collection, 5201–33–17, NAM.

33. "Rawlinson to Kitchener," 1 April 1915, Rawlinson Collection, 5201–33–17, NAM.

34. Haig, *Haig Papers*, May 1915.

35. Edmonds, *Military Operations 1915*, 2:13.

36. Edmonds, *Military Operations 1915*, 2:17–37.

37. Haig, *Haig Papers*, 10 May 1915.

38. Edmonds, *Military Operations 1915*, 2:41.

39. Haig, *Haig Papers*, 11 May 1915.

40. "Butler to Corps HQ," 10 May 1915, WO95/2, PRO.

41. "Rawlinson to Fitzgerald," n.d., Rawlinson Collection, 5201–33–18, NAM.

42. "Rawlinson to Wigram," n.d., Rawlinson Collection, 5201–33–18, NAM.

43. "Western Front in the Great War," lecture series at Camberley, 1920, Montgomery–Massingberd Collection, 114, LHCMA.

44. Edmonds, *Military Operations 1915*, 2:51.

45. Bewsher, *History of the 51st Highland*, 23.

46. Edmonds, *Military Operations 1915*, 2:77.

47. Haig, *Haig Papers*, 18 June 1915.

48. "Note on the Employment of the New Armies," 5 April 1915, Rawlinson Collection, 5201–33–17, NAM.

49. Haig, *Haig Papers*, 7, 21, 22 July, 1915. This is the first mention of the offensive use of gas by the British in Haig's diary. The tone is matter of fact; gas had already become an accepted instrument of war.

50. "Rawlinson to Fitzgerald," n.d., Rawlinson Collection, 5201–33–18, NAM.

51. "Report of Meeting between Field Marshal Sir John French and General Foch," 27 July 1915, WO95/157, PRO.

52. "Joffre to French," 5 August 1915, WO95/157, PRO.

53. "Joffre to French," 12 August 1915, WO95/157, PRO.

54. Haig, *Haig Papers*, 22 June 1915.

55. "Report by Haig with Reference to GHQ," 23 June 1915, Haig Collection, 3155/174, NLS; and Haig, *Haig Papers*, 7 June 1915. Haig's reference to the second line was actually a reference to a line of trenches that the enemy had dug in front of Loos. The true second line lay further back.

56. Haig, *Haig Papers*, 5 June 1915.

57. Haig, *Haig Papers*, 6 June 1915.

58. Haig, *Haig Papers*, 23 June 1915.

59. Prior and Wilson, *Command on the Western Front*, 103.

60. Edmonds, *Military Operations 1915*, 2:114, 116, 133.

61. "Maurice to GOC First Army," 7 August 1915, WO95/157, PRO; "GHQ to GOC First Army," 7 August 1915, Haig Collection, 3155/174, NLS; and Haig, *Haig Papers*, 7 August 1915.

62. "HQ First Army to I and IV Corps," 13 August 1915, Haig Collection, 3155/174, NLS; "Butler to OC I and IV Corps," 13 August 1915, WO95/157, PRO; Haig, *Haig Papers*, 13 August 1915; and "Proposal for Attack by IV Corps," 22 August 1915, WO95/711, PRO. See also "Memo by Haig," 14 August 1915, WO95/157, PRO.

63. "Maurice to Haig," 22 August 1915, WO95/157, PRO.

64. "First Army Conference," 6 September 1915, 2–3, 4–5, WO95/158 PRO.

65. "General Principles of the Attack," 6 September 1915, Rawlinson Collection, 5201–33–67, NAM.

66. "First Army Conference," 6 September 1915, 2–3, WO95/158, PRO.

67. Edmonds, *Military Operations 1915*, 2:125–30.

68. Foulkes, *Gas!*, 61.

69. Foulkes, *Gas!*, 42–44; and "French to the War Office," 16 June 1915, WO32/5170, PRO.

70. "Cubbitt to French," 24 June 1915, WO32/5170, PRO.

71. "French to Cubbitt," 5 July 1915, WO32/5170, PRO.

72. "Notes on Conference at Boulogne," 19 June 1915, 44–46, MUN5/385/1650/9, PRO; and Foulkes, *Gas!*, 53–54.

73. "Rawlinson to Braithwaite," 28 June 1915, Rawlinson Collection, 5201–33–18, NAM.

74. Haig, *Haig Papers*, 5 August 1915.

75. "Notes on Scheme by Gas Advisor," 5 August 1915, WO95/157, PRO.

76. Haig, *Haig Papers*, 21 August 1915.

77. "Maurice to GOC First Army," 7 August 1915, WO95/157, PRO.

78. Haig, *Haig Papers*, 13 August 1915; and "Butler to GOC I Corps and IV Corps," 13 August 1915, WO95/157, PRO.

79. Haig, *Haig Papers*, 26 August 1915; "French to War Office," 16 June 1915, and "French to War Office," 28 June 1915, WO32/5170, PRO; and "First Army Report," 23 August 1915, WO95/157, PRO.

80. "Advance HQ First Army," 23 August 1915, Haig Collection, 3155/174, NLS.

81. "First Army Report," 23 August 1915, WO95/157, PRO.

82. "Notes of Conference held at Advanced First Army Headquarters, Hinges," 24 August 1915, WO95/157, PRO.

83. "HQ First Army to Foulkes," 25 August 1915, Haig Collection, 3155/174, NLS.

84. "First Army Conference," 6 September 1915, Haig Collection, 3155/174, NLS.

85. "First Army Conference," 6 September 1915, Haig Collection, 3155/174, NLS.

86. Edmonds, *Military Operations 1915*, 2:448.

87. Edmonds, *Military Operations 1915*, 2:450.

88. "First Army Instructions," 23 August 1915, WO95/157, PRO; "General Principles of the Attack," Rawlinson Collection, 5201-33–67, NAM; and Haig, *Haig Papers*, 24 August 1915.

89. "Advance HQ First Army," 23 August 1915, Haig Collection, 3155/174, NLS.

90. "First Army Conference," 6 September 1915, WO95/158, PRO.

91. "47th Division HQ to Brigade HQ," n.d., WO95/2698, PRO.

92. "Gough to HQ First Army," 27 August 1915, WO95/157, PRO.

93. Foulkes, *Gas!*, 60.

94. "Butler to Foulkes," 25 August 1915; "Maurice to GOC First Army," 28 August 1915; and "Haig to Chief of the General Staff," 26 August 1915, WO95/157, PRO. See also "Memo from IV Corps to 15th Division," 7 September 1915, WO95/1911, PRO; and Foulkes, *Gas!*, 60–65.

95. Foulkes, *Gas!*, 67.

96. Edmonds, *Military Operations 1915*, 2:160–61. The 4-inch version of the Stokes mortar was specifically designed for use by chemical rounds.

97. "Haig to Robertson," 16 September 1915, WO95/158, PRO.

98. "Haig to GHQ," 13 September 1915, Haig Collection, 3155/174, NLS.

99. Haig, *Haig Papers*, 16 September 1915. The same day Butler asked I Corps and IV Corps to draw up plans for an attack not using gas. See "Butler to OC I and IV Corps," 16 September 1915, WO95/158, PRO.

100. "Rawlinson to HQ First Army," 17 September 1915, WO95/711, PRO; "Rawlinson Diary," 17 and 19 September 1915, 1/3, CAC; and "Rawlinson to HQ First Army," 4 September 1915, WO95/728, PRO.

101. Haig, *Haig Papers*, 17 September 1915.

102. Haig, *Haig Papers*, 18 September 1915; and "Haig to GHQ," 18 September 1915, Haig Collection, 3155/174, NLS.

103. "First Army Intelligence Summary, No. 224," 22 August 1915; "IV Corps Bulletin," 28, 29, 30 August and 4 September, 1915; "First Army Intelligence Summary, No. 237," 4 September 1915; and "First Army Intelligence Summary, No. 242," 9 September 1915, all in Montgomery–Massingberd Collection, 39, LHCMA.

104. Haig, *Haig Papers*, 26 August and 4 September 1915.

105. "Notes in Connection with the Employment of Gas in the Attack," 22 September 1915, Haig Collection, 3155/176, NLS.

106. "Report on attack on Hill 60 on 1 May by Brig.-Gen. Edward Northey, 15th Infantry Brigade," 5 May 1915, Gledstanes Papers, Ref. 13, Liddle Collection, University of Leeds.

107. "Notes in Connection with the Employment of Gas in the Attack," 22 September 1915, Haig Collection, 3155/176, NLS.

108. "Plan of Operations," 28 August 1915, WO95/157, PRO; and "15th Division Draft Instructions for Attack on 21 September," WO95/1911, PRO.

109. Haig, *Haig Papers*, 20 September 1915.

110. "First Report of the Chemical Sub-Committee," 16 August 1915, Hartley Collection, box 41, CAC; "GHQ to Haig," 31 August 1915, WO95/157, PRO; Haig, *Haig Papers*, 31 August 1915; and *History of the Ministry of Munitions* (Oxford: Harvester Press, 1976), 34.

111. "I Corps Artillery Plan," 20 September 1915, WO95/728, PRO; and "I Corps Artillery, Appendix 16," 24 September 1915, WO95/619, PRO.

112. "IV Corps Artillery Operations Order," 24 September 1915, WO95/728, PRO; "IV Corps Artillery Operations Order No. 5," 24 September 1915, and "Instructions Issued by IV Corps Artillery," 21 September, 1915, WO95/711, PRO; and "Instructions Issued to IV Corps Artillery," 21 September 1915, Montgomery–Massingberd Collection, 42, LHCMA.

113. "First Army HQ to Corps HQ," 3 September 1915, WO95/728, PRO; and "Estimate of Ammunition—First Army," Haig Collection, 3155/175, NLS.

114. "Butler to HQ Corps and HA Groups," 10 September 1915, Rawlins Collection, 1162/3, RAI; "Report on Expended, Estimated Need and Allotted No. of Shells for 21–30 September 1915," Montgomery–Massingberd Collection, 42, LHCMA; and "IV Corps, GS 164/3(D)" 10 September 1915, WO95/1911, PRO.

115. "First Army to I Corps," 24 September 1915, WO95/592, PRO.

116. Haig, *Haig Papers*, 24 and 25 September 1915. Foulkes summarizes the decision to open the cylinders in *Gas!*, 65, 68.

117. Foulkes, *Gas!*, 64.

118. "C. A. Ashley Diary," 25 September 1915, Ashley Collection, IWM.

119. They managed to open 2,263 along the main front and an additional 30 in the Indian Corps's sector. See "List of Special Brigade Operations," WO142/266, PRO (hereafter "SB Ops," WO142/266, PRO). The wind also affected the discharge rate. The commander of each cylinder bay, sometimes only a corporal, had the authority to cease the discharge if the wind was incorrect for the attack, and many did so. However, some local infantry officers insisted on maintaining the program, whatever the wind, and compelled the members of the special companies to continue,

with predictable results. One gas officer was threatened with summary execution for his refusal to open the valves. See Foulkes, *Gas!*, 70–71, and Richter *Chemical Soldiers*, 59, 66–68.

120. "47th Division War Diary," 25 September 1915, and "47th Division At Loos," n.d., WO95/2698, PRO.

121. Edmonds, *Military Operations 1915*, 2:191–207; and "Adjutant 8th Seaforth Highlanders to HQ 44th Infantry Brigade," 27 September 1915, WO95/711, PRO.

122. "Narrative of Operations of the 1st Division, 25, 26, and 27 September 1915," Montgomery–Massingberd Collection, 42, LHCMA; and Edmonds, *Military Operations 1915*, 2:191–207.

123. Edmonds, *Military Operations 1915*, 2:226–61.

124. "Report on Operations from 21 September to 30 September by Brig. Gen. M. G. Wilkinson, CO 44th Infantry Brigade," WO95/711, PRO; and "Rawlinson Telephone Log," 25 September 1915, Montgomery–Massingberd Collection, 42, LHCMA.

125. Haig, *Haig Papers*, 4, 6, 7 October 1915; "SB Ops," WO142/266, PRO; and Foulkes, *Gas!*, 85–87.

126. C. E. D. Budworth, "Remarks Based on Recent IV Corps Artillery Operations," 6 October 1915, Rawlinson Collection, 5201–33–67, NAM.

127. See General Staff, *Artillery in Offensive Operations*, 5. For shell gas principles see, General Staff, *Instructions on the Use of Lethal and Lachrymatory Shell* (n.p., 1918), 6.

128. C. E. D. Budworth, "Remarks based on Recent IV Corps Artillery Operations," 6 October 1915, Rawlinson Collection, 5201–33–67, NAM; and "IV Corps to Advanced HQ First Army," 9 October 1915, Montgomery–Massingberd Collection, 42, LHCMA.

129. "Lecture on the Battle of Loos," 27–28, Montgomery–Massingberd Collection, 45, LHCMA.

130. "Lecture on Loos," 27–28, Montgomery–Massingberd Collection, 45, LHCMA.

131. "Report on the Use of Gas on 25 September, 1915," 5 October 1915, Barley Collection, IWM.

132. "OC 187 Company, R.E. to GOC IV Corps," Montgomery–Massingberd Collection, 42, LHCMA.

133. C. H. Foulkes, "Gas Warfare (Offensive) in the Field," p. 7, draft manuscript of *History of the Royal Engineers*, vol. 10, chapt. 20, 1944, Foulkes Collection, 6–61, LHCMA.

134. "Report on Operations of the IV Corps," 22 September–7 October, 1915, WO95/711, PRO.

135. "Rawlinson Diary," 26 September 1915, Rawlinson Collection, 1/3, CAC.

136. "Lecture Series on the Battle of Loos," 14 December 1915–5 June 1916, Montgomery–Massingberd Collection, 45, LHCMA.

137. "IV Corps to Advanced HQ First Army," 9 October 1915, Montgomery–Massingberd Collection, 42, LHCMA.

138. "47th Division at Loos," 9, WO95/2698, PRO.

139. "Report of Operations of 47th Division, 25 September–2 October," 3, Canadian Corps HQ, RG9/IIIC1/3842, NAC; and "Notes on information Obtained From Prisoners," 25 September–2 October, 1915, Odlum Collection, MG30/E300/vol.23, NAC.

140. "Foulkes Diary," 25 September 1915, Foulkes Collection, 2/16, LHCMA.

141. "Lecture Series on the Battle of Loos," 14 December 1915–5 June 1916, Montgomery–Massingberd Collection, 45, LHCMA.

142. Edmonds, *Military Operations 1915*, 2:391–92.

3. EXPERIMENTATION

1. Blue Star was a mixture of 80 percent chlorine and 20 percent sulphur chloride. The latter material is heavier than chlorine and the British expected it to help keep the cloud close to the ground. The mixture, however, had the disadvantage of depositing a pool of liquified gas in front of the parapet pipe and the British feared that its evaporation would injure their own soldiers. They subsequently discontinued its use. See Foulkes, *Gas!*, 90.

2. White Star was a 1:1 blend of chlorine and phosgene. Phosgene has a high boiling point (46° F) and on cool summer nights or during the winter it lacked the vapor pressure necessary to escape its container. The British added chlorine, a more volatile agent, to help propel it from the cylinder.

3. Foulkes, *Gas!*, 52, 94–95; Richter, *Chemical Soldiers*, 109, 112–13; and James E. Edmonds, *Military Operations, France and Belgium, 1916*, vol. 1, *Sir Douglas Haig's Command to the 1st July: Battle of the Somme* (London: Macmillan, 1932), 77–81.

4. Foulkes, "Notes on Phosphorus Smoke Shells and Their Use with the 4" Stokes Mortar," n.d., Rawlinson's Fourth Army Records, vol. 6, IWM.

5. "Cubbitt to Ministry of Munitions," 22 September 1916, WO32/5175, PRO; and "Report by Director of Gas Services on Availability of Stokes Mortar Ammunition," 29 March 1916, Rawlinson's Fourth Army Records vol. 6, IWM.

6. British Army, *Notes on the Employment of 4" Stokes Mortar Bombs* (1917), 5–6. In 1917 improvements in the propellant increased the range to 1,100 yards. Augustin M. Prentiss, *Chemicals in War: A Treatise on Chemical Warfare* (London: McGraw-Hill, 1937), 362. For figures on the gas content of British projectiles see Prentiss, *Chemicals in War*, 453.

7. "Liaison Report of Lieut. Col. Crossley," 13 December 1915, 16–17, MUN5/197/1650/6, PRO.

8. "Haig to Ministry of Munitions," 16 May 1916, MUN4/2709, PRO; "Memorandum by Brig. Gen. H. F. Thuillier, Director of Gas Services, GHQ, on Situation Regarding Bombs, 4" Stokes Mortar," 20 October 1916, WO32/5175, PRO; and "Notes on Gas Shells and T.M.Bs.," Hartley Collection, box 32, CAC.

9. "Memorandum by Thuillier on Stokes Mortar," 20 October 1916; and "Notes on the Failure in Supplies of Ammunition for the 4" Stokes Mortar," 17 September 1916, WO32/5175, PRO.

10. "Notes on Failure in Ammunition for Stokes Mortar," 17 September 1916 and "Notes on Gas Shells and T.M.Bs.," Hartley Collection, box 32, CAC. The Special Brigade's use of the two-inch mortar was minimal, and during the six attacks they fired a total of 488 bombs. See "SB Ops," WO142/266, PRO.

11. 3,000 of the Red Star cylinders had been returned from Egypt. They had been sent to the Near East for use at Gallipoli. Two Red Star was a mixture of 90 percent sulphuretted hydrogen and 10 percent carbon disulphide, and its introduction was not a great success. Although quite lethal, the physical properties of the compound made it hazardous to use as a battlefield gas.

12. For a list of the Special Brigade's operations see, "SB Ops," WO142/266, PRO.

13. Prentiss, *Chemicals in War*, 683.

14. "Notes on Gas Shells and T.M.Bs.," Hartley Collection, box 32; and *Instructions on the Use of Lethal and Lachrymatory Shell*, 6–8.

15. "Minutes of the Chemical Advisory and Scientific Advisory Committee," 24 May 1916, WO142/52, PRO.

16. Haber, *Poisonous Cloud*, 27; *History of the Ministry of Munitions* 10, 35; "Memorandum on Chemical Shell," 4 May 1916, MUN5/386/1650/10, PRO; "Jackson to Addison," 24 February 1916, MUN4/2709, PRO; and "Haig to War Office," 31 July 1916, AWM45/31/16.

17. *History of the Ministry of Munitions* 10, 35; "Memorandum on Chemical Shell," 4 May 1916, MUN5/386/1650/10, PRO; "Butler to War Office," 28 February 1916, "Du Cane to Addison," 28 February 1916, and "Bingham to DMRS," 18 July 1916, all in MUN4/2709, PRO.

18. "Memorandum on the Requirements for Chemical Shell," 1 April 1916, MUN4/2706, PRO.

19. "Memorandum on Steps Taken by the Ministry of Munitions to Provide Chemical Shell," 4 May 1916, MUN5/187/1360/1, PRO.

20. "Probable Resources on 25 June," 4 June 1916; "Estimate of Resources," 4 June 1916; and "Haig to Joffre," 3 June 1916, all in "Haig's Great War Diary," Haig Collection, 3155/106, NLS. The French 75s came equipped with Special Shell number 4 (Vincennite)—a mixture of 50 percent hydrocyanic acid and 50 percent trichloride—and Special Shell number 5 (Collongite)—a mixture of 60 percent phosgene and 40 percent tin tetrachloride. See Prentiss, *Chemicals in War*, 444; and "Notes on 4th Army Conference," 27 June 1916, Rawlinson's Fourth Army Records vol. 6, IWM.

21. "Bingham to DMRS," 18 July 1916, and "Minutes of Discussion on Chemical Shell," 18 July 1916, MUN4/2709, PRO; and "Notes on Conference held on 4 September 1916 Regarding Supply of Chemical Shell and Bombs," and "Supply of Chemical Shells and Bombs," 1 September 1916, both in MUN5/197/1650/9, PRO.

22. Edmonds, *Military Operations 1916*, 1:2, 5, 303.

23. David French, *British Strategy & War Aims, 1914–1916* (London: Allen & Unwin, 1986), 184–85.

24. "Haig's Great War Diary," 8 January 1916, Haig Collection, 3155/97, NLS.

25. "Haig's Great War Diary," 14 January 1916, Haig Collection, 3155/97, NLS.

26. "Haig's Great War Diary," 14 January 1916, Haig Collection, 3155/97, NLS; and "Haig to Joffre," 1 February 1916, Haig Collection, 3155/104, NLS.

27. "Haig's Great War Diary," 4 January 1916, Haig Collection, 3155/97, NLS.

28. "Haig's Great War Diary," 16 January 1916, Haig Collection, 3155/97, NLS.

29. "Haig's Great War Diary," 29 January 1916, Haig Collection, 3155/97, NLS.

30. Tony Ashworth, *Trench Warfare, 1914–1918: The Live and Let Live System* (London: Macmillan Press, 1980), 177–85.

31. "Haig to Joffre," 1 February 1916, Haig Collection, 3155/104, NLS.

32. "Plans for Future Operations," 10 February 1916, and "Haig to Joffre," 10 April 1916, Haig Collection, 3155/104, NLS.

33. "Notes on Conference With Army Commanders," 27 May 1916, and "Kiggell to GOC Armies," 12 June 1916, Haig Collection, 3155/106, NLS.

34. "Note on Special Brigade and Use of Gas and Smoke," and "Note on Wind," 27 May 1916, Haig Collection, 3155/106, NLS.

35. "Note on Special Brigade and Use of Gas and Smoke," 27 May 1916, Haig Collection, 3155/106, NLS.

36. "Note on Special Brigade and Use of Gas and Smoke," 27 May 1916, Haig Collection, 3155/106, NLS.

37. White Star (phosgene) was lethal from only one or at most a few breaths. Red Star (chlorine) and Two Red Star (sulphuretted hydrogen) were less dangerous and required more inhalations before reaching a fatal dosage.

38. "Haig's Great War Diary," 26 June 1916, Haig Collection, 3155/97, NLS.

39. "Haig's Great War Diary," 9 September 1916 and 2 November 1916, Haig Collection, 3155/97, NLS; and "Advanced GHQ to Rawlinson and Gough," 31 August 1916, Haig Collection, 3155/107, NLS.

40. "Battle of Somme Preparations," n.d., Rawlinson's Fourth Army Records vol. 1, IWM.

41. Prior and Wilson, *Command on the Western Front*, 144.

42. "Fourth Army Memorandum," 22 June 1916 and 28 June 1916, Rawlinson's Fourth Army Records vol. 7, IWM.

43. Terraine, *Douglas Haig*, 204.

44. "Kiggell to GOC Armies," 21 June 1916, Haig Collection, 3155/106, NLS.

45. "Fourth Army Operation Order No. 3," 1 July 1916, cited in Prior and Wilson, *Command on the Western Front*, 185–86.

46. "Rawlinson Diary," 30 June 1916, part 1/5, CAC.

47. "Haig's Great War Diary," 5 July 1916 and 6 September 1916, Haig Collection 3155/97, NLS.

48. James E. Edmonds, *Military Operations, France and Belgium, 1916*, append., *Sir Douglas Haig's Command to the 1st July, Battle of the Somme* (London: Macmillan, 1938), 132.

49. General Staff, "Training Divisions for Offensive Action," May 1916.

50. "GHQ to Rawlinson," 27 May 1916, Rawlinson's Fourth Army Records vol. 5, IWM.

51. "Report by Maj.-Gen. Headlam on the Work of the Artillery of XV Corps," 6 July 1916, Haig Collection, 3155/107, NLS.

52. "The Somme: Plan for Offensive by the Fourth Army," 3 April 1916; "Fourth Army Tactical Notes," May 1916; and "Fourth Army Artillery Programme of Preliminary Bombardment," 5 June 1916, all in *Military Operations 1916*, append., 64–65, 137–38, 148–49.

53. *Military Operations 1916*, append., 70. See also, "Battle of Somme Preparations," Rawlinson's Fourth Army Records vol. 1, IWM.

54. "GOC VIII Corps to Rawlinson," 10 April 1916, and "GOC 48th Division to Montgomery–Massingberd," 12 April 1916, Rawlinson Fourth Army Records vol. 6, IWM.

55. "Plan for an Offensive by Fourth Army," 3 April 1916, in *Military Operations 1916*, append., 70; "Notes on Conference held at Fourth Army HQ," 6 April 1916, and "Fourth Army Memorandum," 6 March 1916, Rawlinson's Fourth Army Records vol. 6, IWM; and "Provisional Program," 15 May 1916, Rawlinson's Fourth Army Records vol. 5, IWM.

56. "Conference of Army Commanders," 27 May 1916, Haig Collection, 3155/106, NLS; and "Resources, Appendix C," Rawlinson's Fourth Army Records vol. 1, IWM.

57. British intelligence reports indicated that the enemy would man their parapets in a gas attack. See "Notes on the Employment of Gas and Smoke in the Attack," n.d., *Military Operations 1916*, append., 110.

58. "Program of Preliminary Bombardment," 5 June 1916, Rawlinson's Fourth Army Records vol. 7, IWM.

59. "Fourth Army Operation Order No. 2," 14 June 1916, Rawlinson's Fourth Army Records vol. 7, IWM.

60. "Notes to Fourth Army Conference," 12 June 1916, and "Program of Preliminary Bombardment," 21 June 1916, Rawlinson's Fourth Army Records vol. 1, IWM; and "Amendment to Programme of Bombardment," 23 June 1916, Rawlinson's Fourth Army Records vol. 7, IWM.

61. "Fourth Army Memorandum," 17 June 1916, Rawlinson's Fourth Army Records vol. 7, IWM; and "Summary of Operations," 24 June 1916, Rawlinson's Fourth Army Records vol. 1, IWM.

62. "The Commander-in-Chief's Instructions to the Fourth and Reserve Armies," 2 August 1916, *Military Operations 1916*, maps and append., *2nd July 1916 to the End of the Battles of the Somme* (London: Macmillan, 1938), 26.

63. See "SB Ops," WO142/266, PRO.

64. See "SB Ops," WO142/266, PRO. Also see "Notes on the Use of Smoke," 13 May 1916, Rawlinson's Fourth Army Records vol. 6, IWM.

65. "SB Ops," WO142/266, PRO.

66. Foulkes, "Notes on the Use of Smoke," 15 May 1916, Hartley Collection, box 33, CAC; "Orders 4th Australian Infantry Brigade," 1 July 1916, Monash Collection, 3DRL2316, item 22, AWM; "Notes on the Use of Smoke," 13 May 1916, Rawlinson's Fourth Army Records vol. 6, IWM; and "GHQ to 3rd Army, Reserve

Army, & Royal Flying Corps," n.d., Rawlinson's Fourth Army Records vol. 1, IWM.

67. "Clearing of Dugouts by Chemical Grenades," 1916, WO142/98, PRO.

68. "Clearing of Dugouts by Chemical Grenades," 1916, WO142/98, PRO. See also W. H. Livens, "The Development of the Livens Projector," n.d., WO188/143, PRO.

69. "Lecture Notes on the Offensive Use of Gas," n.d., Gilliat Collection, IWM.

70. "Notes on Fourth Army Conference," 28 April 1916, Rawlinson's Fourth Army Records vol. 6, IWM.

71. "Notes on Conference Held at Fourth Army Headquarters," 6 April 1916, Rawlinson's Fourth Army Records vol. 6, IWM.

72. 3rd Australian Divisional Artillery, "Artillery in Defence," n.d., AWM224/mss4.

73. "Summary of Operations," 15 July 1915, Rawlinson's Fourth Army Records vol. 2, IWM.

74. "Summary of Operations," 15 July 1915, Rawlinson's Fourth Army Records vol. 2, IWM. Rawlinson repeated these suggestions at conferences on 28 April and 17 May. See "Notes on Conference," 16 April 1916, and "Notes on Conference," 17 May 1916, Rawlinson's Fourth Army Records vol. 1, IWM.

75. "GHQ to Fourth Army," 24 June 1916, Rawlinson's Fourth Army Records vol. 5, IWM; and "Artillery Instructions No. 27," 22 June 1916, Uniacke Collection, folder 10, RAI. The British retained 108 French guns into August. See "Haig's Great War Diary," 7 August 1916, Haig Collection, 3155/97, NLS; and "Fourth Army Artillery Programme of Preliminary Bombardment," 5 June 1916, in Edmonds, *Military Operations 1916*, append., 148–49.

76. "Haig to War Office," 17 July 1916, MUN4/2709, PRO.

77. "Haig's Great War Diary," 17 July 1916, Haig Collection, 3155/97, NLS; and "Minutes of Discussion of Chemical Shell," 17 July 1916, MUN4/2709, PRO.

78. "Haig to War Office," 17 July 1916, MUN4/2709, PRO.

79. "Tactical Notes," May 1916, in Edmonds, *Military Operations 1916*, append., 137–38; and "Artillery Instructions," 7 September 1916, Rawlinson's Fourth Army Records vol. 7, IWM. For Rawlinson's comments regarding Aubers Ridge see "Rawlinson to Fitzgerald," n.d., Rawlinson Collection, 5201–33–18, NAM.

80. "Notes on the Employment of Gas Shells," 23 August 1916 and, "Gas Shell Bombardments," 23 August 1916, WO158/436, PRO.

81. "Haig to WO," 31 July 1916, AWM45/31/16; and "Bingham to DMRS," 18 July 1916, and "Minutes of Discussion on Chemical Shell," 18 July 1916, both MUN4/2709, PRO.

82. "Memorandum on Gas Shells," 31 July 1916, Haig Collection, 3155/97, NLS; and "Haig to WO," 31 July 1916, MUN4/2706, PRO.

83. "SB Ops," WO142/266, PRO.

84. O. F. Brothers, "Account of the Development of Weapons Used in Trench Warfare, 1914–1918," 13 August 1919, WO142/275, PRO; and Livens, "Development

of Livens Projector," WO188/143, PRO. Foulkes asked for its production on a large scale. See "Special Brigade War Diary," 24 November 1916, WO95/120, PRO.

85. "Liaison Report of Lieut.-Col. Arthur Crossley," 2 November 1916, MUN5/197/1650/6, PRO.

86. Foulkes, "Employment of Projectors," 26 March 1917, WO188/143, PRO.

87. Foulkes, "Employment of Projectors," 26 March 1917, WO188/143, PRO.

88. "Attack on Thiepval, Conclusions of Conference," 21 September 1916, Maxse Collection, 65/53/7, IWM.

89. "SB Ops," WO142/266, PRO; Livens, "Development of Livens Projector," WO188/143, PRO; and "Orders for Special Section Royal Engineers, Re: Thiepval," 24 September 1916, Maxse Collection, 65/53/7, IWM.

90. "SB Ops," WO142/266, PRO.

91. 3rd Australian Divisional Artillery, "Artillery in Defence," n.d., AWM224/Mss4; "Artillery Instructions, No. 30," 22 September 1916, Maxse Collection, 65/53/7, IWM; and "Handwritten Notes on Preparation for the Somme," n.d., Rawlinson Collection, 5201–33–70, NAM.

92. "Minutes of Discussion on Chemical Shell," 18 July 1916, MUN4/2709, PRO; "Haig to War Office," 31 July 1916, and "Matheson to DMRS," 26 August 1916, MUN4/2706, PRO.

93. "Rawlinson to GHQ," 17 June 1916, Rawlinson's Fourth Army Records vol. 5, IWM.

94. H. Hudson, "Narrative of the Operations Carried Out by the 8th Division on 5 and 6 October, 1916," 9 October 1916, WO158/270, PRO.

95. "OC No 4A Battalion, Special Brigade, R.E. to HQ 1st Army," 12 September 1916, WO158/270, PRO.

96. "Effects of Special Brigade Operations, Summary of Evidence," WO142/266, PRO.

97. "Henry Wilson to HQ 1st Army," 2 July 1916, WO158/270, PRO.

98. C. Barter, "Report on Two Raids Carried Out by the 47th (London) Division in the Angres Section on the night of 27/28 June 1916," 30 June 1916, WO158/270, PRO.

99. "OC No. 4A to 1st Army," 4 October 1916, WO158/270, PRO.

100. Wilfrid Miles, *Military Operations, France and Belgium, 1916*, vol. 2, *2nd July 1916 to the End of the Battles of the Somme* (London: Macmillan, 1938), 544.

101. "Effectiveness Reports—Fourth Army War Diary," 26 & 27 June 1916, Rawlinson's Fourth Army Records vol. 1, IWM.

102. Foulkes, *Gas!*, 157.

103. Livens, "Development of Livens Projector," WO188/143, PRO.

104. Livens, "Development of Livens Projector," WO188/143, PRO.

4. INSTITUTIONALIZATION

1. For a discussion of the advances in British infantry weapons and tactics see Bill Rawling, *Surviving Trench Warfare: Technology and the Canadian Corps, 1914–1918* (Toronto: University of Toronto Press, 1992).

2. See General Staff, *Assault Training*; War Office, Great Britain *Instructions for the Training of Platoons for Offensive Action*; and General Staff, *Training Divisions for Offensive Action*.

3. Paddy Griffith, *Battle Tactics of the Western Front: The British Army and the Art of Attack* (New Haven CT: Yale University Press, 1994), 137.

4. Martin Farndale, *History of the Royal Regiment of Artillery* (Woolwich: Royal Artillery Institution, 1986), 187. For a concise account of the advances in British artillery technique see Jonathan Bailey, "British Artillery in the Great War," in *British Fighting Methods in the Great War*, ed. Paddy Griffith (London: Frank Cass, 1996), 23–49.

5. Bailey, "Artillery in Great War," 23–49.

6. Griffith, *Battle Tactics*, 137–38, 151–52. See also, "Notes on Counter-Battery Work," Uniacke Collection, folder 8, RAI.

7. S. W. H. Rawlins, "A History of the Development of the British Artillery in France, 1914–1918," Rawlins Collection, 1162/1, RAI.

8. "Resolutions of the Chantilly Conference," n.d., "Letter No. 17856/3, From General Nivelle to Gen. Sir Douglas Haig," 21 December 1916, and "London Convention of 16 January 1917," in James E. Edmonds, *Military Operations, France and Belgium, 1917*, append., *The German Retreat to the Hindenburg Line and the Battles of Arras* (London: Macmillan, 1940), 1–6, 16–17.

9. James E. Edmonds, *Military Operations, France and Belgium, 1917*, vol. 2, *7 June–10 November, Messines, and 3rd Ypres* (Passchendaele) (London: HMSO, 1948), 8–9; "GHQ Letter OAD 258," 2 January 1917, and "London Convention of 16 January 1917," in Edmonds, *Military Operations 1917* append., 10–12, 16–17. See also Boraston, *Haig's Dispatches*, 81–85. For the role of the Royal Navy see Andrew A. Weist, *Passchendaele and the Royal Navy* (Westport CT: Greenwood Press, 1995).

10. Edmonds, *Military Operations 1917*, append., 72.

11. "Report on the Effects Produced by Gas Shells on the Night of 8/9 April on the Third Army Front," 19 April 1917, Hartley Collection, box 33, CAC.

12. "GHQ Letter to Second Army," 6 January 1916, in Edmonds, *Military Operations 1917*, 2: 406.

13. "Note on the Strategical Situation with Special Reference to the Present Condition of German Resources and Probable German Operations," 11 June 1917, Haig Collection, 3155/114, NLS.

14. British Intelligence reported reductions in the establishment of German battalions, notices to conserve guns since wastage exceeded replacement, shortages of copper for telephone wires, and the lowering of the ration for the troops. See "Notes on German Resources," 10 July 1917, Haig Collection, 3155/114, NLS.

15. "Note on Strategical Situation," 11 June 1917, Haig Collection, 3155/114, NLS.

16. "Present Situation and Future Plans," 1 May 1917, and "Haig to Chief of the Imperial General Staff," 16 May 1917, Haig Collection, 3155/113, NLS; and "Haig to Chief of the Imperial General Staff," 17 June 1917, Haig Collection, 3155/114, NLS.

17. Edmonds, *Military Operations 1917*, 2:19–20.

18. "Kiggell to GOC Armies," 8 June 1917, Haig Collection, 3155/114, NLS.

19. Edmonds, *Military Operations 1917*, 2:140, 135–38, 151.

20. "SB Ops," WO142/266, PRO.

21. "Record of a Conference held at Second Army Headquarters," 2 October 1917, Haig Collection, 3155/118, NLS; and "Notes on a Conference at Lovie Château," 2 October 1917, WO95/520, PRO.

22. "Fifth Army Order No. 25," 6 October 1917, WO95/520, PRO.

23. "War Diary Entry," 7 October 1917, Haig Collection, 3155/118, NLS.

24. "Statement on Provision of Gas Shell," 26 February 1917, WO32/5174, PRO; and "Notes on Position as Regards Supplies of: Gas Artillery Shell, Gas 4" Stokes Bombs, and Gas Livens Drums," MUN5/187/1650/10, PRO.

25. "Report of Conference on the General Gas Policy and the Chemical Shell Programme," 27 November 1917, MUN5/187/1360/10, PRO.

26. "Report of Conference," 27 November 1917, MUN5/187/1360/10, PRO.

27. Haber, *Poisonous Cloud*, 111–13; and James K. Senior, "The Manufacture of Mustard Gas in World War I," *Armed Forces Chemical Journal* 12 (November–December 1958).

28. "Operations, 28 July to 4 August," WO95/120, PRO; "Report of Conference," 27 November 1917, MUN5/187/1360/10, PRO.

29. See Haber, *Poisonous Cloud*, 114–15.

30. Rawlins, "A History of the Development of the British Artillery," Rawlins Collection, 1162/1, 114, 124, 137, RAI; "Estimates of Special Ammunition Available between 30 June and 21 July," 30 June 1917, Haig Collection, 3155/114, NLS; and "Gas Shell Expenditure, 3rd Australian Division," 27 May 1917, AWM26/195/1.

31. "GHQ to WO," 31 December 1916, WO32/5174, PRO. See also "Army Council to the Secretary, Ministry of Munitions," 20 March 1917, and "Furse to Rogers," 15 March 1917, WO32/5174, PRO.

32. "Notes on Position as Regards Supplies of: Gas Artillery Shell, Gas 4" Stokes Bombs, and Gas Livens Drums," MUN5/187/1650/10, PRO; and "GHQ to WO," 5 April 1917, "Cubbitt to Ministry of Munitions," 12 April 1917, and "GHQ to WO," 19 April 1917, WO32/5174, PRO.

33. "Director of Ordnance Services, GHQ to Director of Artillery, WO," 4 June 1917, WO32/5174, PRO.

34. For an example see "CO 'P' Special Company to XVIII Corps," 24 June 1917, WO142/320, PRO.

35. "Notes on Position as Regards Supplies," MUN5/187/1650/10, PRO; and "Employment of 4" Stokes Mortar Bombs," 26 March 1917, WO95/120, PRO. See also Foulkes, *Gas!*, 193.

36. "GHQ to WO," 13 July 1917, WO32/5174, PRO.

37. PS was pure chloropicrin and PG was 75 percent chloropicrin and 25 percent phosgene, while NC was 80 percent chloropicrin and 20 percent stannic chloride. Phosgene was extremely lethal, while stannic chloride was not dangerous in itself

but did have remarkable penetrative powers. For the composition of these materials and others see, "Symbols for Chemicals," 29 September 1916, WO158/125, PRO.

38. SK had always been in short supply and the British had diluted the active agent, ethyl iodoacetate, with 25 percent ethyl alcohol. KSK was 100 percent ethyl iodoacetate. "Director General Trench Warfare Service to Furse," 6 March 1917 and "Furse to Rogers," 15 March 1916, MUN5/197/1650/10, PRO; and "Hand Written Notes to Remarks on Report of Gas Shell Operations," 6 July 1917, WO158/126, PRO.

39. "Haig to WO," 2 April 1917, and "GHQ to WO," 16 May 1917, WO32/5174, PRO; and "Quarter-Master General, GHQ to WO," 10 July 1917, WO32/5174, PRO.

40. Second Army, "Note on the Offensive Use of Gas and Methods of Gas Discharge," 4 May 1917, Foulkes Collection, 6–13, LHCMA. See also Foulkes, "Lecture Notes," 28 October 1917, and "Lecture to Fifth Army," 4 July 1917, Foulkes Collection, 6–10, LHCMA.

41. "Some Lessons from the Recent Employment of Gas in the Attack," 21 August 1916, RG9/IIIC1/3977, NAC. See also Second Army's "Note on the Offensive Use of Gas and Methods of Gas Discharge," 4 May 1917, Foulkes Collection, 6–13, LHCMA.

42. "Report by Director of Gas Services," 21 December 1917, WO142/98, PRO. Foulkes outlines this attack in *Gas!*, 221–22.

43. C. H. Foulkes, *Report on the Activity of the Special Brigade during the War* (France, 1918), 4.

44. Foulkes, *Report on Special Brigade*, 4.

45. "Note on Offensive Use of Gas and Methods of Gas Discharge," 4 May 1917, Foulkes Collection, 6–13, LHCMA. See also General Staff, *Effect on Enemy of our Gas Attacks* (September, 1917), 18; and "SB Ops," WO142/266, PRO.

46. General Staff, *Gas Warfare*, no. 1 (July, 1917).

47. General Staff, *Gas Warfare*, no. 1 (July, 1917).

48. Foulkes, "Lecture to Fifth Army," 4 July 1917, Foulkes Collection, 6–10, LHCMA.

49. "Lecture to Second Army," 28 April 1917, Foulkes Collection, 6–10, LHCMA. See also Haber, *Poisionous Cloud*, 179–80.

50. Foulkes, *Gas!*, 195–97, 231.

51. "Employment of Special Companies," May 1917, WO95/275, PRO; and Foulkes, *Gas!*, 217–18. Green Star was a mixture of 65 percent chloropicrin and 35 percent sulphuretted hydrogen.

52. Prentiss, *Chemicals in War*, 352. For a summary of the characteristics of British gas shells see "Gas Shell Characteristics," Hartley Collection, box 42, CAC.

53. "Employment of Special Companies," May 1917, WO95/275, PRO; Foulkes, "Employment of Projectors," 20 March 1917, WO95/120, PRO; and Second Army, "Note on Offensive Use of Gas," 4 May 1917, Foulkes Collection, 6–13, LHCMA.

54. Quoted in Foulkes, *Gas!*, 220–21.

55. Prentiss, *Chemicals in War*, 365; and "Gas Shell Characteristics," Hartley Collection, box 42, CAC.

56. "Employment of 4" Stokes Mortar Bombs," 26 March 1917, wo95/120, PRO.

57. Data taken from "sb Ops," wo142/266, PRO.

58. Foulkes, *Gas!*, 198–99.

59. For a list of these attacks see "sb Ops," wo142/266.

60. Second Army, "Note on Offensive Use of Gas," 4 May 1917, Foulkes Collection, 6–13, LHCMA.

61. "Report of Operations," 24/25 May 1917, wo95/332, PRO.

62. "sb Ops," wo142/266, PRO; and "Report on Operations," 25 May 1917 and 29 May 1917, wo95/332, PRO.

63. "sb Ops," wo142/266; and "Report on Operations," 31 May–1 June and 2–3 June, 1917 wo95/332, PRO.

64. "Report on Operations," 3/4 June 1917 and 4/5 June 1917, wo95/332, PRO; and Foulkes, *Gas!*, 217. See also "War Diary O Company, Special Brigade," 4 June 1917, wo95/242, PRO; and Livens, "Development of Livens Projector," wo188/143, PRO. For a list of the oil operations see "sb Ops," wo142/266, PRO.

65. "Report on Operations," 7 June 1917, wo95/332, PRO; and "No. 2 Special Company's Operation Order," n.d., Eggington Collection, 8204–07, Royal Engineers' Museum.

66. Foulkes, *Gas!*, 215, 217–18; and "Employment of Special Companies," May 1917, wo95/275, PRO. See also "11th Australian Infantry Brigade Order No. 73," 6 June 1917, Monash Collection, 3DRL2316, item 42, AWM; "M. O. Circular No. 29, 3rd Australian Division," 21 May 1917 and "Third Australian Division Order, No. 37," 27 May 1917, Monash Collection, 3DRL2316, item 43, AWM.

67. "sb Ops," wo142/266, PRO; and General Staff, *Effect on Enemy of Our Gas Attacks*, 12–13.

68. Numerous smaller gas discharges occurred on other days on Fifth Army's front. "Fifth Army Order No. 6," 7 July 1917, and "Fifth Army Order No. 8," 15 July 1917, wo95/520, PRO; and "sb Ops," wo142/266, PRO.

69. General Staff, *Effect on Enemy of Gas Attacks*, 17–18.

70. General Staff, *Effect on Enemy of Gas Attacks*, 17–18

71. General Staff, *Gas Warfare*, no. 2 (August 1917), 2.

72. Foulkes, *Gas!*, 214; "sb Ops," wo142/266, PRO; and General Staff, *Effect on Enemy of Gas Attacks*, 10–11.

73. General Staff, *Gas Warfare*, no. 4 (October 1917), 2.

74. General Staff, *Gas Warfare*, no. 7 (January 1918), 4.

75. Foulkes, *Gas!*, 238.

76. "Report on Operation, L Special Company, R.E.," 13 September 1917, wo95/332, PRO.

77. General Staff, *Gas Warfare*, no. 4, 3.

78. "Précis of Proceedings of a Conference held at the Ministry of Munitions on [?] May 1917 to consider the Future Policy of Chemical Fillings for Artillery Shell, Stokes Bombs, and Livens Drums, which should be recommended to the Field-Marshal, Commanding-in-Chief, British Armies in France," wo032/5174, PRO.

79. General Staff, *Instructions on the Use of Lethal and Lachrymatory Shell* (France, 1917), 8.

80. General Staff, *Instructions on Use of Shell*, 6–9.

81. "Notes on Training and Preparation for Offensive Operations," 31 August 1917, Monash Collection, 3DRL2316, item 25, AWM.

82. "Undated Lecture by Uniacke," Uniacke Collection, folder II, RAI.

83. "Notes on Training and Preparation for Offensive Operations," 31 August 1917, 3DRL2316, item 25, Monash Collection, AWM.

84. "Notes on Employment of Lethal and Lachrymatory Shell Based on Results Obtained during the Recent Operations," 24 July 1917, AWM25/371/3.

85. "Report on the Use of Gas in Connection with Recent Operations by Fifth Army," 8 October 1917, WO142/98, PRO.

86. General Staff, *Artillery Notes No. 3—Counter Battery Work* (France, 1918), 5.

87. General Staff, *Artillery Notes No. 3*, 5.

88. "Lessons from the 1917 Battle Fighting of the Fifth Army from an Artillery Point of View," December 1917, Uniacke Collection, folder VII, RAI; "Canadian Corps Artillery Report on Passchendaele Operations, 17 October to 18 November, 1917," RG9/IIICI, vol. 3852, NAC; and "Organization and Procedure of Counter-Battery Office, Canadian Corps Artillery," 15 January 1919, RG9/IIIcl, vol. 3922, NAC.

89. "Notes on Counter-Battery Work," n.d., Uniacke Collection, folder 8, RAI.

90. "Notes on Counter-Battery Work," n.d., Uniacke Collection, folder 8, RAI.

91. General Staff, *Artillery Notes No. 3*, 21.

92. General Staff, *Artillery Notes No. 3*, 21.

93. "Notes on Counter-Battery Work," n.d., Uniacke Collection folder 8, RAI.

94. "Second Army to GCO Corps," 31 May 1917, AWM 26/187/10.

95. "Report on Attack at Messines," 26 June 1917, Monash Collection, box 130, folder 962, National Library of Australia; "War Diary, II ANZAC Corps," 6 June 1917, AWM26/191/4; "Summary of Proceedings of a Conference held at Pernes," 20 May 1917, WO95/275, PRO; and "Kiggell to Plumer," 19 May 1917, WO158/215, PRO. See also C. E. W. Bean, *The Australian Imperial Force in France, 1917* (St. Lucia, Queensland: University of Queensland Press, 1982), 589–92.

96. "Conditions to be Fulfilled before the Attack Can Be Launched," n.d., AWM26/193/29.

97. "Report on Gas Shell Operations, Attack on Messines Ridge," 14 June 1917, WO158/126, PRO.

98. "Report on Gas Shell Operations, Messines Ridge," 14 June 1917, WO158/126, PRO. See also "Notes on the Employment of Lethal and Lachrymatory Shell Based upon Results Obtained during the Late Operation," n.d., WO158/126, PRO.

99. "Report on Gas Shell Operations, Messines Ridge," 14 June 1917, WO158/126, PRO.

100. "Report on Gas Shell Operations, Messines Ridge," 14 June 1917, WO158/126, PRO.

101. "IX Corps Instructions for the Offensive of 7 June 1917," Rawlins Collection, 1162/7, RAI.

102. "3rd Australian Division Artillery Memorandum," 5 June 1917, AWM26/195/1; and "3rd Australian Division to II ANZAC Corps," 25 May 1917, AWM26/193/29.

103. "Memo from HA Group," 3 June 1917, AWM26/192/19.

104. "II ANZAC Corps Magnum Opus: Artillery Instructions for the Attack," 25 May 1917, AWM25/191/4; "3rd Australian Division, Artillery Circular No. 3," 29 May 1917, AWM26/195/1; "Report on Gas Shell Operations," 14 June 1917, WO158/126, PRO; and "Gas Program Commencing 3/4 June 1917," AWM26/192/19.

105. Rawlins, "A History of the Development of the British Artillery in France," 122, Rawlins Collection, 1162/1, RAI.

106. "IX Corps Report on Operations for the Capture of Messines-Wytschaete Ridge," n.d., AWM45/18/21; "3rd Australian Divisional Artillery Report," n.d., AWM224/mss4; and "II ANZAC Corps Magnum Opus," 25 May 1917, AWM25/191/4.

107. "Observations by Commander in Chief, GHQ," 24 May 1917, WO158/215, PRO.

108. "Extracts from War Diary 54th and 55th Australian Seige Artillery Brigade," AWM26/187/40; "Extracts from IX Corps War Diary," AWM45/18/21; "Extracts from War Diary CRA New Zealand Division," AWM26/190/23; "II ANZAC Corps War Diary," 31 May 1917, AWM26/191/4; and "IX Corps War Diary," WO95/835, PRO.

109. "10th Australian Infantry Brigade Order No. 48," 4 June 1917, Monash Collection, 3DRL2316, item 42, AWM; and "Attack on Messines–Wytschaete Ridge," 29 May 1917, AWM26/191/4.

110. "MGGS Second Army to CO Corps," 24 May 1917, WO158/215, PRO.

111. "Attack on Messines–Wytschaete Ridge," 29 May 1917, AWM26/191/4.

112. "Revised Artillery Plan, Second Army," 20 May 1917, AWM26/187/10.

113. Edmonds, *Military Operations 1917*, 2:48.

114. "3rd Australian Divisional Artillery Report," n.d., AWM224/mss4.

115. "Second Army Orders," 31 May 1917, WO95/275, PRO; and "IX Corps Instructions for the Offensive," 7 June 1917, Rawlins Collection, 1162/7, RAI.

116. "II ANZAC Corps Magnum Opus," 25 May 1917, AWM25/191/4.

117. Edmonds, *Military Operations 1917*, 2:48–49.

118. "Report on Gas Shell Operations, Attack on Messines," 14 June 1917, WO158/126, PRO; and "IX Corps War Diary," 7 June 1917, WO95/835, PRO.

119. "Report on the Use of Gas Shell During the Operations of Fifth Army up to 31 July 1917," 14 August 1917, Hartley Collection, box 33, CAC.

120. Rawlins, "A History of British Artillery in France," 134, 151, Rawlins Collection, 1162/1, RAI.

121. "3rd Battle of Ypres, Operations of the XVIII Corps on 31 July 1917," n.d., WO95/951, PRO.

122. "Report on Gas Shell, Fifth Army, up to 31 July 1917," 14 August 1917, Hartley Collection, box 33, CAC; and "15th D. A. No. BM/S/24," 28 July 1917, WO95/1919, PRO.

123. "Report on Gas Shell, Fifth Army, up to 31 July 1917," 14 August 1917, Hartley Collection, box 33, CAC.

124. "General Staff Memorandum No. 156, Notes on Recent Fighting," 6 September 1917, Hobbs Collection, 3DRL2600, item 9, AWM.

125. "Amendment No. 2 to Second Army Artillery Instructions No. 2," 13 September 1917, AWM26/274/2; and "Report on the Use of Gas in Connection with Recent Operations by Fifth Army," 8 October 1917, WO142/98, PRO.

126. "Amendment No. 2 to Instructions No. 2," 13 September 1917, AWM26/274/2.

127. "General Staff Memorandum No. 156, Notes on Recent Fighting," 6 September 1917, Hobbs Collection 3DRL 2600, item 9, box 33, AWM.

128. "Report on the Use of Gas in Connection with Recent Operations by Fifth Army," 8 October 1917, WO142/98, PRO.

129. "Report on Use of Gas, Fifth Army," 8 October 1917, WO142/98, PRO.

130. "Notes on Conference held at Lovie Château," 10 September 1917, WO95/520, PRO.

131. "Conference at Lovie Château," 10 September 1917, WO95/520, PRO.

132. Rawlins, "A History of British Artillery in France," 152, Rawlins Collection, 1162/1, RAI.

133. See "Capt. Graf Dohna to Chemical Adviser Armies," 18 October 1917, AWM26/208/29.

134. "Conference at Lovie Château," 30 October 1917, WO95/520, PRO.

135. "Counter-battery Office, Canadian Corps Artillery, Order No. 52," 31 October 1917, RG9III/CI, vol. 3922, NAC.

136. "Counter-battery Office, Canadian Corps Artillery, Order No. 53, Table C," 5 November 1917, RG9III/CI, vol. 3922, NAC.

137. General Staff, *Training Divisions for Offensive Action*, 16–17.

138. "White Star Hand Grenades," 26 February 1917, Hartley Collection, box 42, CAC; and "C. E. W. Bean Diary," 20 September 1917, AWM38/3DRL606, item 164. See also General Staff, *Training and Employment of Divisions*, 57–58.

139. "Gas Operations XVIII Corps Front, during July 1917 to August 1917," n.d., WO95/951, PRO.

140. General Staff, *Training Divisions for Offensive Action*, 16–17.

141. "Von Below to T. H. Adams at HQ First Army, Experience Derived from the Arras Battle," 11 April 1917, RG9III/CI, vol. 3978, NAC.

142. "Fourth Army [German] Headquarters, New English Gasmine Projector," 4 June 1917, Hartley Collection, box 44, CAC.

143. "Extracts from Captured German Document Belonging to 54th Division," 11 October 1917, AWM25/371/21.

144. "Translation of Captured Notebook," 4 July 1917, AWM26/208/36.

145. General Staff, *Gas Warfare*, no. 6 (December 1917), 2.

146. Foulkes, "Gas Warfare in the Field," n.d., Foulkes Collection, 6–61, LHCMA.

5. MARCH TO VICTORY

1. C. E. W. Bean, *The Official History of Australia in the War of 1914–1918*, vol. 5, *The Australian Imperial Force in France During the Main German Offensive, 1918* (St. Lucia, Queensland: University of Queensland Press, 1983), 57.

2. "Munitions Policy—1919 or 1920," 5 September 1918, Haig Collection, 3155/131, NLS.

3. "British Military Policy 1918–1919," 25 July 1918, Haig Collection, 3155/129, NLS.

4. "War Diary," 11 July 1918, Haig Collection, 3155/129, NLS.

5. Although he places too great an emphasis on the role of the tank, Hubert Johnson in *Breakthrough!* accurately outlines the advances made by the British in combined arms warfare. See Hubert Johnson, *Breakthrough!: Tactics, Technology and the Search for Victory on the Western Front in World War I* (Novato CA: Presido Press, 1994), 243–75.

6. "Report on Conference on the General Gas Policy and the Chemical Shell Program," 27 November 1917, MUN5/187/1360/10, PRO; and "Chemical and Smoke Shells Issued to War Office, 1916 to Date," 24 July 1918, MUN5/198/1650/30, PRO.

7. "Report on the Use of Mustard Gas," 27 June 1918, WO142/91, PRO.

8. "Report by Foulkes on Visit to England," 12 February 1918, WO142/98, PRO.

9. "Churchill to Haig," 16 June 1918, Haig Collection, 3155/128, NLS.

10. W. J. Pope, "The Manufacture of aa-Dichlorethyl-Sulphide," 23 February 1918, Haldane Collection, MS20234, NLS.

11. "Report by Foulkes on Visit to England," 11 March 1918, WO142/98, PRO; and "Memorandum on the Delays in Providing Gas Shells," 1 August 1918, MUN5/198/1650/30, PRO.

12. "Report by Foulkes to England," 11 March 1918, WO142/98, PRO. The technical name for the weapon was Thermo-Generator Type M or the M Device.

13. "Minutes of the Chemical Warfare Committee," 20 September 1918, WO142/72, PRO.

14. "Report by Foulkes to England," 11 March 1918, WO142/98, PRO; and F. G. Donnan, "On the Employment of Highly Dispersed Fumes in Chemical Warfare," n.d., Haldane Collection, MS20234, NLS.

15. C. H. Foulkes, "Memorandum on Gas Operations," 1 April 1918, WO142/98, PRO.

16. "Meeting of the Chemical Warfare Committee," 16 November 1917, WO142/71, PRO.

17. "Meeting of Chemical Warfare Committee," 16 November 1917, WO142/71, PRO.

18. "Minutes of Proceedings at a Conference to Consider the Supply of Gas for 1919 as Affected by the Policy of the General Staff," 19 March 1918, MUN5/198/1650/29, PRO; and "Foulkes to OC Special Companies, R.E., First Army," 15 May 1915, WO142/324, PRO.

19. "Scheme for a 'Gas Beam' Attack on the XVIII Corps Front," 6 May 1918, WO142/324, PRO.

20. "Scheme for a 'Gas Beam' Attack on the XVIII Corps Front," 6 May 1918, WO142/324, PRO.

21. "Preliminary Scheme for a 'Gas Beam' Attack on the XVIII Corps Front," 8 May 1918; "Scheme for a 'Gas Beam' Attack on the XVIII Corps Front," 13 May 1918, WO142/324, PRO; "Notes of a Conference Held at XVIII Corps Headquarters, 24 May 1918 on the 'Gas Beam' Attack," 24 May 1918; "Report on 'Gas Beam' Operation on XVIII Corps Front, 23/24 May 1918," 26 May 1918; and "Dawnay to OC Special Companies, R.E.," 9 July 1918, all in WO142/324, PRO.

22. "Report on Operation P/4 on 49th Division Front, 24 July 1918," 26 July 1918, WO95/332, PRO.

23. "Report on Corrosive Gas for Jamming Machine Guns," n.d., WO142/135, PRO.

24. "Minutes of the Chemical Warfare Committee," 14 June 1918 and 18 October 1918, WO142/72, PRO.

25. "List of Substances Examined but Not Recommended for Adoption during the Period October 1917 to June 1919," n.d., WO142/332, PRO.

26. "Proposal by Lieut.-Col. S. W. Bunker, Chemical Adviser Third Army," n.d., WO142/98, PRO.

27. "Minutes of the Chemical Warfare Committee," 20 September 1918, WO142/72, PRO.

28. "Operation Order No. 104, 36th Australian HA, Royal Garrison Artillery," 12 October 1918, and "War Diary of the 36th Australian Brigade, Royal Garrison Artillery," 12 October 1918, AWM26/480/1.

29. "Ammunition Expenditure, 11th Australian Field Artillery War Diary," 7 July 1918, AWM4/13/38/30.

30. "2nd Australian Division Intelligence Summary," 10 July 1918, AWM5/1/44/38.

31. "Summary of Ammunition Expended during Month of June 1918 by Fourth Australian Division Artillery," 1 July 1918, AWM26/410/6.

32. "Fourth Australian Divisional Artillery Administrative Instruction No. 32," 23 June 1918, AWM25/519/28; and "Fourth Australian Divisional Artillery Order No. 167," 6 July 1918, AWM26/410/6.

33. "Night Firing for Night 23/24 June 1918, Fourth Australian Division Artillery," 23 June 1918, AWM25/519/28.

34. "F. J. Wilson to Chemical Adviser Fifth Army," 19 September 1918, AWM27/314/7. "Stinks" was a commonly used slang expression for chemical shells.

35. "W. A. Rigden Memoirs," April 1918, Ref. 80, Liddle Collection, University of Leeds.

36. "GOCRA Canadian Corps to Canadian Corps Artillery HQ," 3 October 1918, RG9/IIIC1/vol. 3924, NAC.

37. James E. Edmonds, *Military Operations France and Belgium, 1918*, vol. 3, *May-July: The German Diversion Offensives and the First Allied Counter-Offensive* (London: Macmillan, 1939), 197–208; and C. E. W. Bean, *The Australian Imperial Force in France*, vol. 6, *During the Allied Offensive, 1918* (St. Lucia, Queensland: University of Queensland Press, 1983), 242–335.

38. General Staff, *Notes Complied by G. S. Fourth Army on the Operations by the Australian Corps Against Hamel, Bois de Hamel, and Bois de Vaire, on 4th of July, 1918* (1918), 2, 6.

39. "Night Firing for Night 23/24 June 1918, Fourth Australian Division Artillery," 23 June 1918, AWM25/519/28.

40. T. A. Blamey, "Lecture on the Battle of Hamel," n.d., Blamey Collection, 3DRL6643, 5/3, AWM; and "Operations by the Australian Corps against Hamel, Bois de Hamel and Bois de Vaire," 4 July 1918, 10, Rawlinson Collection, 5201-33-77, NAM. See also General Staff, *Notes Complied by G. S. Fourth Army*, 5.

41. "War Diary, 14th Australian Field Artillery Brigade," 4, 16, and 19 June 1918, AWM4/13/41/25.

42. "War Diary 11th Australian Field Artillery Brigade," 1 July 1918, AWM4/13/38/30; and "War Diary 10th Australian Field Artillery Brigade," 25, 26, 27 June 1918, AWM4/13/37/23.

43. "Right Group Intelligence Report," 25, 27 June 1918, AWM4/13/27/24.

44. "Fourth Australian Division Intelligence Summary No. 286," 17 and 24 June 1918, AWM26/408/4.

45. "Second Australian Division, Intelligence Summary," 1–4 July 1918, AWM5/1/44/38.

46. "Operations by the Australian Corps against Hamel, Bois de Hamel and Bois de Vaire," 4 July 1918, 10, Rawlinson Collection, 5201–33–77, NAM; and General Staff, *Notes Complied by G. S. Fourth Army*, 6. See also, "General Report on the Action of the Horse and Field Artillery Covering the Attack by the 4th, 6th and 11th Australian Infantry Brigades on Hamel and Vaire Wood and on the High Ground to the East, on the 4th July 1918," 9 July 1918, AWM25/519/28.

47. "War Diary, 4th Australian Division Artillery," 3 July 1918, AWM26/410/6; and "Synchronized Shoots to be Carried Out 3/4 July 1918 by 4th Australian Division Artillery," 3 July 1918, AWM25/519/28.

48. "Fourth Australian Divisional Artillery Order, No. 163," 1 July 1918, AWM25/519/28; and Edmonds, *Military Operations 1918*, 3:201.

49. General Staff, *Notes Complied by G. S. Fourth Army*, 5.

50. Rawlins, "History of British Artillery in France," 204, Rawlins Collection, 1162/1, RAI.

51. "Fourth Australian Divisional Artillery Order No. 160," 29 June 1918, AWM25/519/28. A clinometer is a device that measures angle of elevation.

52. "Operations by Australian Corps against Hamel, Bois de Hamel and Bois de Vaire," 4 July 1918, 9; Rawlins, "A History of British Artillery in France," 207, Rawlins Collection, 1162/1, RAI; and Australian Corps, HA, "Notes on Counter-Battery Work in Battle, 8 August 1918 and the Advance from Villers-Bretoneux to

the Hindenburg Line," October 1918, AWM26/494/2. See also "Agenda for Hamel Offensive," 4 July 1918, Rawlinson Collection, 5201-33-77, NAM; and "Counter-Battery, Australian Corps HA, Operation Order—No. 7," n.d., AWM26/364/12. Figures for the shell expenditure are taken from "Intelligence Summary," 4 July 1918, Montgomery–Massingberd Collection, 71, LHCMA.

53. "Instructions Issued under Australian Corps Order No. 120, Subsidiary Operations," 2 July 1918, Monash Collection, 3DRL2316, item 44, AWM; and "Report on Operations of No. 1 Special Company, Royal Engineers," 4 July 1918, AWM26/358/4; and "III Corps Intelligence Summary," 4 July 1918, AWM26/352/12.

54. Edmonds, *Military Operations 1918*, 3:207–8.

55. "Australian Corps, HA Order No. 143," 1 July 1918, Monash Collection, 3DRL2316, item 44, AWM.

56. "Australian Corps Heavy Artillery Defence Scheme," July 1918, AWM26/364/12.

57. "Counter-Preparation Phase IB," n.d., AWM26/364/11.

58. "Counter-Battery—Australian Corps HA Operation Order No. 8," 3 July 1918, AWM26/364/12; "Australian Corps GOCRA War Diary," 5–10 July 1918, AWM26/365/13; and "War Diary, Fourth Australian Division Artillery," 4 July 1918, AWM26/410/6. See also "Summary of Operations," 5–10 July 1918, Montgomery–Massingberd Collection, 71, LHCMA.

59. "Messages, Right Group, 10:24 A.M.," 4 July 1918, AWM4/13/27/24; "Synchronized Shoots to be Carried out during Night 4/5 July, Fourth Australian Division," 4 July 1918, AWM25/519/28; "Right Group Field Artillery Intelligence Report," 4–5 July 1918, AWM4/13/27/24; and "Australian Corps Heavy Artillery, Daily Tactical Report," 6–7 July 1918, AWM26/364/12.

60. "Summary of Operations," 5–10 July 1918, Montgomery-Massingberd Collection, 71, LHCMA; and "Australian Corps GOCRA War Diary," 5–10 July 1918, AWM26/365/13.

61. "Rawlinson to Cavan," 7 July 1918, Rawlinson Collection, 5201-33-76, NAM.

62. "Cipher CP 502, 11 July 1918; Cipher CP 506, 13 July 1918; and Cipher CP 510, 14 July 1918," all in Haig Collection, 3155/129, NLS.

63. See John Terraine, *To Win A War, 1918: The Year of Victory* (London: Sidgwick & Jackson, 1978), 90–100.

64. "Extracts from Letters and Conferences Concerning the Preparations for the Operations on 8 August 1918," n.d., Monash Collection, 3DRL2316, item 28, part 4, AWM.

65. "Extracts from Letters and Conferences, Operations on 8 August 1918," n.d., Monash Collection, 3DRL2316, item 28, part 4, AWM.

66. James E. Edmonds, *Military Operations, France and Belgium, 1918*, vol. 4, *8th August—26th September the Franco-British Offensive* (London: HMSO, 1947), 30–31.

67. "Extracts from Letters and Conferences, Operations on 8 August 1918," n.d., Monash Collection, 3DRL2316, item 28, part 4, AWM; "Summary of Intel-

ligence," August 1918, Montgomery–Massingberd Collection, 73, LHCMA; and Budworth, "Fourth Army Artillery in the Battle of Amiens, 8 August 1918," 25 August 1918, Monash Collection, 3DRL2316, item 34, AWM.

68. "Australian Corps Heavy Artillery Order No. 150," 6 August 1918, and "Counter-Battery Australian Corps HA Operation Order No. 12," 6 August 1918, AWM26/494/2; "SOS and Counter-Preparation Scheme—SOS 48," 4 August 1918, AWM26/479/9; and "Fourth Army Artillery in the Battle of Amiens, 8 August 1918," n.d., Rawlinson Collection, 5201–33–78, NAM. See also "III Corps Artillery Instructions No. 3," 5 August 1918, AWM26/476/8; and "III Corps, Project of an Operation to be Carried out on 8 August 1918," 31 July 1918, AWM45/23/43.

69. "Daily Intelligence Summary," 1–7 August 1918, Montgomery–Massingberd Collection, 73, LHCMA; and "War Diary Australian Corps Brigadier-General Heavy Artillery," 1 August 1918, AWM26/494/1.

70. "SB Ops," WO142/266, PRO; and "Fourth Army General Instructions No. 37(G)," 2 August 1918, Montgomery–Massingberd Collection, 73, LHCMA.

71. "Lecture, Artillery in Offensive Operations," 29 August 1918, Uniacke Collection, folder 11, RAI.

72. "Telephone Message Log," 8 August 1918, "Artillery Notes on a Visit to the Canadian Corps," 14 August 1918, and "Report on Operations—4th Canadian Divisional Artillery," 8 August 1918, in WO95/1059, PRO. See also, "III Corps Intelligence Summary," 8 August 1918, AWM26/476/8; "Counter-Battery Australian Corps HA, Operation Order No. 12/3," 11 August 1918, AWM26/474/2; and "Fourth Army Artillery in the Battle of Amiens, 8 August 1918," n.d., Rawlinson Collection, 5201–33–78, NAM.

73. For prisoner figures see "Cipher, CP 500," 10 August 1918 and "Cipher, CP 597," 13 August 1918, Haig Collection, 3155/130, NLS.

74. "Australian Corps Heavy Artillery, Scheme for Mobile Warfare," 11 August 1918, AWM26/474/2.

75. For statistics on shell expenditures by Fourth Army during the war's closing campaign see the summary of daily intelligence reports found in Montgomery–Massingberd's war diary located in the LHCMA.

76. Foulkes, *Gas!*, 287.

77. Foulkes, *Gas!*, 289.

78. "Battle Instructions, Series E, No. 2, Australian Corps," 22 September 1918, Monash Collection, 3DRL2316, item 44, AWM.

79. "Battle Instructions, Series E, No. 2, Australian Corps," 22 September 1918, Monash Collection, 3DRL2316, item 44, AWM.

80. James E. Edmonds, *Military Operations, France and Belgium, 1918*, vol. 5, *26 September–11 November, the Advance to Victory* (London: HMSO, 1947), 95; and "Artillery Instructions, Series B, No. 1," 24 September 1918, Rawlins Collection, 1162/7, RAI.

81. Between 13 October and 9 November the British employed BB 12 more times. The expenditure for the Battle of St. Quentin Canal was easily the largest, with the next greatest amount occurring during the night of 13/14 October when the artill-

ery fired 11,000 mustard gas rounds. From 26 September to the end of the war the British fired approximately 44,760 18-pounder and 17,028 6-inch howitzer BB rounds. See "The Use of BB Shell," n.d., AWM27/314/17.

82. "Fourth Army Artillery in the Attack on the Hindenburg Line, 29 September 1918," 23 October 1918, Rawlinson Collection, 5201–33–78, NAM; and "Battle Instructions, Series E, No. 4, Australian Corps," 24 September 1918, Monash Collection, 3DRL2316, item 44, AWM.

83. "Battle Instructions, Series E, No. 2, Australian Corps," 22 September 1918, Monash Collection, 3DRL2316, item 44, AWM. See also "Artillery Instructions, Series B, No. 1," 24 September 1918, Rawlins Collection, 1162/7, RAI; and "Battle Instructions, Series E, No. 13, Fifth Australian Division," 28 September 1918, Hobbs Collection, 3DRL2600, item 19, AWM.

84. "Results of Bombardment with BB Gas Shell on the Night of 26/27 September on Fourth Army Front," n.d., AWM26/474/2; "Artillery Instructions No. 268 by GOCRA Australian Corps," 24 September 1918, Monash Collection, 3DRL2316, item 44, AWM; "Australian Corps Heavy Artillery Order No. 162," 26 September 1918, AWM26/494/8; and "Report on Mustard Gas," 27 June 1918, WO142/91, PRO.

85. "Summary of Operations," 29 September 1918, Montgomery–Massingberd Collection, 78, LHCMA.

86. "Battle Instructions, Series E, No. 4, Australian Corps," 24 September 1918, Monash Collection, 3DRL2316, item 44, AWM; "Fourth Australian Divisional Artillery Instruction No. 7," 27 September 1918, AWM26/495/8; and "Précis of Fourth Army Orders Affecting Artillery for the Attack of the Hindenburg Line, 29 September 1918," n.d., AWM26/474/1. See also "Fourth Army Artillery in the Attack on the Hindenburg Line, 29 September 1918," 23 October 1918, Rawlinson Collection, 5201–33–78, NAM; and "Counter-Battery, Australian Corps HA, Daily Report," 26/27 September 1918, AWM26/494/8

87. "SB Ops," WO142/266, PRO; and "Battle Instructions, Series E, No. 15, Australian Corps," 25 September 1918, Monash Collection, 3DRL2316, item 44, AWM.

CONCLUSION

1. Jonathan Bailey discusses the revolutionary implications of World War I operations in *The First World War and the Birth of the Modern Style of Warfare* (Camberley, England: The Strategic and Combat Studies Institute, 1996).

2. For an example see Martin Samuels, *Doctrine and Dogma: German and British Infantry Tactics in the First World War* (New York: Greenwood, 1992).

3. For a discussion of these tactics see Bruce I. Gudmundsson, *Stormtroop Tactics: Innovation in the German Army, 1914–1918* (New York: Praeger, 1989).

4. Holger H. Herwig, *The First World War: Germany and Austria-Hungary, 1914–1918* (London: Arnold, 1997), 394.

5. For an example of this see Travers, *How the War Was Won*.

6. Senior, "Manufacture of Mustard Gas" and "Report on German Chemical Warfare Organization and Policy, 1914–1918, [Hartley Report]," n.d., Hartley Collection, box 35, CAC. See also "Minutes of Proceedings at a Conference to Con-

sider the Supply of Gas for 1919 as Affected by the Policy of the General Staff," 19 March 1918, MUN5/198/1650/29, PRO.

7. "Weekly Requirements in Chemical Shell: 1918–1919," MUN5/198/1650/30, PRO.

8. See Giulio Douhet, *The Command of the Air* (New York: Arno Press, 1972).

9. Foulkes, *Gas!*, 289. Curiously the Nebelwerfer was initially intended as a multibarrel chemical mortar. See Thomas Parrish, *The Simon and Schuster Encyclopedia of World War II* (New York: Simon and Schuster, 1978), 430.

10. For a discussion of when to innovate see Rosen, *Winning the Next War*, 57–105.

11. Quoted in Herwig, *The First World War*, 400.

12. See Lupfer, *Dynamics of Doctrine*.

Index

Foulkes, Maj. Gen. Charles H., 53, 57, 58, 79, 81, 110, 119, 127–38, 147, 153, 162, 188; appointment to gas command of, 44; gas policy of, 126–28, 133, 135–36, 138, 161; and gas shortages, 124–25; and Livens Projector, 104; and Loos, 59, 60, 63, 68, 74; and Messines, 133; and mobile war, 182, 183, 188, 194; and mustard gas, 158–59; preference for cylinder operations of, 130–32, 160; and repeated gassing of units, 138; and Somme, 98
Frederick the Great, 29
French, Gen. John, 25, 26, 45, 47; and Aubers Ridge, 49; demands for gas by, 43–44; and Festubert, 51–52; gas theory of, 58; on introduction of gas, 43; and Loos, 54–57, 61, 64; and Neuve Chapelle, 48
Fuller, J. F. C., 11, 203 n.16; on doctrine, 12
Furse, Lieut. Gen. William, 124–25, 126

gas, 111, 180, 192; and "annoyers" phase, 44–45; and artillery, 22, 32–33, 72, 115; as barrier to movement, 34; blow back of, 70–71, 74, 78, 129, 130; efficiency of, 1, 22, 36, 75–76, 102, 106–7, 108, 141, 148, 152, 174, 200; experiments with, 44, 162–64; importance in counter-battery of, 141–43, 146–49; innovation of, 2–3, 200; insidiousness of, 42, 175, 185; lessons of, 73, 108–10, 126; limitations on use of, 89, 96, 100, 132, 135–36, 161, 179, 182, 185; and maneuvers, 34, 100, 101, 133; and mobile war, 181–82, 183; and morale, 32–33, 93, 99, 109, 183; and panic, 41–42, 45, 46, 101, 135; pervasiveness of, 113, 194–95; and phases of battle, 21–22, 76, 164; production of, 58, 78, 80–81, 84–86, 111, 121–23, 124, 150,

156, 188, 193; projectile policy for, 83–84, 139–40, 158; rate of casualties due to, 128; selection of agents for, 84–85, 102, 105–6, 122–23, 125–26; shortage of agents for, 124–25; and Special Brigade, 22; and superiority of forces, 110; superiority over high explosives of, 175; and surprise, 175–76; tactics, 89–90, 93, 94, 95, 96, 98–99, 101, 110, 127, 133, 134, 144, 147, 160, 164, 168; theory on use of, 58; and weather, 64, 67–68, 83, 89, 95, 108, 113, 135–36, 140, 156, 175, 186

gas agents (minor): aloxite, 163; bisulphide of carbon, 44; boiling oil, 103, 118, 132, 163; bromine, 44, 58; calcium arsenide, 44; capsicine, 44, 163; CBR, 86; chlorine peroxide, 163; collongite, 214 n.20; corborundum, 80, 163; diphenylaminechloroarsine (DM), 159–60, 193; diphenylchloroarsine (DA), 159–60, 163; diphosgene, 82; hydrocyanic jelly, 44; jellite, 86, 102, 107; KSK, 126, 140, 150–51, 156, 221 n.38; NC, 125–26, 133, 157, 164, 170, 220 n.37; nicotine, 163; PG, 125–26, 133, 220 n.37; phosphorus, 44, 80, 81, 98, 150, 170; poison ivy, 163; powdered glass, 163; silicon tetrachloride, 163; smoke, 61, 63, 68, 80, 81, 98, 101, 108, 116, 135, 165, 168, 169, 170, 187; stannic chloride (KJ), 128, 129, 150, 151, 160; sulphur chloride, 44; sulphur dioxide, 44; thermite, 120, 133, 134, 135; titanium chloride, 163; veratrin, 44; vincennite, 214 n.20. *See also* Blue Cross; Blue Star; chlorine; chloropicrin; gas: selection of agents for; gas: shortage of agents for; Green Star; mustard gas; phosgene; Red Star; SK; Two Red Star; White Star; Yellow Star